Iwenhe Tyerrtye

– what it means to be an Aboriginal person

IAD PRESS

Iwenhe Tyerrtye
– what it means to be an Aboriginal person

Margaret *Kemarre* Turner OAM

as told to Barry McDonald *Perrurle*
with translations by Veronica *Perrurle* Dobson

Contents

Foundations

This Book, *Pipe Nhenhe*   2
    The Wurley-house   4
    We All Feel the Same   6

Born to Be   9
    Aknganeke-arle   9
    Angampeke-arle   12
    Utyerre   15

Relationship of Land   20
    Apmereyanhe   20
    Ilakakeye   22
    Country Marriage   24
    Apmereke Artweye and *Kwertengwerle*   31

The Generations   35
    Kartweye-kartweye-kartweye   35
    Angkweye-angkweye-angkweye   40

Story

Dreams and Story   46
    Cultural Writing Inside   46
    Traditional Country Story   46
    The Three-way of *Altyerre*   48
    Dreams   50
    Dream-Visions   52
    Country Dreams and Story Line   54
    From Dreams to Dreaming   58

Ways of Telling   61
    Painting Stories   61
    Singing and Dancing Stories   66
    Singing and Dancing Just For Fun   69

Ayeye-arle Alheme, Ayeye-arle Apetye-alpeme   72
    Story Goes Out and Comes Back Home   72

Anpernirrentye, Kinship

Angkerrentye Anpernirrentye-akerte   76
    A Dialogue Concerning the Sacredness of Kinship   76

Ikirrentye and Nyurrpe   86
    Nyurrpe   87
    Kwantheme, Nyurrpe-Teasing   92

Touch-feelings   94
    Spouse-feeling   98
    Parent and child-feeling   99
    Crossover-feeling   99
    Body-feeling   101
    Nephew and niece-feeling   102
    Akangkeme   103

Mourning   104
    When Sad People's Fires are Burning   104
    Sorry time   106
    Anpernirrentye and Mourning   107
    Iltyeme-iltyeme, Hand talk   110

Apmere, The Land

What Land Means   114
    A Place Everywhere   114
    Irrerntarenye and Arremparrenge   116

Recovering Our Land   122
    We Had No Title   122
    We Who See the Beautiness   125
    Grandfather's-Stories Land   131

Healing   132
    Plants Grow With the Power of the Land   132
    Powerful Little Medicines   135
    Healing With Song   142
    Sacred Punishment gives Peace   145
    Let Homeland Heal You   146

Our Nature

Plants and Trees   152
    Ancestor Trees   152
    Food from Plants   156
    Stories from Plants   158

Animals   163
    Respect For Animals   163
    The Eaters get Eaten   166
    Help from Animals   167
    A Tale or Two   172

Once the White People Came   176
    And Here They Still Are   176
    Where Are Our Foods Now?   181
    The Food Chain is Breaking   187
    What's Happened To Our Water   189

Language And Learning

Language   194
    From the Flesh of Our Land   194

Teaching And Learning   198
    Teaching is a Really Sacred Thing   198
    And I'm *Still* Learning   199
    Land is the Real Teacher   207

Akngerrepate Mape, the Elders   211
    They Were the Very Highlight to Us   211

Iwerre Atherrame, Two Cultures   215
    When Shadows Measured Time   215
    Urekethureke, it's a Problem Life Now   216
    Two Cultures Can Hold Each Other   219

Foundations

"We are part of the Land.
The Land *is* us, and we are the Land.
That's how we hold our Land."

This Book, *Pipe Nhenhe*

The pipe nhenhe intelhe-ileme atyenge aperlele awetyenhenge, ipmenhele awetyenhenge, arrengele awetyenhenge, atyemeyele awetyenhenge, alerele awetyenhenge. Ayenge-arle angkerne yanhe marlele-arle urreyele-arle awetyenhenge. Itne akaltye-irretyeke anpernirrentyeke, itne apmere nthenhe-arenye, itne itelarelhetyeke iwenhe-apatherre itne. Iwenhe-apatherre mikwe, anyikwe, apmarlikwe, atyikwe, ipmenhikwe, arrengikwe, aperlikwe. Alakenhe-arle akaltye-irreme tyerrtye urrperle-kenhe iwerreke.

Alakenhe-arle arrwekelenye mape anetyarte. Alakenhe-arle itne akaltye-irreke. The mpwareme ayeye nhenhe alkngwirreketye. Ampe ingkernenye mape Angkelethe-ante akngerre angkeme. Alakenhe ikwerenge pipe nhenhe the intelhe-ileme ampe tyerrtye-arle akaltye-irretyenhenge. Tyerrtye angkentye-arle aparlpe-ilekele itne-arlke akaltye-irrirtnetyenhenge. Ayenge angkentye angkeme anwernekenhe angkentyeke mwerre akaltye-irretyeke. Tyerrtye arrpenhe mapele awetyenhenge akaltye-irretyeke. Pipe nhenhe the mpwareme ingkerreke anthurre akaltye-irretyeke. Pipe nhenhe-arle read-eme-iletyenhe-arle itelaretyeke nthakenhe-nthakenhe anwerne anintyeke. Alhernterele anwernekenge warrke-arle-irremele awetyenhenge alakenhe itne akaltye-irretyenhenge nthakenhe iwenhe tyerrtye. Atyenge-akerte-arle the ayeye nhenhe ileme. The ayeye ileme atyenge artweye-areyele ilintyeke. Tyerrtye urrperle anwerne utnenge rlterrke antirrkweme. Alakenhe itelaretyeke.

I'm writing this book so that it can be read and understood by all my grandchildren, and also my nieces and nephews – by all those boys and girls. So that they can learn about kinship and rediscover their own Land-origins; trace the kinship roots running through themselves, their mothers, their fathers, their great-grandparents, their grandmothers and their grandfathers; and become aware of the nature of the long path we Aboriginal people have travelled, from the beginning.

I'm writing this book so that the young *Arrernte* kids will learn more about the old ways. They'll learn about how our Ancestors lived. I'm writing this book so all that won't be forgotten. The young people of today use a lot of English in their speaking.

This Book, *Pipe Nhenhe*

But there are *arrirtne arrpenhe mape*, another sort of old-style, strong words, you know. People don't use those words much now, *arrirtne yanhe* use-*eme-ileke*. Today's kids should be learning them, 'cause some of the old names of words are not used properly now, and that means other knowledge gets lost. Any *Arrernte* people who have forgotten some of their language can learn it back, and I'm using a lot of *Arrernte* words in this book so that our language can continue to be learned properly.

Other Aboriginal people can also read and learn from it. I'm making this book so that everybody can learn. Reading it will show to people just how we have always lived. Non-Aboriginal people who work with us can learn what being an Aboriginal person really means. In doing this, I'm telling only my own story, about how I see things as an Aboriginal person, I'm not speaking for anyone else. But I am telling the story that my families have told me from the beginning. We Aboriginal people hold a very strong spirit, and that should be kept in mind always.

Alherntere mapele nthakenhe-ame arelhe urrperle iwenhe-ame arelhe urrperle nthakenhe-ame itne aneme kwenhe. Nthakenhe itnekenhe iwerre iwenhe itne itelareme alakenhe, and so that's why I bin *mpwarerle pipe nhenhe atyenge nhenhe-akerte.* So people *itne* can *arerle, nthakenhe-akenhe arelhe urrperle aneme-arle. Iwenheye itne itelareme. Iwenheye itne itirrintyeke. Iwenheye itne itelareme. Nthakenheye itne aneme layake mperlkere uthene apmere* town *anyentele. Nthakenhe itnekenhe* way *itne antirrkwerle-aneme kwenhe. Arelhe urrperle-kenhe* way *antirrkwerle-aneme, iwerre, urrperle-kenhe* way *antirrkwerle-aneme kwenhe. Iwenheye itnekenhe lterrke anthurre aneme kwenhe, urrperle mape-kenhe antirrkweme lterrke kwenhe. Alakenhe itne aretyenhenge,* you know? 'Cause they might think that "oh *kele, urrperle mape* town-*werne apetyeme-arle mape angkentye-arlke itnekenhe aparlpe-ileme.* Oh *kele, itne mantereke-arlke irrpemele.* They can't *alakenhe awethe mpwarirtnerle kwenhe".* Or sometimes they say "*itne* town-*werne apetyeke-arle, ngkwarle-ante antywele-aneme itnekenhe utnenge itetheke alkngwirremele kwenhe".* But *itne antywele-aneme prape alhwarrpe-arle itne antywelte-aneme,* you know? *Ante* also *arrwekele itne aneneheke aneneheke* just like *nantheke-ante antyemele* like *artwe mape,* you know *nantheke, pweleke-ante warrke mpwaremele, ampe arntarnte-arenhemele,* not only *itne alhetyarte layake* two or three weeks, some used to go like one year *apeke uyerre-arle. Ampe itnekenhe imernte aretye-alpemele akngerre-ante aneme. Alakenhe itne alhelte-iwetyarte. Arelhe akenhe arlwekerele anemele apeke ampe apeke ingkerne apeke itnekenhe amangkerle-anaye. Kenhe ikwerenge-arle aneke apeke kenhe arlenge re anteme alhepe-alhelenge nanthenge.*

Non-Indigenous people often wonder just how Aboriginal people really are, just what it is to be an Aboriginal person. How Aboriginal people live, what their way of life is, what their knowledge is. That's one reason why I'm writing this book about my experience. So people can see how Aboriginal people approach life. How they understand the world. How we think. How we can live side by side with white people in the one town. How we keep our traditions, hanging on to our customs and beliefs, keeping on holding so strongly. So that those white people can see things through our eyes. Because they might think that, "oh well, Aboriginal people who've moved into town, they're losing their language. Oh, they're wearing clothes now. That must mean they've lost the old ways". Or sometimes they might say, "these town mob, they're just drinking, and they've forgotten about their living spirits, they're killing off their souls". But the reality is that they're drinking because they're so sad and lost, so they just keep on drinking. Because in the early days they had lots to do, riding horses and working with cattle on country. And not only a little bit here and there, but sometimes they might go droving for a whole year. They'd come back and their kids would have grown up. They don't have that work to do now.

The Wurley-house

Itelaraye ilthe apeke-arle arteme ilthe-arle arrwekelenye arterrirretyarte ante when they *ilthe arterle-ante* they used to *mwerre anthurre mpwarerle. Nhenge arne akartenge iltheke-arle tneme akwete anetyenhenge lterrke,* they used to *iperte tnyele imernte arne renhe ngkernemele ikwerenge-ntyele imernte arne ikwere-arleke apwerte arrernemele apwerte mape.* They didn't *arrekwerlkwerle iwenhe apeke ilerle ahelhe* first

This Book, *Pipe Nhenhe*   The Wurley-house

iwenhakweye ilerle apwerte first *arrernerle. So apwerte yanhe mape-le kine antirrkwerle arntape nhenge layake arne pmware-pmwarele apeke, interrkele apeke arlkweketye. Ilthe nhenge atnartenge lterrke akwete anetyenhenge. Alakenhe.* So that the *nhenge arne atnartenge lterrke akwete anetyenhenge. Tnertnerle-arle-alpeme re,* you know. *Arne arrpenhe-areye ampeke-iwetyenhe-arleke ikwere-arleke. Alakenhe.* Because they made that *ilthe lterrke anetyenhenge layake kwatyele anhelenge apeke, uternele amperlenge, nhenhe arne ultakelhetyakenhe anekerre, itelaraye, atnartenge-thayate.*

I remember when the old people used to build traditional shelters, the ones that were put up in the early days. They built them really well. They'd put the posts in so that they would stand strongly for a long time, for generations. They would dig a hole and put the post in, and then they'd get rocks and pack them into the hole around the post to keep it standing up strong. They didn't fill the soil back into the hole until after they'd put the stones and rocks in, so that these would squeeze the bark tightly and stop beetles and white ants getting in and eating those posts. That way the framework that was in the ground would stand firm and secure, the posts all in a row, stretching out straight over generations, a lasting structure for whatever branches and leaves people might lay over the top of that wurley in the future. That's how it was. The old people made the wurley strong to withstand the rain and the summer heat, so that it wouldn't break down, but would stay standing like that always, as a solid foundation.

Women's camp at Telegraph Station, Alice Springs, 1895, photographer F. Gillen, Baldwin Spencer Collection, courtesy Museum Victoria

In the same way, these words that I'm setting down will make a foundation like that wurley-house. *Angkentye, angkentye nhenhe-arle the mpwareme alakenhe lterrke anetyeke*, I'm building this foundation on strong language. We don't want to put down groundwork that's going to disappear, *angkentye arrernerle uyerrenhetyenhe-arle*. I'm building this foundation so that people will have *angkentye*, some of those solid words that was used before so that, like the strong posts, they will always be there. Foundation language. Together with all those other words that were spoken every day, those that people use in different ways; the words that just come and go, like the brush roof you put on that wurley. *Angkentye mwerre anthurre* people-*le itelaretyenhenge*, some good strong language for people to keep in their minds. *Angkentye arrwekele-arle angkentye lterrke ane angkentye lyete-arle angkerreme*, both the good strong language from the Story times, and everyday talk as well. In doing this I've got to *aratye anthurre ilerle*, I've got to speak honestly, I've got to be really true. That's the way I learned from my parents, and my parents learned from their parents, and their parents were learned by *their* parents. Because I don't want to tell my kids wrong stories, so that when they grow up they can be telling wrong stories. I want whoever reads this book to learn properly, and get more of understanding of the good things, the really true ones.

We All Feel the Same

I'm writing not only for my own kids, but for all Aboriginal kids, all Aboriginal peoples. If we see an Aboriginal people, all our culture is all the same. But also it's different in languages, other languages play a part in different ways, but really they're all the same. In hunting experience, talking experience. Singing is different in different languages, but it means still the same. And in understanding. But most of all, see an Aboriginal people, they *feel* the same as that person, and he probably feels the same as *that* person. Even though he's from another country or from another area. Every Aboriginal people, families, they still feel the same thing. Like in sadness, happiness, exciting things, and serious things. And we feel all that in the same way as those other people. And like meeting people from down there, we make sure they're still part of us.

We as Aboriginal people, we see ourself as like brothers and sisters, or aunties and uncles, you know. Like Aboriginal people from down south or anything, they call us "brother" or "sister", and we call them back "sister", because they're still part of us. Or aunties – they're not really our aunties but we still call them aunties. And also they still call other childrens their children, and other people from other countries they still call us, you know, by relationships. I see a lot of Aboriginal people and I say, "ay, well, *arelhe urrperle anwerne-arteke*, he's an Aboriginal person like us, but he just comes from a different area". He might be really fair, or he might be really dark, but we still call them Aboriginal people, just like myself.

It doesn't matter where I might be in Australia, I could see the sacredness in this or that Land, and all the sacredness in the members of that Land. I could feel it and I could see it, what is the sacredness in that Land to those people. No matter where they are, no matter where they're from. How they see it, and also how I see it to them, how I see it to myself, how I relate. I see what is really important to those people, in their own Land. And not only how they see it, but how they feel for it, how they guide it. Also their spirit of touch, sacredness, how they see it in that way. I relate through the people. That's how every Aboriginal people sees every Aboriginal people. Not only seeing, it's a touch. It's like a feeling-touch, that's how we know it. It's just like giving the goodness, seeing the goodness inside each other. Seeing it, feeling it, and really looking inside those people. What it means to them is also what it means to us.

We as Aboriginal people, we *always* relate to other people, connect with them, no matter who we are. If I see an Aboriginal person I wouldn't just say "oh, he's another language speaker, different from me". No, I'll always say "that person is one of us, he's part of us". And no matter who that person is I still relate in whatever they are, no matter where you're from, you know? Like, whether you come from the southern area, or the north area, or the eastern side, or from the west, Aboriginal people always got the similar way of doing things, saying things, and the way they act, and the way they relate, and how they're part of Land, and how they're part of people. All those people that hasn't got skin names or anything, they still have that connection, the same as the people who have got skin names. If they don't have skin names they still know what their relationship is, how they see it. That's how Aboriginal people are. And that's most important. Aboriginal people, we hold the Land, our Land is real sacred to us, and in that Land, for us, is something that only Aboriginal people can see. No matter who they are, people from anywhere, they can see what's in that Land, even if it's built, if the buildings been built on it. They know what has always been there, and it *is* always there. Because we have our own Landmark in us, and that's really special to us. The Land *is* us, and we *are* the Land.

Born to Be

Aknganeke-arle

Countries have got all names on it. Not given today, when non-Aboriginal people came, it was given in Traditional Creation Time. And that name has been remained centuries and centuries ago. Ancestors, as we know. The names are part of the Story for that Land. The names tells that Story, one part in this area, another part of it over there. *Alakenhe ikwerele-arle arrwekelenye mape anenheke* – Stories and names is how when the people in the Creation have lived. And shared.

We relate to people in our kinship, and we also relate to other Beings. 'Beings' is like, countries. Like from our country, we relate to those people in the next-door country, we've just got like a jigsaw puzzle or patchwork of Lands we relate to. How we got our Land, and how we relate to the next people on that other Land. We gotta call them by their skin name whose those groups are. And also that Land is related to us just like those people's skin names are.

Animals and other Species are in the kinship too. These come from our Land, and they're what our 'totem' is, as English calls it. And what those kids call that Species is by their grandfather, or their mother, or their father's father, or their mother's father. That's how we relate.

My father is related to the Rain, so we are related to the Rain. And our relationship is to *arrenge*, the father's father, because that's his totem, that's a Creation Name of his. He's the Rainmaker. And the End of the Rainmaker, *Akertarenye*. Only all my brothers could have talk about that, but not me. Brother-Stories and sister-Stories is different. I can tell stories to kids about who belongs where, but women can't talk about Species or any other details about Land. Some of my nephews, my brothers' sons, can talk about it. Because they are *ikwerenge-ntyele*, they are male-descended from my father, their *arrenge*. All I can say is that we are from that place. We are *Akertarenye*s, and that's only the name that I can use. I can't do any more explaining, because I'm a woman.

My parents got their own skin groups, and we've got different names from my parents'. And they got different skin names from us. Skin names are very sacred, they come from the Land itself. That's our traditional names. Before, people used to call us through our traditional name, which comes from the Land. Not like Sally, or Roslyn, Judy and Betty and May and Rosie and Polly – they were the popular station names of people, *alherntere-kenhe arrirtne*, white people's names. No, we were called names from *apmerenge-ntyele ware*. Our names came from our Land. And from that *apmere*, that *arrirtne*, it's always respect. The name for and from the Land, it's always held in respect by other people. Because it's a sacred name for those groups, and because some people are the guardians of that name. Like *Akemarre Akertarenye*. That's my proper traditional name. *Akemarre* is my skin name, and the Land, *Akerte*, is where my traditional site, where my grandfather's country is, where he originated from, like *aknganeke-arle*.

Aknganeke-arle means like what that name was really named. And also it's like where they're from. *Aknganeke-arle* means that he is really the traditional owner, he's the Ownership of that Land. And where his Traditional Stories came. It's like how the Creation *begun*, you know, *was*. My grandfather could call himself, or be called, *Akerte-arle Aknganeke*, 'that's where I was originated from'.

And people used to use your skin name like a second name. And all that's related to your Land, that's related to your waterhole, that's related to your trees, everything what's in that Land. And people will relate you to those things through that skin name. And it's really sacred, and really has reverence, you know, because it comes from your Land, and comes from your Story.

That's how people used to really *know* people from different countries, by their Story-names. And all the *Akertarenye*, other people used to know about them, they'll know the sons, and the daughters, and the grandsons, *Akertarenye mape*. And also the children of *Akertarenye*, like the daughters' kids, they'll say "*Akerte-arle atyakeke*, those ones call *Akerte* their mother's father". And they'll relate to them as that. If you tell 'em who your family is, as soon as they know, if they know the families, they know straightaway which country and which totem you belong to. Straightaway, *alakenhe*. And they relate to you in that particular way, from your father's father's Story, *alakenhe*. Your *aknganentye arrengenge-ntyele*.

Skin name is who you are, and where you're from, what is your country, what came out of your country and named himself and then became yourself. *Arrenge atyinhe aknganeke Kemarre. Kwatyeke artweye.* My father's father-Ancestor arose as a *Kemarre*, owning, originating, responsible for, and beholden to our part of the Rain Dreaming. Well, *arrenge atyinhe-kenhe aneke*, my grandfather had a son, and he's *Perrurle*. And *anwerne imerte aneme-arle akngeye atyinhe-kenhe, arrenge atyinhe-arteke* skin-*nge*. From my father, we kids turned out *Kemarre*, just like my grandfather. We didn't *anerle Perrurle*, we didn't become *Perrurle*, we became *rayateke* skin because *ikwerenhenge anpernirrentye*, my grandfather's kinship name was different to my dad's. So that's how my grandfather-Ancestor named himself, and that's how we became who we are.

Anpernirrentye-arle apmereyanhe anperneke iwenhe-apatherrenge. The kinship system relates to the Land by skin name. And *iwenhe-apatherre mape-kenhe apmereyanhe re*, by whatever the skin names are of those people from that Land. *Anyenhengenhenge angwenhe-kenhe apmere yanhe re.* Those people are whoever is the father-and-son cycle for that country, fathers and sons, those people. *Anyenhengenhenge* – father-son, father-son, grandfather, *arrenge, akngeye*, and *ampe ikwerenhe*, and their children, *ye*. *Anyenhengenhenge-arle apmere yanhenge arrateme.* The father-son cycle arises out of that Land. And the Traditional Beginning is how you call father's father, *alakenhe akngeyenge-arle rarle aknganeke*, he's the Beginning of the country, that *apmere*. And *aknganentye* is a name that means your totem, the Symbol for that Land. That name comes from *aknganeke*, and means 'Beginning Story'.

So that's that word, *aknganeke-arle*. *Aknganeke-arle* is for *apmere arrenge*, the country of your father's father, and how you arose and arise out of that country, with everything that's in it.

Angampeke-arle

There's another word too, called *angampeke-arle*. It's like, *ileme*, it tells how you yourself came to be, to grow, wherever you came from. *Angampeke-arle, nthenhenge-ntyele unte apetyeke. Ilerlenge iwenhe-arle unte aneke re*, it tells you how you were, right from the beginning; *iwenhe apmere yanhenge-arle arrateke*, tells how you emerged from your own country; and *angampeme-arle apmere ikwerenge*, how you continue to arise from that Land. That's how it is, it tells you where you're from, like where you really originated from; it tells about your group of people.

Angampeke-arle also tells the way that we all are as Aboriginal people: *Tyerrtye mape alakenhe akwele tyerrtye mapeke kele angampintyeke re akwele yanhe*, the way that it's really always been for Aboriginal people, from Creation onwards to right now. *Alakenhe-arle angampeke ane alakenhe-arle anintyeke tyerrtye mapeke ane tyerrtye mape-kenhe*. Just how it all arose and will always be for Aboriginal people. How it's always been *performed*. How it named ourselves and always will be. And how it grew. *Angampintyeke* is like, that's how the eyes of Aboriginal people saw us and it always will be that way, eternally. 'Cause it's not gonna end.

Just like *anpernirrentye*, the kinship system. *Anpernirrentye anwernekenhe alakenhe-arle anwerne anintyeke ane anenhetyenhe*, that's how our kinship-and-us-in-it always was and always will be. And also it tells you about *nthakenhe-nthakenhe-arle aneme*, what our living style is, how we live. That's what that word tells us – *angampintyeke-arle* – we became what we are and also who we are and where we're from. That's that name.

Angampeke – "what is what", and *angampintyeke* – "what will be". When we first came into existence, it takes us to where we are going to be. *Ye*, that's how it is. And there's a real big feeling that people can get back to that place, that original place, *in the future*. Like, *apmere nhenhe-arle angampintyeke* might be for how we are living to be in it, you know, how we are living to be in our own Land, on and on into the future.

And for us, *angampintyeke* for *apmere nhenhe-arle aknganeke mapeke* – for the ones who relate to the Land of our father's father, the Rain Dreamers – well, *kwatye-arenye mape, kwatyeke artweye mape-arle angampintyeke apmere nhenhe-arle*, that's how it will say: "The people of the Rainmaker, that's how they were originated for. To relate to this; this; and this; and to these people". And how we, not 'describe', but how we *relate to be*. That's what it really means. How everything came up together to *be*. How we need to see it, how we need to live with it, how we need to relate with it, and that's how we learn from it. That's that word.

Anwerne-arle angampintyeke arrirtne nhenhe ngkwarle nhenhe, merne nhenhe, we arose together with the proper names of things, like for different foods, the correct names. We didn't *angamperle* to put "hey, *ngkwarle-arle nhenhe*", we weren't born to call grog *'ngkwarle'*. That *ngkwarle* is really the label for something else, for sweet foods like honey. We didn't *angamperle* for that, it's a wrong way of doing it. *Iwerre apale-arle alhetyeke, ane iwerre apale-arle anetyeke, ane iwerre apale akaltye-irretyeke*, we didn't *alakenheke angampintyele*. We weren't born to go the wrong way, to live out our way wrongly, or to learn the wrong way, we weren't created for that. *Anwerne alakenheke angampetyakenhe-arle* or *alakenheke anwerne angketyakenhe*. How we say things is really important. We didn't arise out of the Land to speak the wrong way. *Angkeme*, talking and naming things, is part of how we arose, grew up to be. We weren't to be, or grown, for that sort of reason. *Angampeke-arle* relates to those sort of wrong ways and right ways. *Ye*, that's right *alere*, my nephew, its mean something like 'destiny', *ye*.

Angampeke is like if it tells you, "*unte-arle angampintyeke, arrenge ngkwinhenge-arle unte angampintyeke* to be *this*". *Angampeke* is like, born into it or add to it. Add to the Story. *Alakenhe*, "that's the way it is". You were created out of your Ancestral country to be who you are. And this is what you are. You gotta look at these sort of straight things. That's what it is. And you gotta relate to this, that's how the people held the Law very strongly in the Land. And keep the culture, and kept their living style, and kept their sharing style, and also looking at it, looking at it really in the distance – not today, not just there, but *looking in the distance*. *Alakenhe-arle, angampeke-arle yanhe-arle*. That's what *angampeke-arle* is all about.

Not only *lyete*, but *anintyeke-arle, angampe-arle-intyeke re alakenhe ikwere*.

Not only today or yesterday, but right out of Creation you're born to become just like that. You're born to be for that, and you come in to learn to be who you are, as that. It tells you, it's a whole lot of Stories: "Do I have to live like that?" Or, "I shouldn't live like that, because that is not right". You're born to be this, and this is how you should be. And you've got to really spread it out, you know, spread what you are to all those other people, and they spread their ways of living with you too. And the whole thing became a whole spread together, *arlkethe mpwarerle*. Like a big blanket, a patchwork of a living style. On one country-ground, or even when families from other countries join together. *Alakenhe*, it's like that. 'Cause you were born to be somebody special for all those other people.

Angampeke. Some people say *angampeke-arle* is for how you become, you became into this Land. Like *intintyeke itelaraye*, like how you became to be in existence on this Land, you know. That's another way of putting it. *Intintyeke*, means like you 'flew in'. *Unte intintyeke*, like if you shot out from your mums. *Intintyeke*, that's how it is, *intintyeke-arle*. "*Alakenheke-arle unte intintyeke*", they say that, *ye*.

Angampeke. Born to be. *Alakenhe ikwere-arle anwerne angampeke.* Just for that we were created into the Land. *Kereke unthetyeke alhetyeke, ampe arntarnte-aremele anetyeke*, husband *arntarnte-aretyeke*, wife *arntarnte-aretyeke*. And share-*eme-ilerretyeke*. *Alakenhe. Rlkertele aneme mape arrpenhe iwenhakweye-aretyeke…arntarnte-aretyeke. Alakenhe.*

To go hunting for animals, to care for our children, for husbands to care for their wives, and wives to care for their husbands. To share everything, and to look after the ones that are sick. These are just some of the things we were created for.

The First People are called *angampintyeke-arle*. And from them we know our Rule, what is the Rule we were made for, *anwernekenhe iwenheke anetyeke*: *Akangketyeke, wantetyeke, arntarnte-aretyeke, itelaretyeke, angkentye apale angketyale, angkentye akurne iletyale, ane itelaretyeke unte iwenhe-apatherre. Alakenhakweye* respect. *Ye.*

To be joyful and loving, to share our food, to guide and care for our loved ones, to understand, to speak only in the correct way to people, and to bear in mind always our kin relationship and obligations. That's respect. That's the way our Rule is now, and that's the way it's always been.

Trying to break away from your relationships as an Aboriginal person, to achieve something in a good job or something like that, well, you're that same person always, and you can never really change anything. And it wouldn't achieve. You might think it can achieve something for yourself, but it wouldn't. You'll always bend. And you wouldn't know where to start. Well, you might start, but there's no any further things will hold you.

So you'll still bend the rules back, but it's really hard to say "no" to your families. Unless you think you can sit up by yourself somewhere, *apwerte akertnenge anerle anyente anthurre*, sitting alone on the top of the hill, so that you don't want to be known by people. If you're that Aboriginal person from that Land, you can't be different, there's no way that you can change, not really change deep down. We can't bend it, we can't put things in it, we have to do it exactly in the way it was done before. Other people'll tell you, "you're not that person, you're this person, you belong to these people, and you're connected to these people, and you're *this*". If you're that person, you can't be different, there's no way that you can change. Unless you're a minister. Aboriginal people are part of every other Aboriginal person in a deep way, and with a deep recognition. There's a lot of people used to say things about many, many people, "but in the end they'll turn back". And many people *have* turned the wheel back, they have come back to be who they really are. *Angampeke-arle. Alakenhe.*

Utyerre

Apmereyanhe, our language-Land, is like a root or a tie to us. It holds all of us. The only way that we can translate into English how we see our relationship with the Land is with the words 'hold', and 'connect'. The roots of the country and its people are twined together. We are part of the Land. The Land *is* us, and we are the Land. That's how we hold our Land.

And it's really important for our kids to know why we want our Land to live on, to go back to. Because we've got a strong tie to it. It's like a big twirl of string that holds us in there with our families. That's where all our culture, and our names, our skin names come from. That's why we hold a big treasure of Land for us. And we have a special name for that tie or string, it's called *utyerre*.

Utyerre can be like, *utyerre-arle*, you might say, "*utyerrenge aweke*, I'm hearing a message from that line". And that *utyerre* means a telephone. And when he's hearing on the telephone, that person can see – in his mind he knows it – what that line runs, they can see it, where the message's coming from, like a string. And *utyerre* also is like a vein, a vein in yourself, and in your country. And how you relate. One time I was talking to this person here, and I was describing it: "It's like when we used to dig yam. When you dig for yam, you find a yam, it's like a bean in there. But also there's another string coming from it that lays further down, that's *utyerre*. And when you follow that *utyerre* you find another yam". So that's how we call *utyerre*. It's like those lines that go straight and connect to this, and connect to this, and connect to this.

I was talking to my little grandson down in the township one day. He said, "oh, who's that old lady come from?" And I said, "That's my cousin". "How come she's your cousin?" And I said to him, "Don't you say anything about that old lady. That old lady's *utyerre* runs from her to me to you". And he said, "How come?" "Because her father and my mother is brother and sister. So her bloodline, *utyerre*, runs into me, and runs into you".

And he looked really hard at her. "Am I really related to her?" His eyes were just about popping out! That's how you've gotta describe what's your relationship, and what *utyerre*'s all about. Like if you have *utyerre*, you have a bloodstream or bloodline or, what do you call it? A string of blood inside your body. But you don't have an empty vein running in there, you have blood running through you, 'cause it runs in there. So that's *utyerre*. *Utyerre*'s got that message, and also it's got a tie to it. *Because it keeps you alive.* So that's *utyerre*. *Utyerre* contains something running through it. It carries a message and also keeps you alive. It looks after and guides the family who you are connected to. Even your wayback grandchildren.

Utyerre has a message in it. You have to follow that back to where you really belong. A lot of people say, "*utyerre ngkwinhe apentirtnaye, nthenhenge-ntyele unte apetyeke*. You've gotta follow your *utyerre* back, because that's where you really originate from". Or "*utyerre ngkwengenge-ntyele-arle apetyeke-arle yanhe*". Or "*utyerre ngkwenge artweyenge-ntyele apetyeke*". Like that string comes from your father, or your parents. You gotta follow your straight line, where your string is, where your bloodline lays in the country. Like what country you're really tied to. What is really your connection. What line, what stream runs in from you to there.

Utyerre connects you, ties you back. That's how we say, "*utyerre intintyeme*", it 'lays'. *Intintyeme* is like if you see a 'plane, *laying* across the sky. Or when you see somebody is up on the other side of the river, and their reflection floats over. We say sometime it 'runs'. But *intintyeme*, I mean you can't lay across the Land, but that's how the meaning we see when we're talking about it, describing it. Like when you put down a line, and it lays across. That's how we say *intintyeme*. The string lays in the Land. A person's relationship lays, stretches out, where it lays to. But also it can stretch and stretch and stretch in all directions: "Well, I call this place this, and I call that place over there that, and I call that place over there this relationship". And it can also go on and on and on, down and around, with her children and grandchildren as well. And those people over in the other places will know straightaway, "that's how that line and that *utyerre* is to us. What those people are related to us is by this *utyerre*, where that string lays to us". You know when a person she talks about things "*atyemeye atyinhe-kenhe*", belonging to her *atyemeye*, her mother's father? Well another person'll know straightaway, 'cause her *utyerre* lays into that grandfather. And his connection is tying this other person to her. Or him to him. Or him to his grandchildren. *Utyerre anwernekenhe-arle apmere yanhele inteme*, that's how our country-lines stretch all around us. That grandfather is just like a big plant, a plant of a tree. When you grow a tree, you have lots and lots of roots. From those, other roots goes up and grows another plant. Then more roots, and so on. Well that's how it is to us, how we see it in Aboriginal eyes.

Father-and-son line, *anyenhengenhenge*, is also called *utyerre*. *Altyerrenge-arle aneke utyerre*: That's how the Traditional Story was created in each of them persons, through *utyerre*. And in the Land. And in the people. And "*apmere utnenge*" and "*utyerre anwernekenhe*", they say. Because our spirit and also our streamline runs in that Land. That's how people see it, and that's how we know it.

We can also say that the Land is our mother, when we talk about *apmereyanhe*, which is a bigger patch than just our father's father's homeland. It means like, we are created from that bigger patch of Land. Because my mother comes from there, my grandfather comes from there, *arrenge atyinhe*'s from there, all of them from that patchwork of Lands. And my mother especially. And that's how mother is our Land. It gave our mother birth, and also, she gave us birth. *Alakenhe*: The Land is our mother. Skin name stays in there, with that, for the Land to be known by. That Land is this skin name because it's a mother, and we relate from that skin name for that Land.

Anpernirrentye, the kinship system, became a person, *ye*. Well, a person, that person, *anpernirrentye*, that *anpernirrentye*-person, it's from that *apmere*. Because that Land is the name of that person. *Kemarre ahelhe*, that country-ground, means a *Kemarre* person. Both ways. *Antirrkwerreme*, like you know, holding one another, Land and person. *Anwerne antirrkwerreme-arle apmere nhenhe atnyenetyeke*. And we connect with each other to hold the country. The country is us.

"Let's hold each other, and be with this country". Like if a tree gets pulled out, "let's *antirrkwerrerle arne nhenhe atnyenetyeke*, let's be as one to support this tree; *antirrkwerreme-arle*, to hold one another to hold this place". As if you're an anchor on that, and you anchor yourself with that person, and that person sits on it and holds it down, something like that. Dreams and stories and trees and songs and animals and ceremonies, all holds in that one big patch, that *apmereyanhe*, just in that one big country-ground it holds the whole pile. And *utyerre* holds all those people together to do all those things, to make all those things, to get all those things, and to make it happen, and to keep it happening, so it just goes on and on and on.

The Land next to you is a relationship through *utyerre*. Two homelands next door to each other are like two living things laying, one on this side, one on that side. We're on this side, they're on that side. And the bloodline between them, *utyerre*, you know, *apmere utyerre intetyakerleme*, it ties them together in one spirit. The spirit of each country goes deep into the ground and joins up with the spirits of all those other countries in *apmereyanhe* to make one big root down there. Aboriginal people knew that for ever since, and they grow up with that, and they learn for that, *angampeme*. It all grew up together, *aknganeke*.

People really cry for it if they see a tree chopped down. It breaks their heart – *mape-arle angkeme* "ay, *Arne Akngerrepate atnyene-arle*, it's part of us". They cry bitterly when they see one of their own Ancestor Trees that's been fallen. And they *iwenhakweye ilerle*, they make a protest and they ring up and complain. "That's just an old tree", the whitefeller might say, because he doesn't really know what it is. Now today we've got rights to stop what tree they can chop off, what tree is not there, you know? There's a bit more of understanding now, from people *lyete*.

But still only a bit. These words were things we never used to fully describe to the professional people when we had Land claims. Our people thought that it's not really necessary for an anthropologist or somebody to know about. Because they weren't asked about it. "Why are you really wanting to have this country?" People might say, "well, this is my father's country, and my grandfather's country, and I'm *apmereke artweye*, the traditional owner". But there's no any other further questions.

You've gotta talk, and really analyse words like *utyerre* or *angampeke-arle* to really get a full meaning of it. You've gotta analyse it. You cannot say anything without doing that. You gotta describe it, what it means, how it is, and why. All those words you gotta put in it. Like if you're going out and, "oh, I'm gonna go and put a bore down there", well, you gotta go and see where the bore's gonna be. Which is the right spot. You gotta bring those equipments around, and work out how you gonna bring it over, connect them together. Well that's how it's like explaining *utyerre*, you've gotta connect all those words to become that what it is. And that's how many, many things we as Aboriginal people have never described. Because it's really hard to describe to others the picture that we've got in our head. If they can't see that good picture, then there's no answer. Sometimes non-Aboriginal people go away with no answer then, and we're left with no answer as well.

people live out at Harts Range, *yanhe mape*. *Apmereyanhe-arenye mape ingkerreke anthurre*, those are all people living on their homelands inside that *apmereyanhe*, and they all speak the same language, but they look after their own boundaries. Also, each one's got their own totems, their own *aknganentye* – different totems, you know, from the Rain, which is ours, *anwerne kwatyeke artweye*. Those other mob, *arrpenhe mape* might be some other things they might *itnekenhe anerle. Itnekenhe aknganentye*. Different totems they have, and we still all speak the same language. *Alakenhe*.

Ilakakeye

You're related in a special close way to the countries and the people inside *apmereyanhe*, even though they're other totems. That's really our own *anpernirrentye mape*, our 'private' kinship circle. These people's countries are related to us just like the people's skin names are, and also the countries relate to each other, just like people do.

Apmereyanhe-arenye mape, they are other Dreamings for them, other Species of Creation, but we're all same-language speakers. And we relate to them as mother's

---

Land and Women Together, 2002, acrylic on canvas, photographer Barry McDonald
"This is how women's Stories are told. These blocks of Land are six countries in my *apmereyanhe*, and this is how the Sacred Stories are told. These six countries are joined as well. The symbols are the Stories for each group and country; Fly (*amenge*), Ant (*yerre*), Euro (*arenge*), Emu (*ankerre*), Mistletoe (*ingkwerrpme*), and Fuchsia (*atnyerlenge*). The six women at the bottom of the painting are from four different skin groups. At the top sit six women from the four remaining skin groups. Next to the women are the tools that they use to grind pigments for their painting. The story that I'm telling here, this is my own story".

fathers or mother's mothers, or uncles, those sort of relationships we have, from our own mothers and from our husbands and wives.

In *apmereyanhe anwernekenhe*, we have two groups of skin names which describes us one from another, describes our father's side from our mother's and uncle's side, or from our husband's or wife's side. And there are four skin names in each group. We call the other-side group a special name which I don't want to say here, and they call us that same name when they're talking about our side. And we can also call ourselves "*ilakakeye*", and they call themselves "*ilakakeye*" too. *Akeye*, you know, is how you call somebody, what relationship you call them. *Ilakakeye* means you call yourselves "*ilake*"; like father and son, *anyenhenge*. People say "*ilake*" for 'us two' when they talk. Father says "*ilake*", and son also says "*ilake*" when he talks about himself and his dad. Father and daughter can also say "*ilake*". *Anwakerrakeye* means 'us mob on this side'; same thing, but more than just two people talking.

My father's *Perrurle*, and our Land is *Perrurle/Kemarre* skin. That's *anyenhenge*, the father's and the son's skin names put together to call that homeland. My father and all my brothers. Every homeland has *anyenhenge*, only they are called by different skin names. So there's *Perrurle/Kemarre anyenhenge*, and there's also some homelands called *Ampetyane/Angale anyenhenge*. Some are *Penangke/Pengarte anyenhenge*, and other Lands are *Peltharre/Kngwarraye anyenhenge*. And that's father/son skin in each Land, *alakenhe*, four different sorts of *anyenhenge*.

Inside our *apmereyanhe* we have two groups of homelands. Our *ilakakeye* side has *Angale/Ampetyane*, and *Kemarre/Perrurle* Lands in it. And the other side, that special-name side from me and my brothers, it has the *Kngwarraye/Peltharre*, and *Pengarte/Penangke* countries. So I call those *Perrurle*, and *Kemarre*, and *Angale*, and *Ampetyane* people on our side "*ilakakeye*" or "*anwakerrakeye*". And the *Peltharre*, *Kngwarraye*, *Pengarte*, and *Penangke* people on the other side in our *apmereyanhe* I call that special name. And they call each other "*ilakakeye*" or "*anwakerrakeye*", and they call us that special name too.

The Two *Arrernte* Landowning Skin Groups in *Apmereyanhe*

Mrs Turner's Landowning group

Perrurle/Kemarre anyenhenge
Angale/Ampetyane anyenhenge

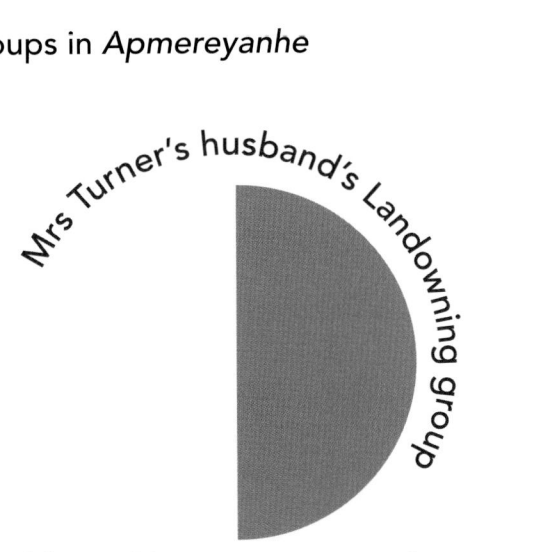

Mrs Turner's husband's Landowning group

Peltharre/Kngwarraye anyenhenge
Pengarte/Penangke anyenhenge

These two skin groups of countries, and all the people in them, they help to look after each other's Lands inside their *apmereyanhe*, and they help with other things too. One side helps the other side, both ways. Like the other side are the people who can talk about any sacred and punishment things for us, and also when there's death in the family. We've gotta get the right people to do the right sort of things. We can't do things just only us, and they can't do things just only them. They've always gotta have the opposite-side country skin groups to do jobs like singing songs, or decorations, things like that. And getting the right people together. It's the right thing for them mob to do the jobs for us, and for us to do the jobs for them.

Country Marriage

Arrwekelenye aneke apmere kantreye itweke-itwe, apmere itwekele aneme mape antirrkweme ante anpernirrentye ingkerreke-akerte. Alakenhe arrwekelenye mape arratye anewe-akerreke. One time, during history time, all people lived in these next-door country groups, and all their skins were bound closely together, the Land with the people. And that's how proper marriage was done, through skin groups in that Land.

The marriage, the two people who married inside that *apmereyanhe*, they marry from the strong of that Land, they marry through the flesh of that skin group, and also through *utnenge*, the flesh of that Land. That's country marriage.

Apmereke artweye atherre anewe-akerreme apmere kantreyenge ane utnenge apmere-kenhele ratherre antirrkweme ane ampe itnekenhe antirrkwintyetyenhe. Alakenhe-arle apmereke artweyele arintyeke. Alakenhe-arle anpernirrentyele antirrkweme.

When elders and other people see those two marry through their own country, they know that the children that will come from that marriage will always be strong in that Land, will always look after the Land, will be the best leaders of that country. The flesh of that country goes into those people for generations. That's how people have always looked on it, and that's how kinship holds, that's how those eight skin groups will always hold.

To hold the Land like this is in those right people, the right people in that Land that's supposed to get married. And who do they marry into? Well, they marry into the people who live next door to them, they're the people, the ones they call "*anpernirrentye mape*". *Anpernirrentye mape* are all those people who live inside *apmereyanhe*. *Apmere mape aneme anpernirrentye*, these are the kinship group, and those people gotta marry in that big dialogue thing, you know, around them. This, this, this, this, and in here. They run in the channels of those people, and they've gotta marry one another, and that's how people keep their culture really strong and keep their family really strong. Because that's how it was. Never and never used to go across on the other language side to marry, because you can't marry a wrong language speaker from that way-over-there side. All northern *Arrernte* people used to marry northern *Arrernte* people. All *Ikngerrekwiperre mape* married *Ikngerrekwiperre mape*. All *Warlpiri* people used to marry *Warlpiri*. *Pitjantjatjara*s. You name it, everywhere. Probably Top Enders married other Top Enders, because then they can have their own culture, they can have their own Law, they can have their own skin groups.

Alewanthe,
Penangke/Pengarte

Rltewepangke,
Kngwarraye/Peltharre

Arunthenatye,
Angale/
Ampetyane

Irlpalkerunthe,
Perrurle/Kemarre

Ureyelwenhe,
Kngwarraye/Peltharre

Awelhapmere,
Angale/Ampetyane

Anewelarle,
Perrurle/Kemarre

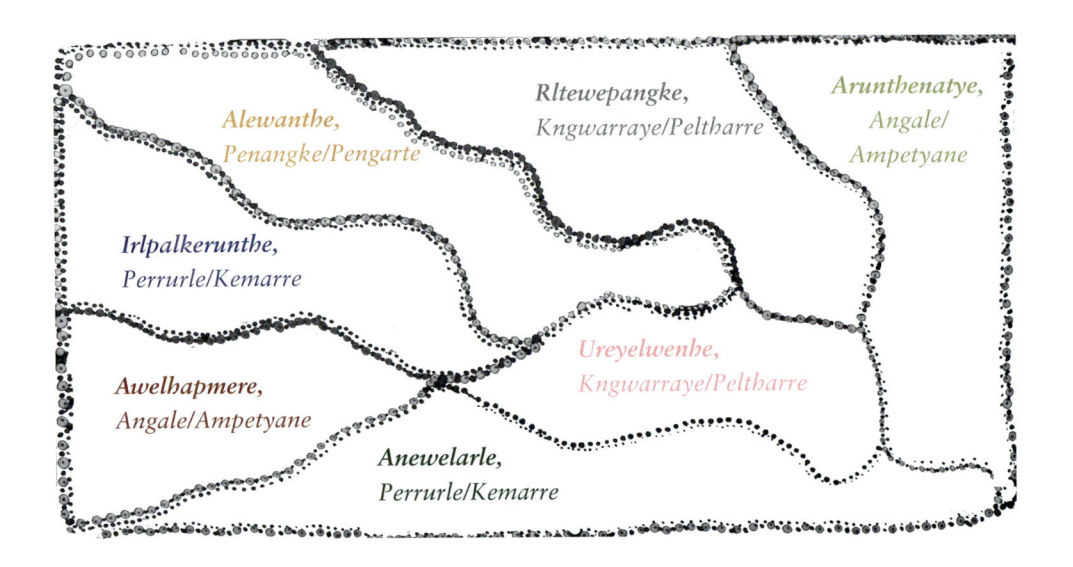

I'll talk about marriage in one *apmereyanhe*. Well, *apmereyanhe mape*, they was from seven homelands, there was seven homelands in that *apmereyanhe*. There was people from *Awelhapmere*, they're *Angale/Ampetyane anyenhenge*; there was people from *Irlpalkerunthe*, that's *Perrurle/Kemarre anyenhenge*; then there was *Penangke/Pengarte-anyenhenge* people from *Apmere Alewanthe*; and there was people from *Rltewepangke*, the *Kngwarraye/Peltharre anyenhenge* mob. And there was also the *Angale/Ampetyane* people of *Apmere Arunthenatye*; also *Kngwarraye/Peltharre*s from *Ureyelwenhe*; and the *anyenhenge* from *Anewelarle* was another *Perrurle/Kemarre* country-mob. Well, that's all the people and countries *apmereyanhe-arenye mape*.
It's all connected in that. Well, only those people could marry into each other. The *Ureyelwenhe mape* would choose from only those families outside *Ureyelwenhe*, but still inside their own *apmereyanhe* boundary. They can marry from any of those families. *Anpernirrentye. Apmere kantreye anyente-arenye, itne-arle arrenge-akeke, atyakeke, ipmenhe-akeke, aperle-akeke.* Because it's really one country-group, and the homelands relate to each other as grandparents, all the four grandparents for everybody are there. But the marriage skins should match up, right skin with right skin.

Relationship of Land   Country Marriage

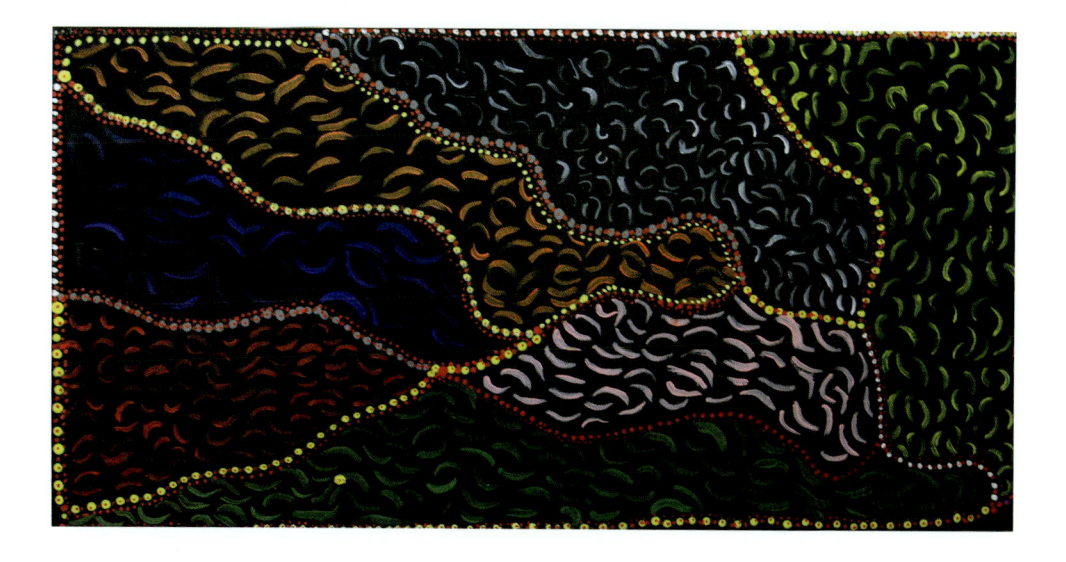

So in all those countries in that group, well, *Irlpalkerunthe-arenye mape*, those *Kemarre mape*, will marry a *Peltharre* from *Ureyelwenhe*. And *Kngwarraye Ureyelwenhe-arenye* can marry an *Angale* from *Arunthenatye*. And *Ampetyane Awelhapmere-arenye* would marry *Pengarte* from *Alewanthe, alakenhe*. *Peltharre Rltewepangke-arenye* can also marry a *Kemarre Irlpalkerunthe-arenye*, and a *Perrurle* from *Anewelarle* will marry a *Penangke* from *Alewanthe*. And so on it goes, *alakenhe*.

People used to marry outside their own homeland because there's other countries everywhere inside that *apmereyanhe* that's got all those right-marriage skin names. It always works out equal for everybody, for *Pengarte, Kemarre, Ampetyane, Kngwarraye, Angale, Perrurle, Penangke, Peltharre*. They're all in that, 'cause it's come out from those countries. In that *apmereyanhe* dialogue area, there's always connection-marriage. *Alakenhe*.

Leading With The Channel, 2002, acrylic on canvas, photographer Jason Gibson
This painting shows seven countries in *apmereyanhe* joined and bounded by *utyerre* and creeks. "The creeks separate us, but they join us also. We live together, the streamlines of the valley are all connected. We say 'northern', 'central', 'southern', but really we're all connected. The bend in the creek tells us where we live. The circles tell us who we are. The flow of the channel is the connection".

It's always the children of first cousins who have to marry. First-cousin people. Well, if you're a woman, and your aunt – your father's sister – had a daughter, then she's your cousin. That aunt came from your own homeland, but she married a man from a next-door country. And daughter *yanhe*, that daughter from them might herself have a boy or a girl, next-door country *kine-arenye*. And you might have a boy or a girl of your own. Well, those two kids married, yours and hers.

Cousins are me and my father's sisters' children, or me and my mother's brothers' kids. Those are cousins, that's some of the cousin-ways. We can't say "cousin", like non-Aboriginal people do, to *meye ngkwinhe-kenhe ampe mape*, your mother's sisters' children – they're your brothers and sisters, because all our mother's sisters are our mothers too. The same thing goes for your father's brothers' children, they're also your sisters and brothers, because your father's brothers are really your fathers.

Ankelenhenge atherre-kenhe, or *altyelenhenge atherre-kenhe* are the children of cousins. It doesn't matter whether they're men cousins or women cousins, their kids can marry. And that's a real proper system in *anpernirrentye*. That's how you follow the skin system, and that's how people in every *apmereyanhe*, in every *anpernirrentye* used to follow their skin system and kept all those kids, and all those young fellers, and all those men and all those women together. And their kids will always follow that, always. And then the Land is healthy, and the people are healthy, and the life is healthy, *alakenhe*. That's how *alakenhe irreke* people *arrwekelenye mape anenheke*, how they always did it before. *Alakenheke itnenge*. That's just what it was like with them:

Akaltye-irrenheke, constantly learning;
arintyeke, seeing it as forever ongoing;
imernenheke, being shown continuously.
That's how it was.
That's how it was *and is*.

Alakenhe, ye. So people used to just marry in their own area. *Apmere itweke-itwe anewe-akertele aneme, altyelenhenge, ankelenhenge,* people married their next-door neighbours, the children of first-cousin lines getting together. Kids of cousins like *Kemarre* and *Pengarte.* We're from *Perrurle/Kemarre* country, and my brother's kids'll be *Perrurle*s. And there'll be another place nearby, our cousins' *Pengarte* country might be next door. The kids from that place will be *Penangke*s. Well, my brother's daughter will marry one of them. And when they have kids, they'll have *Pengarte*s. And those *Pengarte*s'll marry another next-door neighbour, from *Ampetyane* country *apeke*. There is always a marriage between all those countries inside *apmereyanhe*, from that same patch of Land. That's true marriage, the right way, country-married. Flesh-and-blood-country-marriage.

In that *anpernirrentye*, you can have three marriage choices. First choice is always with the right skin name from the other-side Land-owning group, *alakenhe*. But three choices gotta be in your own line, you never cross that *nyurrpe* line. I'll talk more about *nyurrpe* when we get to describing other ways of kinship. For *nyurrpe* things, we have a *different* two sides of skin name, different to the two groups in *ilakakeye*. Well, you can't cross over that *nyurrpe* line because those four skin-people on that other side, it's not you. They are your parents. That's run in your parents' bloodline. *Nyurrpe arrpenhe* and *nyurrpe arrpatye* – two separate lines, *alakenhe*. And the four on your side are in your grandparents' names-line, and that's the names-line you can marry into. That's in your *arrenge*'s, your father's father's name-line, that's in *ipmenhe*'s, your mother's mother's name-line, that's in your mother's father's *atyemeye*-name-line, and it's also in your *aperle*'s name-line, your father's mother's name-line which is also the same as your proper wife's name-line.

So a *Kemarre* really should marry a *Peltharre*, which is first-choice, or *Kemarre* can marry *Ampetyane*, or even *Pengarte*. I know one young couple who both came from my area, and who got married and now have kids of their own. He's a *Kemarre* and she's *Ampetyane*. Just second-choice, but it's in the same country. And they're still the children of cousins, because his father's a *Perrurle* and her mother's *Kngwarraye*, *arrwempenhenge atherre*. Which is the right way to get married, because they come from the same great-grandparents, which is the Law. The way you say it is *unte iwenhe unte angampintyeke alakenheke. Alakenhe anpernetyeke, ante alakenhe aretyeke*. Just that is what you were born for. In just that way you have to relate. And just like that is how you have to see it.

Marriage between the Two *Arrernte* Landowning Groups in *Apmereyanhe*

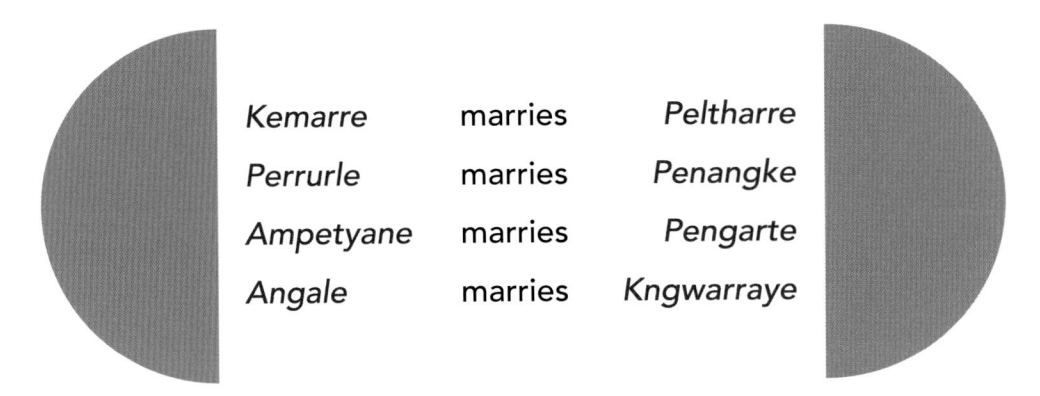

Kemarre	marries	*Peltharre*
Perrurle	marries	*Penangke*
Ampetyane	marries	*Pengarte*
Angale	marries	*Kngwarraye*

Lyete-arle aneme anwerne anpernirrentye anwernekenhe akwete itelaremele. Anwerne arrpenhe nyurrpe ane arrpenhe nyurrpe; nyurrpeke-nyurrpe. Alakenhe-arle the itelareme. Today we still know our kinship system strongly. And we know about the two skin group moieties that holds everybody in our society. That's the way I recognise it. And even though life has really changed for me in recent times, I've still got good strong culture, and I believe in my skin group, what my skin group is, what my children's skin group is, and what my grandchildren's skin group is. I follow that very strongly, and that's how it is for every Aboriginal people, and that is the proper way of relating. Even though things have changed, and even though you might have married into the wrong skin group, your own skin name will never change, and your children will always be this or that skin name. That's how Aboriginal people are very strong, and have that strong skin group in them. Most important is that you can always ask who you are: "What is my grandmother's skin name?" And "what is my grandfather's skin name?" You can ask all your families what that is, and that's not shame, and then after that you can talk on the behalf of your own countries. And children when they grow up, they always have their own skin names, and they will always have their country-names. In the old days, people married other people from just the countries close around them. But today is different, because there's a lot of different people marrying into each other's cultures. So there are now a lot of different cultures and languages in our skin groups. But I still keep my skin group very strong in my way for my grandchildren and my children. And that's very important for every family to hold.

Apmereke Artweye and *Kwertengwerle*, Landowners and Land-guiders

When people talk about owning Land, they mean that they belong to Land that they get from their Ancestors. *Apmere arrekakerrenhe* – yours and your father's Land, and that word also tells about your grandfather, your father's father. That's what 'owning' and 'own country' means. Another name you can call it is 'homeland'. And *apmereke artweye* means those people who can speak for that homeland – father, grandfather and children, you know, *anwakerrakeye mape*, those on their own side of the fence. But we Landowners also have relationship in those other countries as well, next door or across the way a bit from us in our *apmereyanhe*. You know, with those other-side Land-owning mob, the ones in the opposite line to *anwakerrakeye*. We relate to them as mothers' fathers, or grandmothers, or uncles, or cousins. From our parents and our joint parents. 'Joint parents' is all those people next door, through us. For as we know, people *apmereke artweye mape* just only owns the Land where their fathers' fathers are from.

And when you're *apmereke artweye*, if you're a Landowner, if any totem Species goes from next-door people through your *apmere* to another country – across the boundary line and stops in another homeland – well, you cannot follow that and make that into your relationship. You are just part of that other Land, you're just part of those families, you're not the owner. But you can help guide them.

One skin group holds the Land alright, they are the owners of the Land, *apmereke artweye mape*. That's on my father's side, that's *Perrurle mape*. But what about my mum's family, where do they fit in? You know, *Penangke mape*, where do they fit into all us *Kemarre*s, *Kemarre* kids, the ones who have the Land from Dad? You've gotta have two lots of families, all the time. And then there's all the *Peltharre*, my husband's mob. How do they fit? And where's *Kngwarraye*'s family, coming out of my children? Where are they, where's all the *Ampetyane*, my grandkids? Well, *those* kids gotta come out! Because there's no such a thing as a country with only one or two skin groups, like how the *anyenhenge* name says it, 'cause they got all different groups coming out from those two people who got married. And those mothers and those wives and children got to relate to what that Land is to them, and to their grandchildren and their great-grandchildren.

Sometimes the wife goes to live on the husband's country, sometimes the husband goes to the wife's country. It follows. Either way they follow one another. To Lands next door to each other, or across the way. 'Cause you've got father's Land and mother's Land as well, then you're in with those mothers' group too, with mother's Land she got from her father. There's those four grandparents, *ye*, in every *apmereyanhe*. *Anpernirrentye nhenhe mape ingkerreke-arle ante arntarnte-areme, apmere nhenhe mape-kenhe*. And you're related to the families of three of those grandparents in *guideness*, in a guiding sort of a way. You're related to their birds and their fires, whatever is there. Hunting patch where the water lays. You're related, but you can't talk for those Lands, those other totems, you can just *guide* the Lands of those other three grandparents. You're the owner of just your own Land which you get from your father's father.

I want to make it clear that it's only the women I'm speaking about here, I can't talk about the men's side, only my brothers or nephews can do that.

'Talking for Land' means like if you're talking on the behalf of your parents, or really your father's father. That sort of talking is like, "well, this is my country, this is my grandfather's country, that's how I fit into this Land. And that country holds everything that belongs to us. And I can talk about it because I'm this person, I'm related to my father's father". They might talk to anthropologists like that, they might talk to people in Land Council, they might talk to a lawyer. So that those people can see what that person's

Relationship of Land   *Apmereke Artweye* and *Kwertengwerle*, Landowners and Land-guiders

utyerre is to that place. But before the time that the *alherntere mape*, the white people came, elders and groups knew who all those owners were. Aboriginal people knew who those people are to talk on the behalf of what that ground is to them.

The Land must have people through whom it can talk. It's like a person, talking for Land, it's like when you relate to a person. As we see it in our own eyes and how we feel, it's just like a live thing when we talk about it.

And when you go to see people, if you've gotta talk to people about their own country, they don't say "well all right, we are the owners of the country". No, they say "but where's all the managers? You gotta talk to the managers too". That's how we look at it. "Who guides this place? We own it. Who looks after it, who does the guiding of it?" It's just like having a manager. If you're an owner, you always have a manager to run everything. To run the bores, to run the fence, and run the cattle, and where the cattle are put, where they're moved around for the feed.

So this is where the mothers and the wives fit into their children's and husbands' Land, or where the husbands fit into their wives' Land. Because if you have a Land, you can't have only owners, *apmereke artweye mape*. There's a Land-guider there too, which is called a *kwertengwerle*. And those Land-guiders will be the owners' uncles – their mother's brothers – or they'll be their mothers, and also their cousins. Mainly the cousins of my father, they are our own guiders. My father is *Perrurle*, so our guiders are all the *Kngwarraye mape*, his mother's brothers' sons, and the *Peltharre*s too, his mother's brothers. His uncles and his cousins look after us, the ones from the next-door *Peltharre/Kngwarraye* homeland. That's how it is in women's way too, that's how us women look at it. They're *kwertengwerle*s for us, and we're *kwertengwerle*s for them.

Apmereke artweye can talk for the Land, and they also know who can witness for them, who are their Land-guiders. *Apmereke artweye* and *kwertengwerle*s. Talkers and witnesses. Owners and managers. We as owners, we gotta have somebody to manage it, so this one manages it. Not by going 'round, "we gotta do this and that", but just through a Stories-manage. Manage by the Stories. Like, "they sing their song, well let's see what tune they sing". Something like that. *Alakenhe*. On woman's side – I'm talking only woman's side here – well, those women have the song for these women here, those women know the song also. Well, they're *kwertengwerle*s from that place there, all the girls from there. And they do all the paintings, they do the symbols on these ones. And the same skin names, their children've got the same skin names as these ones here, like the *kwertengwerle*s, they paint their mums and aunts, *ye*. Mother *mape-arle-areye*, and *ampe anwernekenhe mape-arle*, mothers and kids, 'cause they're *kwertengwerle*s for each other. *Kwertengwerle* next-door-*arenye mape*. They can join in with our kids who've got the same skin names, they can join in and do the women's work. Like *Perrurle mape ane Kngwarraye mape*. They can work together, *kwertengwerle mape*, *ye*. *Anwerne altyelenhenge intelhe-ileme itne altyelenhengele. Alakenhe.* That's how they paint the designs, our children will be paired up with their cousins to paint the designs on us, cousins will paint cousins. *Altyelenhenge mape, altyelenhenge-arle kwertengwerlele-arle mpwaretyeke. Irlterle-arelhetyeke, arntengenhenge mape. Arntengenhenge, ye.* Sister-in-laws will be in cousin-pairs too, same thing, and their children will be in cousin-pairs, and so on. Or *arntengenhenge ipmenhenhenge*, they'll be granny-type skin, and also cousins too. And they'll do it, like *nyurrpeke-nyurrpe-arle*. That's how we all do it, *ye*.

    They're the guiders, we sing it and they sing it too, when they're doing the symbols. We can't do it on our own. *Arethape-arteke mape. Arethape mape.* That's how *itne-arle angkerretyarte* to describe it. How the old people discussed it, as if the owners are like a tiny helpless newborn baby, and can't do anything for themselves. So *apmereke artweye* and *kwertengwerle*s sing the songs together. The owners of the song sing it, and they are joined by the other family groups. That way all the skin groups are singing all the songs. But those guiders are also *apmereke artweye* for their own Land, and they've got us mob, or their *kwertengwerle*s from the Land over on the other side from them to help them with their work.

    And all that's what's in that marriage between two people from countries next door. Cousins are *kwertengwerle*s for each other, and their children are the right ones to get married to each other. 'Cause then they learn, and they know the richness, and they know the strong what is comes around.

The Generations

Kartweye-kartweye-kartweye

I'll tell you another thing marriage does for people and for Land. Well, if there's two people married in the right way, in a right relationship with the people who are in the same area, then that marriage grows people. It grows families, it grows generations like their great-grandmothers, like their great-great-grandfathers. They can have all their grandparents, their great-grandparents, from the same country. And that's how all those children from the marriage will get their name called you know, in the image of their great-great-grandparents.

Apmere kantreye anyente-arenye mape ampe marreyete-irremele, ane ampe itnekenhe arrateme layake grandparents *mape-arteke-anteye. Arrenge ikwere-arteke, ipmenhe ikwere-arteke, atyemeye ikwere-arteke, aperle ikwere-arteke, meye ikwere-arteke.*

This keeps the country going. You can't have just old people still living there without no children or no other generations. That's how traditional country marriage is most important. 'Cause those kids' names'll be called after that couple's grandparents, their own great-grandparents. And it just grows up like from a bottom branch to the top. And all those branches are all called names after all those great-grandparents, or the grandparents, or their fathers, or their mothers.

That's the Law that the old people had, and that's why people will not really want to move out of their own country, and if they can, will stay living in that country and grow their own children up. So they can have proper marriage, proper relationship. They can learn about Land, what Land is to them, for them, and what Land *is*. They can know who they are, what their skin name is and how they're related to the Land. Like the parents, you know? And that's the most important thing that our Aboriginal kids, *ampe tyerrtye mape akaltye-irretyeke,* can learn about.

Because there's not many people learning about it now, you gotta tell them about things, you know, kids. I was brought up in a different way, on a station where there's old people there all the time. Now I've gotta teach my own grandchildren who they are, how to relate, talk to them every day, tell them about it. If I don't teach them now, they won't learn when they get their own children. Or when they're grandparents themselves. I always tell my grandchildren about marriage. And my kids. Young mothers. I talk to them about who is the right person, about their own proper ways.

Some non-Aboriginal people might say "this is just an old worn-out country". But as Aboriginal people, we see the Land as *areme apmere anwernekenhe prape apmere anwerne-arteke renhe-arle* relate-*irreme*. It is so close to us, and it relates and is related like all of us are. Because our grandfather-Ancestor is the leader of that country, and our Land is part of him, and we're part of him too. It holds us all. So Land is beautiful to us, and that's why a lot of people like going back and having funerals in their own homeland, because he knows that he's going back to rest in that place where he belongs.

People have always gone back home to pass away. Then that soil makes maybe two more people the same as the one that died. *Apmerele aherne irrare-werne akngirtneme apmerele utnenge athenetyeke.* The Land takes the spirit back to its own cemetery to lay it down to rest, so that the spirit can look after the place and the people who come from there. Because our Land holds the roots and veins which tie us in. That's how we Aboriginal people all know and understand together. *Anwernekenhe alkngenge-ularre.* That's how it is through our eyes.

Your country is your country, that *apmere* is *arrantherre* – it *is* you mob. And because that place is part of you and yourself and the rest of the family, then generation *ingkerrekele-arle antirrkweme*, all the generations hold each other. Like *itnekenge alakenhe angkeme*, "*kartweye-kartweye-kartweye*", people refer to that as 'generation to generation to generation', *alakenhe. Kartweye-kartweye-kartweye* means relationship to relationship, or really, 'round and 'round, as the generations go 'round. Your own Land-Rule comes from your *arrenge* and *akngeye*, grandfather, father, and yourself. All those generations have the one Law from that country. That's how Aboriginal people see it when they know who they are; what their skin name is, what is their father's

The Generations   Kartweye-kartweye-kartweye

skin name, and what is the *arrenge*'s skin name, and what is *arrenge*'s father's skin name. That's why we say "*kartweye-kartweye-kartweye*".

Anpernirrentye...relationship.
Rlterrke...strong.
Always...*akwetethe*.
Anintyeke...always been.

When we're on our own country, we feel really at home. Not only at home, but we really relate to the place itself, to the country. Because the country is part of us, part of the generations, *kartweye-kartweye-kartweye*. We feel so happy, we can do things, we can sit outside, we can listen to the birds, we can listen to our kids running around. We can have inner peace in our own Land.

Aboriginal people don't worry about themselves as one person on their own, *iknge. Anwerne arelhe tyerrtye urrperlele areme*, we see that we're not just the one person. *Anwerne aneme tyerrtye atherrame-kenhe*. We come from the spirit of our mother and father, and that spirit, *tyerrtye atherrame*, has got a lot of connection. We know that we've got two people in us, in ourselves really. And from that two people, it's just like a big root of a tree comes out. That's how we see it. That's why we don't really think about just ourselves. Also, if we're gonna be thinking just of ourselves, you might as well go and live up on the hill, or live somewhere in the never-never where nobody will know you, or see you. 'Cause that's not the way that *arelhe urrperle* is. *Anwerne rarle* people *atherrame-kenhe-arle, tyerrtye atherrame-kenhe, utnenge atherrame-kenhe*. We're born of the spirit of two people, and they themselves came out from the spirits of two different countries, *ahelhe yanhenge arrateke*. And it's not only one person who came to it from each of those places either. Two parents and also four grandparents and eight great-grandparents and so on and on and on.

An Aboriginal person is always a part of a team, is held by that team, that group. This goes right back into *apmere ahelhe-werle* like *angkweye-angkweye-angkweye*, right back into the Land, like how the little ant lion goes. An Aboriginal person knows this because they have seen it from the day they were born, and they knew the Story even *before* they were born. *Itne-arle itelareke urreke-arle intetyenhenge* means they knew it before he was existent. My family knew what my brothers and sisters will be holding before they were born. In teaching, cultural, hunting, discipline, how it was held. The discipline comes from the heart and from the Land. They held it in that journey, and now we hold it in the journey *ingkernenye mapeke*, for those following after us. *Ingkernenye mape* means the kids who come after, the grandchildren, the new generations. These young kids of today, and their kids, and further on.

It just came out so many roots in that ground, *apmerenge*. So we don't really put ourselves just, "today I'm just going to be myself", or "next year I'm going to be myself". There is no such a thing as 'myself' for *urrperle mape*, because we are so connected to one another. Because we are so close to one another. To our Beings – what comes from our Creation, what comes from our Land, what animals, hills, trees, it's close to every one of us. How could we think of being alone? And we as *tyerrtye urrperle mape*, we don't *itirreke nkwenge-arrpe* or *atyenge-arrpe*, we don't think in terms of 'just you', or 'just me'. You might *itirrerle*, "oh, why don't *ayenge anyente aneme intetyenhenge*, why don't I just go and stay somewhere on my own?" But you'll still have people coming to you. You'll still have people *ngkwenge interle-aneme* or *ngkwenge anerle*, sleeping and eating and drinking around you. *Inemele arlkwemele, irrwe antywemele kere arlkwemele, alakenhe*. Getting things to eat, drinking tea, having a feed of meat, things like that. That's why *arrpanenhe anyente anetyeke arrangkwe* 'cause they can't *anyente anerle*. They just cannot live by themselves. They can *anyente interle* but *alakenhe anwerne arntarnte-arerreme*, they might stay on their own, but we always care and look out for each other. Like, we have to be looking after other people, because there's no such a thing as "I'm going to be myself". That's how the spiritual guideness is in us.

I used to think a lot about *anwerne*, my people, you know, about how some people used to say "oh, *kele ayenge-arrpe anetyenhenge*, oh well, I'm by myself now". But there's no such thing as "*ayenge-arrpe anetyenhenge*". You can't be alone. I mean you can say, *angkerle* "*kele, ayenge-arrpe arntarnte-arelhetyeke*, it's all right, I can look after myself", but that doesn't still happen, because we Aboriginal people've got a lot of relationships in a different way from another people's society. Because we've got kinship, *anpernirrentye*, we've got Land, *apmere*, we've got feelings, all that. And we see that which is really part of us. *Alakenhe-arle anwerne itethe anintyeme, ane itethe anenhetyenhe.* That's how life's always been and how life always will be.

Only thing that we can use to 'be myself' is like to be brave, to be strong, and to know who we are, that's the only thing that we know just to be yourself. Like *itelarelhetyeke*, your memories and understanding, and also *itirretyeke*, your thoughts, and *aretyeke*, how you see things. That's the things that you can be yourself. But if you're gonna be just yourself, only yourself, then there's a lot of loneliness in you. You'll have a big pipe with no joints in it. Or a big string with no knots in it. *Alakenhe.* Never, never go and stay just to be alone, to be yourself. Because you'll always have a deep broken heart.

Utnenge atherre is the two spirits in me. There's two spirits of life in me, from my father and my mother, *akngeyenge-ntyele, ane meyenge-ntyele*. And also sometime we can see it from *utnenge apmere ahelhenge-ntyele. Alakenhe.* That the spirit comes into us from the Land also. But that Land is already in those two people, to *be* a person, you know. I just *apmwerrke-ulkere ware ayenge akaltye-irreke*, I just learned about that lately – mother and father-*akerte*. How I lived with them in my growing-up. And also *ratherre apmere arrpenhe-arenye atherre*, how they combined from two different countries and became me. And how those two became one spirit *utnenge anyente aneme mpwareke ratherre. Utnenge anyente yanhenge-ntyele aneme prape arunthe anthurre aneme.* And how there's a lot of people made from that one spirit. That's how we know who we are. And also from those two spirits lots more came, because there's a root in those two people's spirit, it's like a big plant down there, not from them but from the other families, *utnenge arrpenhe mapenge-ntyele akeke akngeyenge-ntyele, akngeye ikwere atherrenge-ntyele*. From those two people's *akngeye*s, from mother's father, and from father's father. That became *utnenge atyinhe arrateke* from my parents, that's how my soul arose. And *ikwere atherre artweyenge-ntyele*, it goes on and on and on and on, generation upon generation, *kartweye-kartweye-kartweye*.

Angkweye-angkweye-angkweye

Land gives us, Land takes us back. Not only *inirtnemele utnenge, re ikwerenge-ntyele arrpenhe-areye anteme arratenhelte-iwemele*. Not only taking the spirit back, but out of that one person lots of others appear, springing up out of the Land. There's a lot of little ones goes out from the other tunnel. *Alakenhe-arteke*. That's how we see it you know. *Arrpenhe-areye ampe arrpanenhe*, look at all the kids there today, look at all my grandchildren. *Arrwekelenye mape-arle anintyeke-arteke lyete aneme – Angale-arlke, Penangke-arlke, Kemarre-arlke, Perrurle-arlke, arrpenhe mape anemele.* A whole new mob of skin names for that Land has come out, the same names as their Ancestors.

And for my dad's Land there's another *Perrurle, Kemarre, ane Pengarte, ane Peltharre*, there's another mob coming out. That's how the Land is, you know. *Arrpenhe-areye uyerrenheke ane arrpenhe-areye arratenge-ntyele*, one mob fades out and another mob appears. It's a real recycle, and when you see that *anpernirrentye*, you see that name, and you can say, "hey! Like *Ampetyane, ane Angale-arlke aneme. Ampetyane mape anemele*, well, those little ones, those new *Ampetyane*s and *Angale*s, that was all the ones that was *mame atyinhe-kenhe* mother *mape-arle* – my mother's mother mob. And those little *Pengarte mape aneme, ampe atyenge alere mape-kenhe*, those *Penangke*s, those little children of my nieces, well they were those fathers or aunties of my Mum". And so on, new people taking the old ones' place.

That's why people used to marry other people in the same *apmereyanhe*. They never married out from that Land, so they kept all their families in One Land. And in One Land, all the skin group came. And all the names of those kids came named after every individual grandparent and great-grandparent – *arrenge, atyemeye*, and *apmarleye. Apmarleye* is a daughter type of name, and people use it to call their great-grandparents. Like if my mum was still alive, Jacinta and them, my grandchildren, would call her "*apmarleye*" or "*malyeye*", same name again. *Malyeye* means their daughter. And my mum will call those great-grandkids "*mame*", 'Mum', because they're *Ampetyane*s, and she's *Penangke*. That means those kids'll have the same

The Generations   *Angkweye-angkweye-angkweye*

skin names as their grandmother's mother's mother. And my brothers' *atyemeye* grandchildren, *Pengarte*s, they'll be the daddies for my mum.

And going further down, my mother and Jacinta's son, my great-grandson, both have the same skin name, *ampetyele-atheke anthurre*, reversing right back. They're both *Penangke*. That's what he became. And little Lazarus also came over from all those generations. From his mum, then to her mum, to me, and to my mum. Reversing right back home, right back *alakenhe-arle ampetyele-atheke alpeme*. Just like *angkweye-angkweye-angkweye*, like the ant lion that goes 'round and 'round, digging himself backwards into the ground. So that little boy Lazarus became my little uncle.

Alakenhe, ampetyele-atheke anthurre got to *alperle* you know, you've got to follow back the cycle right to where it began. Just like *angkweye-angkweye-angkweye*. Well, *angkweye-angkweye-angkweye, ampetyele-atheke tyenelhirtneme*. So the merry-go-round always turns back as well. It comes out, and also goes back. *Arrwekelenye-kenhe arrirtne mape-arle ampetyele-atheke alpeme*. The Ancestors' skin names always come around back home. Like *Angale* became Taia, my grandson's daughter. Taia's *Angale* now. She's the one takes over, going back to old Lena Turner, her great-great-grandmother. *Alakenhe*. Right back to my husband's mother.

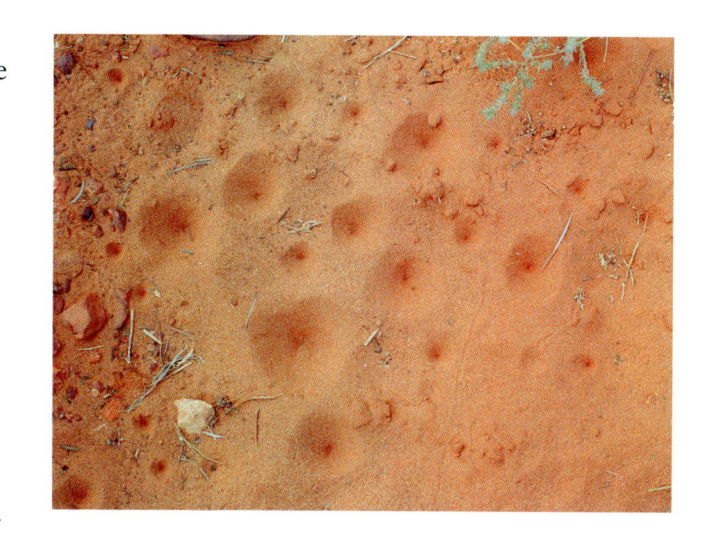

And when you're thinking about marrying somebody, *ampetyele yanhe-arle alperle*, you gotta see what's on the other side too you know, going backwards and backwards. 'Cause *arrirtne nhakwe mape alpeme layake nyurrpe arrpenhe mape-kenhe arrirtne. Arrirtne yanhe-arle ampetyele-atheke apentirtneme*, 'cause they're going back

---

Angkweye-angkweye-angkweye, photographer Barry McDonald

to the other-side mob's names as well. From them, the other-side-Land people from yourself, you know? So somebody became another *Penangke* from that other side. *Angkweye-angkweye-angkweye-arteke* gotta *anpernirrerle* too, you know, you've got to follow that *angkweye-angkweye-angkweye* too, all the way, both sides. That's kept all the rules tied in. *Alakenhe*. Like those kids now are *there*, they're going backwards right *kwene anthurre nhakwe-werle* – right down into the bottom of the Land, right back into the Stories.

We all have our own Stories. We don't talk about other people's Stories, we can tell just our own Stories. Because our Story is connected to our Land and also is connected to us and to our children and our children's children. We belong to the Land, and the Land belongs to us. We live on it, we go back to it, we go back and get buried there. And that is our Story. Every little thing in that place, in that area, is ours. We talk about the hills, the trees, the rocks, mountains or waterholes, any birds, any living creatures in our Land. We talk about all that. And we get things from our own Land. We eat, sleep, get up from the Land itself. And also we have our own Stories to tell. We tell the night Stories from our Land, we tell the morning Stories from our Land, day Stories. Because it's all related in our own country, in our own place. So every individual person has got all that in them.

And people from next door, they got *their* own Stories, and people from the other next-door, they've got *their* own Land. And also we got our own skin group, in our family group, in father, son, daughter, grandchildren, great-grandchildren, and grandmothers' names. And they got their own names as well, on that other side, and those kids there goes right back to the generations' names also, the skin names. They come like their father's father, *arrenge*, they come like their father's mother, *aperle*, they come like their *ipmenhe*, their mother's mother. Like their *ipmenhe* was, and became this and that, but all comes from the Land itself.

But we don't talk about other peoples' Land, we just talk about our own Land. I can't go and tell Story about that person's Land over there, because it's not right according to our Law, according to the Aboriginal ways. Our ways of living is just to

The Generations *Angkweye-angkweye-angkweye*

talk about your own place. For Land and your children, you and your husband's side. And your kids and grandchildrens that belong to that country. That's how the Story holds every one of us, every individual people. Every individual group from that Land, all that comes in from the Story for all the people who belong, and who they are. For me that'll be all my *Akertarenye* family. All the *Akertarenye* people's Land. Like my *atyemeye*, my *ipmenhe*, my *aperle*, and my *ampe atyinhe-areye ante arrenge atyinhenge-ntyele, aperle atyinhenge-ntyele*, all that, all related in there – all my grandparents, my grandchildren, their children, and so on. All them kids became them names then, and the recycle keeps going, *layake ampe atyinhe mape-kenhe ampe-arle aneme kraneye atyinhe-kenhe-arteke aneme arrirtne ampetyele-atheke anteme anpernirrirtnemele*. My children's children are the same as my mothers' mothers' names, reversing right back into those relationships. It turns back that wheel, but it turns from those great-grandchildren, not from their great-grandparents. That's how they get their name-opposite, *alakenhe aneme*. And my kids become like my great-grandparents' names. The great-great grandchildren. From their great-great grandparents, that's how they get their name. And that's all that Story, and all the skin names and the Story, and life and living and holding and guiding and watching, that's all in that Land itself, *apmere anwekakerrenhe*, in the country that connects to us. 'Cause *anwakerre*, me and my families, we cannot *angkerle arrpenhe nhakwe-arenye mapeke*. Can't *angkerle nhakweke*, we simply cannot talk for those other people's country. 'Cause *anwakerre-kenhe atnyenerle ayeye anwernekenhe-arrpe renhe itne-arle arntarnte-arentye mape*, we hold our Story on our side, and that other mob are the guardians of our Story. 'Cause *itne-arle arntarnte-arentye mape-arle*, they're our guiders, *alakenhe-arle itne ilerrerle-aneme*, and that's the way the Story is told to one another, both sides all the time, that's the way the system has always worked.

Story *nhenhe*, it's not only today, and it's not only long time ago, it's written in people – in *tyerrtye mape-kenhe* History. We don't have a book for it, but *anwerne itelareme impatye*, we know and recognise the Story by its track in the Land. It's like written in the Land itself. It's all written there in the Land. And you're born into it, and you know it straight out. You read those writings. *Alakenhe*. But that writing's been

43

written. From generation to generation. Who you are going to be. Who your kids going to be. What they're going to be called. *Alakenhe*. It's like a big History.

Look at the writing coming across here *alere*, look here nephew, outside this window. *Alakenhe*. So that's how it is in the Land itself, *apmerele aneme*. For all those people, that's the Rule, in that country, *apmere anwekakerrenhele*. Really describe-*eme-ileke* people *arrwekelenye mapeke*, you know. It was described really clearly for the early-day people by the Creation Ancestors. That's how people see it. They have it there, and they have it in their heart, and they have it in their mind. But also eyes can see it, like if it's there, you know? *Alakenhe*.

The Land brings love for two people getting married, because they know they come from the Land. That relationship and that skin name, and the right group, and the right respect for people all come from the Land. That's why they've *gotta* marry them, because of the sacredness of that person. The Land gives them that love, and also people, *ye*. People is really important to them. They love the people, their generations; they love their Land; and their Story is precious like jewels. That's how people get married, and that's what it is to have relationship in the Land. *Alakenhe*.

Story

"The Story *is* the Land, and the Land *is* the Story.
The Story holds the people,
and the people live inside the Story.
The Story lives inside the people,
and the Land lives inside the people also.
It goes all ways to hold the Land."

Dreams and Story

Cultural Writing Inside

That's how you got to protect that country, you know? You got to go back and live on the Land, you got to go back and protect it, by knowing your Story, by living inside your Story. Even though it's run-down the whole place, it's a Sacred Land for us. We see the beautiness of what's in it – that Story is written in it, *intelhe-ileke nhenge yanhe anwernekenhe*, it's written there in that place – that's how we see it. "Hey, oh that place is old now, you can't now *awethe inirtnerle*, you can't relate back to it any more". We don't say that sort of thing. You know, *warlperle mape* might *angkerle* "oh, this is an old station; never mind, *kele*, we'll give it back. Let's give it back, we don't want it, they can deal with it". But we see the writing inside. Cultural writing *kwene*. That's what we see there, *alakenhe-arteke-arle itne areme*. Never mind the surface, the part that looks worn out, *akertne nhakwe kele-arle*, that's washed every day, every year, that's *kwatyele-arle arlkngerle-aneme*. Rains, *alhwerrpe-arle arnerle, uternele amperle*, the rains scour it, winter winds sweep over it, and the sun scorches it in summer. *Ye*, that's washed every day. But not what's down in there. *Alakenhe*. You can chip the wood off *akertne-thayatenge*, from the top, the surface, but the solid wood is inside – that's where the beauty is.

Traditional Country Story

When the old people called our *Altyerrenge* Stories "Dreamtimes" to the first *alherntere mape*, they probably said it in a way that the *warlperle* could understand it. Because those *alherntere mape*, the white people didn't have that Traditional Story, *arrwekele atnyenetyakenhe-arle aneke*. But we didn't realise that by putting it like that, "in the Dreamtime, that's how that happened", that *warlperle*s would see our Traditional Stories as just like their own fairy stories that begin "once upon a time". But they're not like that. Like *Ulkerte uthene Arlewatyerre uthene-arle intelhe-ilelheke*, the Perentie and Goanna painted each other, and went down to the water to look at themselves in the reflection, *kwatyeke arelhetyeke*. And that's a True Story, how we see it, and how they, *arrwekelenye mapele-arle areke, kele ingkernenye mapele aneme arintyeme, ane ayeye nhenhe ileme,* you know. How the old people saw it, and how those who follow behind them are seeing it coming back, and how they in their turn tell the Story. It was told by those people in the past, and now today people still tells that Story.

It's not a dream, like a fairytale dream, it's a Traditional Story, and that is *in* us. You know, if people want to tell a story of 'away back when', or the histories of today, like 'then and now', then that's just olden-day stories. And to tell Traditional Stories of like how it arose in this Land, well a better way of putting it, people must've thought, was to say "that's in the Dreamtimes, in the Dreamtime Stories how it is this and that". But it's not in the Dreamtimes. It's our Land Histories, our Traditional History Stories. *Altyerrenge* doesn't mean the olden days, it means always was, and nowadays as well. 'Olden times', well when our people say "olden times" they mean "in our story, in the olden-time story", just surface story. In that olden-time story they talk about what happened when like the first settlers came, and when the first settlers saw them. And at that time what was happening, what things were happening in their time. Like 'olden day' means *mape anetyarte*, like *atneme, ane ilye, ane alkwerte-ilye ware itelaremele.* How people lived before with digging sticks, and boomerangs, and boomerang-shields, just things like that they understand by 'olden day'. 'How It Was', and then came this and that and this – "then the horse came, and the pony came, and then the goats came, and the sheeps came" and whatever, *itelaraye? Layake arrwekelenye mapele arntarnte-areke* means like the first Aboriginal people to get in touch with white people as shepherds or stockmen, they were those people who just left behind all their shields and their spears, *irrtyarte*s and things like that, and they learned a bit of English, the little bit they was learned and was given, and all the wrong names became labelled to things, on both sides.

But when our people say "*Altyerre ante Arrwekelenye Mapele-arle*", *itne ileme nhenge layake,* that means the First People. That's what they mean. Those First People, part of them's in the Land itself, here now, not just in the olden time. But only people there can *arerle*. *Apmereke artweye mapele ware alhengke-arerlte aneme*. Only the people belonging to that Land can recognise them there. Like it tells you in that map there, that Story map.

But we just got used to saying "in the Dreamtime". I think maybe 'Traditional Country Stories' is one of the best names for it. "Oh, this happened in the Dreamtime when the tree stood there". But it wasn't in the Dreamtime. That tree there tells us where, in our Traditional Country Story, how it came and how it cuts off, like where the Story reached, you know, something like that. It tells that sort of Story. Putting it in a way for people to know it and to understand it is to put it into 'Traditional Country Stories', that's a better way of putting it for *alherntere mape*. And also it's a good name for it for us. Traditional Country Stories are about now. And it belongs to now. It's today's Stories, there's nothing old about it.

Arrwekelenye yanhe rarle alpeke rarle.
Alpeke-arle rarle ayeye angkweye-arle
alpeke-arle rarle yanhe re akwete aneme.
It was back;
it went back a long time ago;
it's still today.
People hear it and see it.

The Three-way of *Altyerre*

The words we use to say that we see the Story is *Altyerre areme*, *ye*, we say *alakenhe-arle anwerne "Altyerre areme"*, that's the way we see the Story, and that's how we say that we see it. And we also say *altyerre areme* to mean a dream. That *altyerre*, it's when you're asleep you see that *altyerre*, a dream. That dream *altyerre*, it's just *altyerre* in the dream, any dream. Like you might dream something like the man fell off the horse, or my kids went and tumbled over – that's just a guideline. But it's still the same name as that other *Altyerre, urrperle anwernekenhe* way, which tells you how this Traditional Story came. How this *Altyerre* travelled. So that's *altyerre* too. And another *altyerre* is related to the *altyerre* which is your relationship to your mother's father's Story. *Yanhe-arle*, you're related by that Story too, *unte altyerre akeme*. That's *altyerre* in that way, for my mum's *Altyerre*, the name became what my mum is, that's my mother's father's Story.

And that mother-*Altyerre* relation is really important now, because after *alherntere mape* came along, kids of ours started getting born who didn't have traditional father's side any more. People have always named themselves from their father's father's Land, always followed that Story. Father-son-father-son it's always gotta be, *anyenhengenhenge*, unless you're not connected to any father country, then you can relate to your mother. *Alakenhe*. If your father's line is white, *akngeye mperlkereke artweye*, you're always connected to your mother then. *Unte-arle altyerre akeke*, you relate to your mother-country Symbol. *Altyerre* is a name for *apmere atyemeye*, mother's father's Land. *Aknganentye* is for *apmere arrenge*, father's father's Land. *Rarle altyerre akeke*. That *altyerre* is your mother's Traditional Symbol *ikwerenhe*. *Altyerre*; like, that's her Traditional Story, from father *ikwerenhe*.

Altyerre is really important for when somebody has to relate just to the mother's side of the Story, mother's *Altyerre*. Like, "my mum might *Altyerre anerle iwenhakweye*, she might have a Story relating to whatever. And, well, I don't have a father's side, an *arrengeye*, so I'll follow my mother's Story, her *Altyerre, ye*". *Atyemeye ngkwinhe-kenhe-arle*. *Atyemeye ngkwinhe-kenhe* you can *apenterle*. You can follow your *atyemeye*, 'cause he's the father of your mother. *Atyemeye* is mother's father's Country Story. If there's no father's side there, well you can always follow that person almost as well. 'Cause that person he is part of you. But *atyemeye-kenhe*, it's not as strong as *arrenge*. When you're *arrengeke artweye*, relating to your father's father's country, you're a really owner of whatever *apmere* Land is you. But *atyemeye-kenhe apmere*, your mother's father owns another Land. Because when *atyemeye* owns his Land, his sons are the ones who owns those with him, you can just guide. His sons, that's your uncles and their sisters, and his sons' sons, your cousins, them mob on the other side, *ye*.

We say *aknganentye* when we mean the Symbol of your *apmere arrenge-kenhe*, your own Land, the one coming from your father's father to your father, and then to you. Well, you might have a dream about that, and a dream about your father's father's Story can be called *altyerre aknganentye*. "I seen that dream, *ayenge-arle aknganeke-arle the altyerre areke*", you know? "I seen a dream about my father's Story". And I might *altyerre arerle kwatye-akerte apeke*. For me, it would be something about water, and "hey, *Kwatye anwekantherrenhe, anwekantherrenhe aknganentye tharle altyerre areke*. Hey, there might be something for us, maybe a good thing or a bad thing, we've gotta just see, 'cause I saw a dream and I saw the Water Dreaming belonging to us mob". Might be a good thing, might be somebody coming, might be somebody going, or maybe a bad thing, somebody might be sick. In the same way, you can have a dream about your mother's *Altyerre*, her own Traditional Story. And you can call that dream *Altyerre altyerre*!

So that's the three-way of *altyerre*. There's *Altyerre* means the way that the Traditional Story travelled, then there's *altyerre* that means any dream you might have when you're sleeping, and there's also *altyerre* means your mother's father's Land Story. *Alakenhe*.

Dreams

When somebody sees a dream, sometimes it's for them, or sometimes that represents a dream for someone from another skin group, other-side Landowners. That's a dream *arrpenhe mapeke*. Nowadays people say that dream is for your *nyurrpe*s, but that's not really the right way of describing it. Even I use that *nyurrpe* word now, when sometimes it might be better if I said that other, special name I talked about before. Anyway, I might have a good dream, and that good dream might happen, might come true not for me, might probably happen to my children. Or if I see a good dream about my kids, well that dream could be for *their* kids. And that's an *anpernirrentye* dream. It relates to people and skin names in *apmereyanhe anwernekenhe*, our patch of homelands.

Sometimes that dream can tell you maybe that a certain thing might happen, you know, just to be aware of it. And maybe a dream you might see might be about my mum visiting, and also my brothers might be coming, or my brothers' children, something like that. And it relates into *anpernirrentye*, it's an *anpernirrentye* dream.

Whatever it is you dream about, the dream itself won't tell us the meaning, we gotta guess, and then wait and see. And later on that dreamer might say "hey, *arratye re, altyerre nhenhenge-arle tharle altyerre arekenge*"; "didn't happen *irrekaye*"; or "*altyerre-arle akekenge araye*". They might say "hey, it was true, just like in the dream I was having", or if it didn't happen, then "maybe it was for somebody else who was related to another place". It mightn't be them who comes, the people you thought would arrive, it might be somebody else, someone from the opposite-country skin name might come. Or "hey, *tharle altyerre areke*, oh, *ayenge-arle atnyeke kwenhe*, hey, I had a dream, and I fell over in the dream" or something. Some people would probably say "oh that's for your *ampe ngkwinhe mapeke*", for your kids. But might not be only for my kids, it might be for somebody else *apmereyanhe-arenye* who's got the same skin name as my kids. *Alakenhe*.

You might not see dreams only about people either. You might dream the hill, or maybe a cliff, or a bank of the river, *arnkarre*. Well, you'll realise that *arnkarre* connects to people of this skin group. Or you might see a cliff, *apwerte antherrtye*, and that represents another family. Or you might see kangaroos, which will represent some other families. They might be having problems, or they might be coming. That sort of things we see in dreams, in relation to *anpernirrentye*.

Because the dream itself can't explain, then it's good for us to tell people about it, what it really means, the meaning of the dream. *Akngerrepate* people like myself and other elders who know the Stories and the skin names and the people, they can know who the dream is for. And then I'd tell my family what it was really concerning, you know? This is just a legal way of talking about dreams and the people they're meant for.

A dream is not just a dream. It's a real happening Story, or a real happening picture given to you. That's how we see it when we tell about a dream of something's going to happen, or somebody's going to arrive. It all comes out of that Story, that Traditional Country Story. It's in our skin names, in our *anpernirrentye*, and the skin names follow. Like who'll be coming, or might be there'll be a cloud coming up, or rain. People who knows about Traditional Stories, well their Story might be linked to the rain, or maybe for animals, like might be for kangaroos or emus or something like that. And you might find something on the road; "hey, I dreamt about these people here – there look – that's their traditional animals, their *aknganentye mape* are out there", like kangaroos or emus or something. And they know straightaway because it comes from all the skin names, skin-name people, *anpernirrentye mape*. *Anpernirrentye*. That's why and how Traditional Stories always come through that. *Atnengkarre-arle alheme*. That's the way Story goes.

You told me a tale yourself once, *alere*, about a woman staying on somebody else's country. And that *arelhe* wasn't respecting that Land, and in the night she had a dream where some women came to her and told her to go away. Well, when she heard that somebody telling her to go back, that's not just the dream. It's real. 'Cause the People are real there – the People of that place, the ones that represents that country and its Story, and the ones who told that Story in its beginning. 'Cause *apmereke artweye mape arratye rarle angkeme*, it really is those Ancestors that were talking. And that *Altyerre*, that Traditional Story for that place, it comes *arrwekele*, in front of us, from the Beginning. It's really true when they say it you know, *alere*; *altyerre arratye re*, they say that *altyerre areme*, dreaming dreams, is right at the heart of Aboriginal culture.

Dream-Visions

A dream *means* something on that Land, wherever it is. It's not just a dream, it's a true thing they see it, if you're in that Land – it's like a vision. If somebody sees a dream, "*anwerne-arle akwele ingke alhelte-iweke kwatye akngerre aretye-alheke. Ay, anwerne-kenhe areke apwertenge-arle anwerne-akerte areke-arle, mape alhelte-iwerlenge*. Hey, I dreamed about that we went along on foot and came upon lots of water, and we also saw from the top of the hill people – our mob – walking".

Well, they'll tell the person, those Landowners will tell her, "*ye*, that dream you had, that means that people-*arle arratye renhe apmere nhenhe*, you know, around here, the *apmereke artweye*, those Ancestors really did used to go up the hill and see people walking in the distance. And also you seen that dream because that Dream is belong to this country. *Apmere nhenhe-arenye-kenhe Altyerre-arle yanhe*. That Story belongs to the people of this country. But it's just put into you so you can see, *arerle*, what the Land was like". They give a dream *iwenhe-arteke-arle aneke* – about what it was like before. They see *themselves* in that dream because it just shows them how their parents, or their *aperle*, or *arrenge*, or *atyemeye-arle untheke renhe*, how their grandparents walked around at that time in this area. But it's them too, they're connected. People say "*oh, ayenge kantreyele-arlke apmere altyerre mwerre anthurre aremele anetye-alheke kwenhe*; hey, when I went to that country I just dreamt about lovely things in that place".

Ye, altyerre, that just tells you the Traditional Story, in a dream, of that Land. You can dream about other places where you're staying, *ye*, you can dream about motorcars, you can dream about anything. Or if you're in your own country, they'll give you a good dream about your own Story. But anybody can see any dream, it doesn't have to be just on your own country. Might be *apmere nhenhe-akerte* dream *arerle*, you can see a dream about this country too. But *apmere nhenhe-akerte* dream, but you just dreaming about their Dream, you dream about the Story of the owners of the place you're staying at. *Apmereke artweye mape-kenhe altyerre ware-arle unte arerle-aneme*, you dream about the Dreams belonging to this place that you're on. And if you're in another place, you might be dreaming about those other people's Stories, you're dreaming about their Dream. You're just dreaming about their Dream, their Stories, their Traditional Story Dreams. The way they see it and the way the People of the Land gives you, "oh, this is what our Dream is, this is the Dream of all these people here, the *apmere nhenheke artweye mape*; I'll give you a dream, *kwenhe, alakenhe*". And you dream-*irrerle*, you dream it then. And that's how it is, that's most certainly how it is.

People never used to talk about these things, *alere*. But this is good you know, *ampe mape akaltye-irretyenhenge*, so that the younger people will learn. And maybe remember also, "*ay, apmere nhakwenge the prape mwerre akngerre altyerre areke*; hey, that's right! At that other place I had a beautiful dream, *apmere nhakwele anemele the altyerre mwerre akngerre altyerre aretyarte*. And when I lived at that other one place I used to have beautiful dreams too. It was *really* beautiful, *mwerre akngerre*". Well, those dreams was given to you by the *apmereke artweye*, the Traditional Owners, the Little People of the Land. Might be you were sick, *rlkerte apeke aneke*, or maybe you might've had worries or something. They can give you those sort of dreams to relax you.

Even a dream about a green sports car might be a dream for certain people *apeke mutekaye atnyeketye*, maybe their car might have an accident. It sometimes tells that story for the future; if you see those dreams it can be protection too. "*Ay, mutekaye-arle atnyeke-arle the altyerre-areke* you *mape mwantye alhele mutekaye ngkwinhe*. Hey, you mob, you should drive your car real carefully in case you have an accident". Sometimes it guides you, *nyurrpeke apeke, ye*. For those other-side people in your *anpernirrentye*.

Even you might have a dream about a cat when you're staying in Sydney or Melbourne. Well in that *apmere yanheke artweye*, the mob that belong to that Land, there might be a person who had a Cat *aknganentye* or a Fish *aknganentye*. So you dreamed about their Story down in that country. I don't think there *is* a dream that you don't call *Altyerre*, Traditional Story. In Aboriginal way there is always Traditional Dreams, no matter what it is. If you dream about a house, well it represents a wurley or *ilthe*. Shell *apeke*, it might be somebody who's related into the Shell, Shell-*ke artweye*. Every little creature, there's a dream about everything. It's all connected in with somebody's Traditional Story. But not every dream is going to be one that *you* relate to. *Alakenhe*.

Country Dreams and Story Line

So, when people dream, sometimes they dream inside their Story, sometimes they dream outside their Stories. Sometimes outside their Story too. They might see a dream which is other peoples' Dream, which is not theirs, you know? That's the outside dream, inside somebody else's Story. You can see your own Stories, dream your own Dreams.

That dream might represent that they're coming, or that they're gonna be appearing today. Or sometimes is a good-luck or sometimes is a bad-luck stories. And you can dream that story for outside people as well, outside stories, outside dream, *arrpenhe mapeke*. That inside Dream, you can dream about might be you go hunting, or might be people might come and see you, or you might be given something, or might be the rain might come. *Alakenhe*, part of your own Story, on your country. If you're living on your country you can dream about these things.

And you can dream about outside people, people of outside skins' Stories. You mob might dream about other skin, and that other skin, and other skin, you know? And might have an effect on skins on people on that other-Land side as well, in your *apmereyanhe*, who might have the same skin names as in your group in your inside Story. 'Inside Land' really. Because it's in that Land, that Story. So that can relate to all the people on the other, that other-Land side as well.

Not only on the other side in our own patch of homelands, *apmereyanhe anwernekenhe*, but also from further-down country. We know how *Ikngerrekwiperre*, our *Akarre* language, is related to all the other different-language speakers that live around us. We've got *Alyawarr* people living north of us, we've got *Akityerre* people living beside us to the west, we've got southern languages living next to us. And some of those mobs are the same totem people as us, you know, *kwatyeke artweye*. And that Rain Story tells how they relate to us and to the Land itself. We might *anpernerle*, relate with them like *makeme, altyerrakeme, aknganentye*, you know? Like through mother Symbol, or through father Symbol. And we might call them distant relations, because they have the same area, they are on the same line where the *kwatyeke artweye ingkerreke apeke*, where the Rain Ancestors travelled. We're related even to *Warlpiri* people in that way. They're associated with us as well, but we're related to them in a different way than we are to the people in our own *apmereyanhe*, our own private kinship circle, *anpernirrentye*. Like it's through where the Story is laid, *Atnengkarre*, the line of the Story, that Rule. *Intintyemele*, you know. That line lays in the same direction as it did whenever it came to be *Altyerrenge* towards our way, still laying in the same direction as when it started. *Alakenhe. Layake nhakwenge-ntyele intintyeke anwerne akwelathe kwatye aknganentye arrpenhe mapenge-ntyele.* We ourselves lay – as I've been told by my elders – in a line that stretches from that other Rain Dreaming mob over all that way. And that line, *ye*, it spread all around *kwatyeke artweye mape arrpenhe-areye*, around all the Rain Dreamers. But that's just...we might just leave that because it covers some other difficult things too. It's better to talk about just languages than to talk about *aknganentye*, totems. That might be connected more with men.

Those different-language speakers, those other distant relations, as soon as they find out what your skin name and who your family is, they know straightaway how to relate to you. They see what your country and what your totem is, and they relate straightaway and they follow that track, that line, that place where it came from: "Well, this is what I relate to you". *Alakenhe.* Your *aknganentye arrenge-ntyele*, from your father's father's Story.

If they're *Anmatyerr* people, if they're *Kaytetye*, if they're *Alyawarr* people from my mother's side, or if they're *Ikngerripenhe*, if they're Central *Arrernte-arenye mape*, or if they're Western *Arrarnta-arenye*, if those skin names, if they know who you are, they'll relate to you exactly the same as they relate to any other close families of their own. But maybe in a more distant way. And you yourself could always know. About how your relationship might go into *Anmatyerr* way, it might go into *Alyawarr* way, might go into *Warlpiri* way, Southern *Arrernte* way, *Ikngerripenhe* way. Or maybe even *Warumungu* way. 'Cause it can go a long, long way, that line. Into all the ones that's got identity with skin names. But even every Aboriginal people's got relationship system, or skin names, or what their totem is, and that's what they are.

Story language changes from place to place. Like Central *Arrernte* might change to Western *Arrarnta* and that changes to *Anmatyerr* then. But the Story of those distant relations is still the same, how what Species travelled through their country. And that makes those people special to those other people further along the line, no matter how far away. And also how they relate to *all* those other different-language people, *apmere arrpenhe-arenye mapeke*. Like *alturlenge-ntyeleke, ikngerrenge-ntyeleke,* or *antekerrenge-ngtyele, ayerrerenge-ntyele*. For those people from the west, those from the east, those from the south, and from the north, those four directions bring in a lot of relationship, but not in a relationship like, "you're my uncle, you're my whatsiname". It's more distant, it's a relationship of Stories, a connection through Symbol. And how you can just relate to them, but you can't be part of them, not really part of their Land. Those people and their homelands have 'further skin names', same like us, and also the Story that is connected to us, like the Rain Dreaming mob. They've got similar Stories as our inside Stories. They might even have the very same inside Stories like ours again, and with our skin names as well! Further-down-country-way relate, *ye*. That's how that is. Because that Story is really still being handed along that line, from one language group to the next one. Even with dreams. Maybe my niece *Perrurle* here can tell something more about that.

<u>Veronica *Perrurle*</u>: *Apmere nthenhe-ame-nthenhe-amele-arle Altyerrenge anpere-irrenheke renhe ilemele itelaraye Alterrenge angwenhe-kenhe-akweye nhenhele alheke kwenhe*. No, *Altyerre yanhe nhenge ngkernelhetye-alhelenge, apmere arrpenhe ngkernelhetye-alhelenge pwathe-irreme apmere arrpenhe yanhe itne-arle* take-eme-over-*ileme kele. Altyerre yanhe itnekenhe anteme ileme nthenheke-atwetye renhaye. Alakenhe-arle arrwekele aneke.*

Whichever country the Story passes through, that was the Story that was *related* for those particular people, the Story that is and passes through their country. When the Story continues over their boundary and stops for a while at another place, those original people aren't the boss of it then, and they can't tell the new chapter. No, the people from the next country take the Story over. That part of the Story becomes theirs then, up until the next boundary it reaches. And so on, that's how it is in the Creation. Stories are handed from the people of one language boundary to another, and onwards from there. That's how Story travels.

From Dreams to Dreaming

With our dream, that's why people *nhenge* dream-*irreme* and you know, that's why we've got to keep that dream into a Traditional Story, a Traditional Country Story. As I said before, "in the Dreamtime the Perentie and the Goanna painted themselves", but it wasn't in the Dreamtime, it was in the Traditional Story. And then they put a curse on one another, and today one of the animals still gets strike with the lightning. Because of the curse this animal said.

It's like *thipe nhenge yanhe mape itelaraye, thipe akatwengatwenge. Thipe nhenge yanhe mape akaperte atwerreke-arle-arteke arelhe atherre-arle Altyerrenge ake atwerreke.* Well, *thipe yanhe apeke ake athetheke akwete rarle anintyeke. Arelhe atherre-arle Altyerrenge atwerreke. Apmere* there's one over there at *Arltangke, Akarle Atwerreke. Layake Altyerre yanhe-arlke-arteke*, now you see all the *thipe akweke akaperte-arle atwerreke.*

It's like that little bird *akatwengatwenge*, the redcap robin. Their heads are bright red, just like those two Women in the Creation who drew lots of blood hitting each other on the heads with sticks. These little birds have always been that way. The Women hit each other in the Creation, you can see one of them over there near Arltunga, at a place called *Akarle Atwerreke*. Just like in the Traditional Country Story, you now see all those little birds with bright red heads, just as if they've been hitting each other.

Thipe Akatwengatwenge, photographer Barry McDonald

That's how it's always been, that's how we've all seen it and still see it, right from the Creation, *arrwekelenye-arle anintyeke*. Them birds describes how those People was. Well, they got hit, and those birds too are part of those Women, and became the redness on the top of their head. The birds are part of the Women, they represent the Women, the birds *were* and *are* those Women. And they're showing what it was like *arrwekele arrwekelenye Atnengkarre apmere ikwerenge-arle aneke re*, you know? They show about the Ancestors from that place and in that time and about their Law, the Traditional Stories that are *aneke re*, always was there, still are there, and will always be there in that place.

And today you see *arelhe mape ake atwerrerlenge*, you always see women hitting each other on the head with sticks. You don't see men doing it, *artwe akaperte atwerrerlenge*. And women also cut their heads, and you don't see men doing this either. Only women do it to each other, *arelhe atherre-ante-arle nhenge akaperte atwerreke. Arelhe atherre akaperte atwerrele*, women hit each other in a special way, through sadness, *angkwetye-angkwe*, a special mourning, especially for when a child passes away. Mostly cousins do it to each other, *altyele mapele*. When sadness comes, women'll hit themselves, *arelhe akaperte atwelhele*. Thing, you know, nowadays you see people hit themselves *akaperte atwelhele, Altyerrenge re atwelheke re*, because *Altyerrenge-arle atwelheke re*, that's how it tells in the Traditional Stories, how it's laid down there. That's the sacredness of healing.

When you don't do that, don't hit each other on the head, then you're not that traditional person. If you want to be that real traditional person, you've gotta be like a mirror of that *Arrwekelenye* Person, that Ancestor *who you became* when you came out of the Land, *arraterle*. What it was, and what it is today. You cannot like, if your parents and your sisters and cousins are in sadness, you cannot walk around wearing this or that type of clothes, just anything *mantere alakenhe-akerte apeke unthele*. Or, "oh! My sister's over there, I'll go and see her". No, you've got to be exactly the same as them in their mourning. It's from the Traditional Stories.

The Traditional Stories give our kinship, *anpernirrentye*, the body and the colour and the meaning – and that colour is like *Kemarre* and *Perrurle*, *Ampetyane*, *Angale*; *ye*, that sort of colour. It keeps the colour in the traditional people – not like green or yellow, pink or blue, *alakenhe*, but it's the colour of relationship. The colour of Law. The colour of who you are, and what you are. *Alakenhe*.

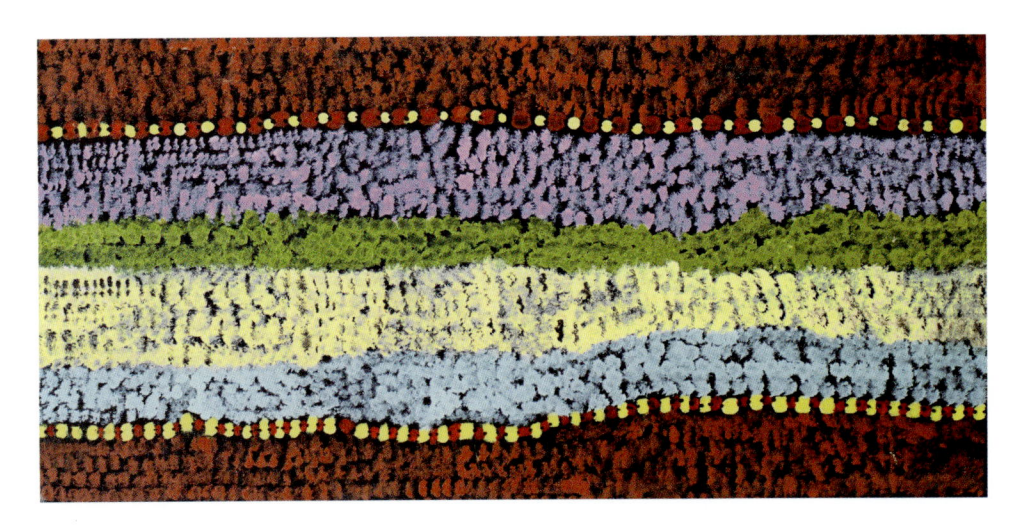

That's how it is, *anpernirrentye* holds that colour, and we got to describe that to people you know, what it is to be *you*. What it is to be you, you've got to follow that colour. And that fits into the Land, of what it is, your relationship, your close guideness, and also close memories. You got that *memory* of those People in you, the colours of those, who they are, *alakenhe*. You got to know it, you got to know that to be *really* you, *itelarele iwenhe unte re*.

Skin Groups Dancing, 2005, acrylic on canvas, photographer Barry McDonald
"*Anthepe* is the *Arrernte* name for the dance women perform at initiation ceremonies. The brush marks represent the patterns left in the sand by the dancers' feet. The different bands of colour show the different skin groups dancing together; cousins and sisters in different skin-groups dance together in pairs, grandchildren dance with grandparents. The red and yellow dots represent *inernte* seeds strung together in necklaces with human hair string. This dance has been handed down from generation to generation. These are the things we paint to teach our children and to keep our culture strong".

Ways of Telling

Painting Stories

    I just like to *angkerle* you know *ayenge tharte-irreke* painting *apmwerrke ware. Arrkene mpwarerle-aneme arne-arlke apere-arlke, arne apeke, apwerte apeke ilerrtye apeke ante ilemele nthenhe-nthenhe-ante-arle intintyeme-arle nthenhe-nthenhe-ante-arle akngakeme* people *mape-kenhe apmere. Alakenhe mape-arle mpwareme nhenge ilemele merne-akerte iwenhe-arle arne aneme-akerte ante kwatye nhenge pmwarele-arle itne atnyeneme alakenhe-akerte, alakenhe-arle* the *mpwareme ilemele-ante ilemele.* I don't *arrpenhe mape-kenhe ilerle*, I'll always *ilerle ayenge-arle akaltye-irreke*-way. *Atneme-arlke-akerte, iwenheye atneme, atneme kwenhe layake kere tnyenhe-tnyenhe* or *kere akiltye-ilenhe, alakenhe-akerte meyele mpwarerle atneme*. That's why I put *atneme* in my painting. And also about grinding stones, I put grinding stones *ntange-arle atheme-akerte. Ntange ulyawe,* might be *ntange arlepe-arlke-akerte apeke*, or *artetye-arlke apeke*, you know, those sort of things-*arle atweme*. And people-*arle-le apwerte atnyenewarretyarte*, they used to *iperteke artetyarte kele imarnte apwerte arrpenhe akertneke arrernemele.*

    Ante arelhe-kenhe arelhe-arle aneme, altyelenhenge-areye-arle aneme, or *angkwerenhenge-areye-arle aneme* the *ilerle* story *ayeye* painting *atyinhe*. And also *angwenhe-arle-ante-areye-arle nhenge, layake arelhe-kenhe urrpme* I used to *ilerle arrernerle. Ante arelhe-arle nhenge* paintings like colours *mape arrerneme atheme-arle-iperre-arle arrerneme. Ante kere impatye layake arlewatyerre-arle alheke*, I always like *arengke-akerte apeke-arle arelhe alheke kere ingkentemele, ingke impatye; arengke-kenhe impatye*, or *ankerre-kenhe impatye* you know, those sort of things I always *mpwarerle ante ilemele.*

    But most-*ulkere* I always *ilerle layake nthakenhe-arle arelhele-arle akaltyele-antheme, arelhele-arle akaltyele-antheme ampe. Iwenhe-ante-areye mpwaretyeke. Itneke-arle ilerle-aneme* anything like *atneme-arle ineme*, or *apwerte athere-akerte*, or *ntange-akerte*, or *kwatye-arle urtnele inteme-akerte, merne-arle urtnele-arlenge atnyeneme*, or *merne iwenhe apeke atwakeye apeke, arrutnenge apeke, awele-awele apeke. Alakenhe-akerte. Ingkwerrpme-akerte,* maybe *anweketye-akerte apeke,* or maybe *atyankerne-akerte. Alakenhe-akerte* I always *ayeye ilerle. Alakenhe anyente renhe meye mpwarerle anelhe-ilemele. Ante lhere-arle intintyeme-akerte, lhere nhenhe-arle akngakeme, nhenhe-ante-nhenhe-ante, lhere arrpenhe nhareye nhenhe-ante akngakeme. Ante apwerte-arle aneme-akerte. Alakenhe.*

Painting *alakenhe meye mpwaremele ilerle.* So people can *ilerle, ante nhenge arelhe-arle aneme ulyepere intelhe-ilemele,* or *arelhe-arle inwenge-arle intelherle-aneme. Alakenhe.* Patterns on the women. About patterns, and colours of ochres, *ante layake, ingkwerlpe-akerte apeke* draw-*eme-ilerle*, paint-*eme-ilerle, alangkwe-akerte, arrwekele ayenge angkerne alangkwe-akerte, ante atwakeye merne iwerrarrkwe-arlke-akerte apeke. Alakenhe. Ante ngkwarle aperaltye urtnele atnyeneme.* I always *alakenhe ante ware ilemele arrernerle* 'cause *arelhe mape-arle alakenhe ware akngernewarretyarte ilerrirretyarte ayeye. Ante iwenhe merne utyerrke, yanhe areye-akerte.* And I always *ayeye mwerre ilerle* so people can *arerle, ayeye alakenhe ileme* 'cause *akaltye-arle-irreke mape-arle ilerle-aneme. Ane merne-arle arlwileme* – like gathering foods, that's the one I talk to people about. *Ye, alakenhe-akerte*, and I bin doin' a lot now, painting *mpwarerle anemele akweke-arle-akweke-arle*

Digging Sweet Potato, 2006, acrylic on canvas, photographer IAD Press
This painting is about the sweet potato that is dug during certain times of the year. Winter is the best season to dig for them as they are young and sweet.

Ways of Telling Painting Stories

ilerle-aneme mapele atningke-arle painting *atyinheke-arle paye-eme-ileme. Ayenge-arle akaltye-irretyarte mape merne mape-akerte ware the mpwarerle-aneme merne tharle arrwekelenye arlkwenhetyarte mape-akerte. Ante ayeye nhenhe the ilemele atyenge-arrpe-akerte. Nthakenhe-arle ayenge amangkeke ikwere-akerte, ante nthakenhe-nthakenhe-arle the arrwekele arenhetyarte arenhetyarte renhe ayenge amangkemele.* That's why *the ayeye nhenhe ileme.*

Apmere aherne-arle alheke kwenhe anwerne akarelhepe-alheme. So *ayeye alakenhe nhenhe iletyenhenge.* But that's how *arrwekele ayenge angkerne* painting *atyinhe-akerteke*, and then I moved on to how people worked and how they lived – their living style is changed.

I would just like to talk now about how I started painting, not too long ago. Just as a hobby, painting different things like red gum trees, or hills, gullies, or rivers, telling about where these lay, without picking out where any particular people's country is. I mean, by just making up places in my head. This is how I tell it when I'm painting, about foods and what type of plants there are, and water that they hold in scoops – these are the type of things I paint about. And I don't tell about other people's places or things in my painting. I'll always tell about only the things that I was taught. About digging sticks, and what a digging stick is; like it's a digging tool for hunting burrowing animals, or it can be used to cut up meat, sometimes it's really sharp. You can cut the rib bones from the kangaroo, or you might break the two hips apart with it. That's the digging stick, and you can use that to

Knock-off Time, 2006, etching, photographer *Irrkerlantye* Arts

dig honey ants, or dig goannas, sometimes dig perenties out, or dig witchetty grubs. And that's just part of the tool, the way Mum made them. That's the type of things I paint about, that's why I put the digging stick in my paintings.

And also I paint about grinding stones. I put grinding stones in, the ones for grinding up seeds. Pigweed seeds, prickly wattle seeds, or mulga seeds maybe; you know, those sorts of seeds that you pound. People used to treasure their grinding stones. They used to bury them in a hole, and put another rock on top of it. You know they'd dig a hole and they'd dig that grinding stone and hide it away and put a round stone on the top, and people when they come along through the season, they'll know, and, "hey, this must've been a big edible seed country here, hey there might be a stone here somewhere". And they dig underneath and they find another stone, might be they put two or three stones, or they might put it under the tree, and they might just leave the stone outside, and "oh yeah, well the stone's chucked outside, there might be a flat stone somewhere in here". Those sort of stories, *ayeye*, I always tell, *ilerle*.

And I paint about where women sit, where the cousins are supposed to sit, or where the sisters are supposed to sit, I tell that story in my paintings. And I describe the women's body-painting designs, I put that in my pictures also. What colours the women put on themselves after they've ground them up. And also tracks, like where the goannas have been. I always paint the tracks of women following kangaroo tracks with a dog – dog's tracks too, emu tracks, those sort of things. I always paint and tell about all these different sorts of things.

Mostly I show now about how women teach, how they teach the kids, teaching whatever the story might be that I paint about. Telling them about how to get a digging stick, or about grinding stones, or about seeds, or water lying in a scoop maybe, or food in a coolamon; whatever foods it might be – wild orange, wild passionfruit, bush tomatoes, that sort of stuff. Maybe I'll paint the different sorts of mistletoe fruits or maybe even conkerberries, those are the sort of things I paint and tell about, things that my mother did when I was with her. And about where the creeks lie, how they branch out from each other – just picking them out of my imagination, no particular river in mind. It's the same thing with whatever hills I can make up in my head.

That's how I go about telling stories in my paintings. So that people can see from my canvases how women paint themselves up for dancing, paint their thighs and their chests. About the women's patterns, the colours of the ochres. And the bush tobacco, I'll draw and paint about that too, and maybe bush bananas. I talk about the bush bananas that grew around when I was young, and wild oranges of different types. And about the sweet manna from gumleaves that was carried in a coolamon; I always put that in my paintings 'cause that's how the women used to carry it around. And also about bush figs. I tell these stories so that people can really see just how the knowledge was learnt from the old people. Especially about gathering foods, that's what I've mostly been talking to people about.

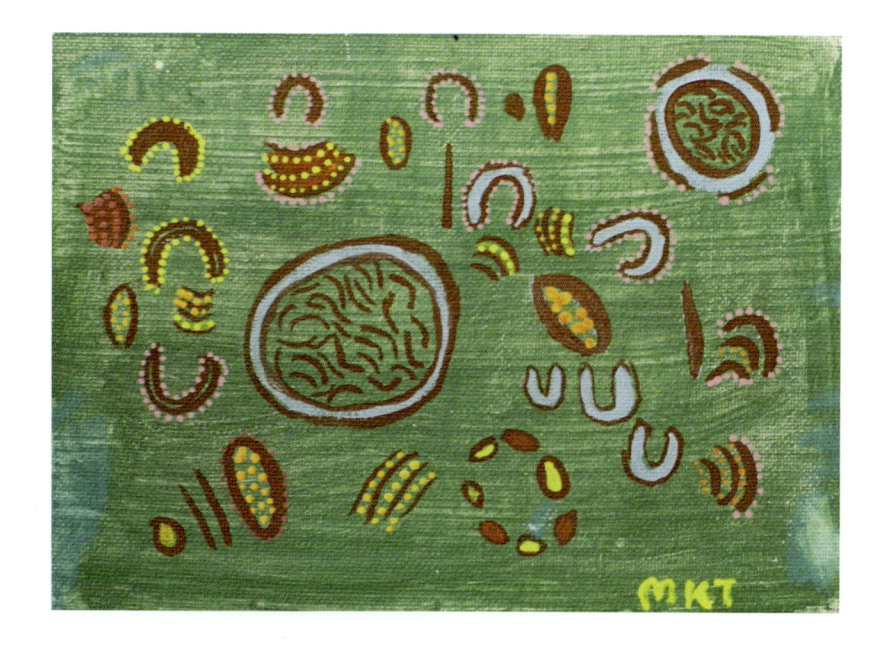

I've a lot of those sorts of paintings, and little by little, people are starting to buy my work. Mainly the ones about the foods that I learnt about and ate in the early days. I only tell stories about my own experience. About how I grew up, and how I saw things in that growing time. That's how I tell stories. Early on, my paintings were all

---

Young Girls Learning From Grandmothers, 2001, acrylic on linen board, photographer Barry McDonald
This shows young women being given knowledge by their grandparents. The large circles represent the Land and its knowledge. The stripes, *imperre*, represent the Symbols for that Land. The circle of stones represents ochre, while the *urtne* contains ground-up pigments. This is the time of preparing for ceremony. There are grindstones shown in the painting also.

about how we moved through the landscape, about bush foods and women's customs. But lately I've shifted to how my people worked and how they lived – how their living style is changed now.

But to us as Aboriginal people, we often come back in. When we go back to our old community, that traditional lifestyle, it goes back into us and changes us. Sometimes people like to stay in the homelands, while some other people don't like to stay there 'cause there's not many activities in the homelands for them. But when they feel sad, they make sure that they go back, they really fit into that Land. And that's the time a lot of people goes back and really settles in. But whatever it is I paint about, painting these stories is really good for me. It really helps me, and I tell my kids about it. I always teach my children and grandchildren about it, about what it is that I'm painting.

Singing and Dancing Stories

This is a story that was told to me: We'd taught dancing to all these *Pertame*, Southern *Arrernte* girls, they were doing *anthepe*, women's-side song and dance. And on that *anthepe* songs, it had all *Arrernte* people singing, old men singing. And when they took it down to Canberra – they did that dance traditional down there – well, they reckon all those Little People from that country, when they went to sleep they heard them People singing! All these People came talking to them in the Dream they reckoned, *akwele angketyekewe, apetyewarreke, alyelhewarreke, alyewerle*, talking, and singing their own songs in that country. That's how people learn their own songs, you

---

Washing in the Wind, 2008, etching, photographer *Irrkerlantye* Arts

know, when people go and dance. *Irrerntarenye mape*, the People of that Land gives you them songs from your own place, wherever it might be. Anyhow, they could just hear all the Old People singing, and dancing, sitting around. But those young women didn't understand the language. It wasn't any of their language, so I think that the other language must be still alive *itethe ahelhele*. They couldn't understand them because it was different. And it's still there, the language and those songs and dances are definitely alive in the ground somewhere 'round there, Canberra-*thayate*. It's good to know that.

When they got back here, those girls told me "hey, our dancing just brought back the lives of those Old People from that country at Canberra!" I think that young woman, that *Kngwarraye*, she's the main one heard all that People singing, I think she must have seen them too, I think they must've painted themselves. And it's really wonderful that all those people down in the southern countries, they got everything there, even they got that Seven Sisters, you know, and that Three Sisters, you know that Three Sisters hill? *Apwerte nhenge* Three Sisters *Mape anerle-aneme*? *Angkwerenhenge Urrpetye*. And I think somebody should take that dance down there again, 'cause that's the same public Traditional Story we got.

If people *ampe mape-arle alyelhetyeke ante anthepe-irretyeke alhele* there with them, if young people from here went down there to dance and sing, then it might wake up those Old People again to sing for the people there so they can understand what their own songs would be. What the tune of their song will

Two of the Seven Sisters Making Frost, 2002, acrylic on canvas, photographer Barry McDonald
This is part of the Seven Sisters Story. Two of the Sisters are sitting behind a windbreak. The upper circle represents an *urtne* with food in it, and the lower circle represents their fire that is dying down, causing them to get cold. The grey swirls represent wind and cold weather. After sitting there for a long time, the Women finally get up and move away from the fire to urinate, thus creating the Frost (*ilweltye*).

be. And they'll probably teach them what it was, they might show them what Symbol, what it means, of those Three Sisters. I think we should really ask them, as people who's related to the Seven Sisters, and also to the Three Sisters down there. Because I was really shocked when they came back and told me about that.

Well, them people will start singing their own songs again then. If they had local Aboriginal people to join our other Aboriginal people for that dance, it could be really good, so that they can be able to hear their own songs for themselves. But it was just all *Arrernte* kids dancing that time. They should join them other girls from there. Then they could hear their songs of their Ancestors – their own songs – and they must've seen Symbols or something too, I don't know. All them Old People were dancing, but sometimes when you go they can show you Symbols too. What sort of designs on body painting, if you're *apmereke artweye*, for women. Same as the people here when they go back to homeland, they can see their own Symbol.

Some people think that country songs is just only for men. But women have songs of their own, as we know. Women told songs in the Stories, or Stories in the songs. Well, they used to sing it for young girls, young mums, young sister-in-laws, young daughter-in-laws. And whenever they sing, they always tell the people the Stories of their songs. But never sing

---

Land Power Ceremony, 2001, acrylic on linen board, photographer Tamsyn Jones
This painting depicts women's ceremony. The pink-red stripes are the body-decorations, *imperre*. These *imperre* are the same designs that the women make in their sand-paintings. The 'horseshoes' show the women painted-up and dancing. The yellow dots represent cockatoo feathers used to shoo away evil. The green dots represent flower-bunches used, together with feathers, to draw up the power of the sand-painting into the bodies of the dancers through their painted chests. This painting symbolises the dance that serves as a necessary preliminary to other women's ceremonies – to draw the power of the Land into the dancers.

other people's. Your mother, your grandmothers taught you their songs, you've got to sing it because it belongs to them. And you can't sing other people's songs and claim it as your own. You just learn from it, because the Story is just sung for the close families to hear. But you can learn from it, and you can relate to it, but you can't claim it for yourself, because it doesn't run in that guidelines. *Ye*, the women tell Stories and sing Stories through songs.

Today they sing it on tapes. Now they've got it on videos, how they sing it. Before, it used to be really sacred. But now it's they want to show what is really the goodness of the song, and things like that. They want to tell it to the world. Like when they're having Land claims and things like that, they sing all that Story. To show what it means to them of that Land they're going to get, or Land they own. *Ye*, that's the sort of Stories that the women sing. Singing and telling. Today they still do it. They do it in public for public singing sometimes. Other singing is just only for the women themselves. They've got…no, I don't want to talk about that, because some of the songs that they can see and hear is not legal ones for me to say. Because they sing that other sort of song to show what is part of the Histories and Stories, and what lays in the soil of the Land itself.

Singing and Dancing Just For Fun

Some other women's songs is just for entertainment you know, and they're not Story songs. They just used to sing these sort of songs for fun, and one I remember was about belt buckles and *mwekarte kwerralye-kwerralye*, men's starry hats, those ones with silver ornaments around the hatband. These are the jokey songs they used to sing, even about the whip cracking! They made them up in fun, and they used to just muck around, being cheeky and a bit flirty, and it becomes their really popular songs then and, *iwenhakweye*, joke stories. *Alakenhe*.

Apere arne apere artnangkwe-artnangkwe. Arne artne, the thick red gum scrubs, that's how it was before on the Todd River here, *arrwekele-arle alakenhe aneke*. Right up to, maybe to *Thereyurre*, the Alice Springs Telegraph Station. But today it's not like that, only the south end of the creek looks still the same, thick like that, *apere artnangkwe-artnangkwe*. I'm telling a story about how people used to sing – like *apmere iwenhakweyele anemele*, what's the name of that place they were at? – oh yeah, they used to be at Clarabelle Station. And all the old ladies used to see all the men, they used to see these men taking all the cattle in the creek, *lherele-arle itne anetyarte, pweleke mape*. And the old ladies used to tease one another, "hey, let's sing this song here, *nyurrpe yanhe mape tnarlkwemele kwenhe*. We'll sing about all the *nyurrpe*s". My mum used to sing that song, and my cousin used to sing it. And all their sisters. I used to hear it later on, after the song got a bit older and they used to sing it just for fun. They used to sing like this, *arrkene ware akwele-arle, arrkene urrayurre*:

Ay, apere artnangkwe-artnangkwenge ilaye

Ay, apere artnangkwe-artnangkwenge ilaye

Wipe ltare altwetye-irreme

Wipe ltare altwetye-irreme

Ay, apere artnangkwe-artnangkwenge ilaye.

All that word just means 'under the gum tree scrubs you can hear the sound and the cracking of the stockwhips!'

Then they'd have a big laugh and go "*hehehehehe, ye!*" And you know, they'd poke each other in the ribs and "*kweye kelekatyaye*! My goodness girl!" And then they'd have another big laugh and fall on one another. They used to sing that all the time, but they never used to tell all the men about it, what the song was about, which was really about them mustering bullocks and cracking the whips. It was a fun sort of a song. And the women'd get together at night-time and sing that when all the blokes were gone. "C'mon, we're gonna sing that song now. *Kweye mpe! Apere artnangkwe-artnangkwe akweke alyelhetyekaye!* C'mon girls, let's sing about the gum tree scrubs!" And then they'd start singing and another mob'd start laughing, and everyone'd have a big old giggle about it because it was a really funny song. It was some sort of entertainment for them when the blokes had gone away, you know? They'd just get together and make up songs, and that's just one song they used to sing. *Ye*, those old ladies used to sing that as part of the entertainments that people used to have. We would listen and sit around windbreaks *apmere arlwekerele*, at the ladies' quarters, the women's camp. The women used to stay in one big *arlwekere* when the husbands went away. And when they came back, they could go and live with them again then. And they had all these funny songs that they used to find and sing.

When we was still only little kids, me and my cousin used to sing that *apere artnangkwe-artnangkwe* song sitting up in a tree. But it didn't mean anything to me, I didn't know what they were singing about, I didn't know what was the meaning about it. And my mum used to say "hey, you shouldn't sing like that! That's a grown-up woman's song!" I didn't know that by singing it they were teasing my uncles and them. Teasing them about how they'd crack the whip, and how they'd run amongst the cattle; that they was really praising them up in a teasing way!

They really enjoyed themselves them days, *akangkemele itne anetyarte*. And sometimes *arelhe mape*, all the women used to just get up and go and dance for fun, you know? Dance in a big pile just for a joke dance. *Putye-arenye mape-arle aneme ampe mape* used to *akaltye-irrerle*, and they used to teach by that sort of dancing.

Ye, we dance for fun, or for teach. Sometimes when we teach the young women the non-sacred dancing, we teach them when the time comes along for the young women's singing, when the really new teenage girl comes out. That's when we teach them how to dance, how to paint themselves, how to shake your legs, what type of clothes to wear. How to dress themselves, how to make and wear the headdresses. How to stand in a row or a line, a straight line or behind one another, *akerte-arratye*. Or to learn to recognise whatever song that certain people sing when it's their turn to come out onto the dancing ground, their country song. When it's time for that *apmere* to come out. Teaching time is fun time. But they can teach only their own children.

When there's a fun dance, everybody gets in, *akaltye-irretyeke*, for learning. Even *anthepe-irretyeke akaltye-irretyeke*, you know? That's how people used to teach dancing, just by doing it. The old people, they used to just go in and dance, and that's the time you learn, by watching the old people dancing. Then as they're growing up they know about it themselves then. Not many young people are learning that nowadays.

Ayeye-arle Alheme, Ayeye-arle Apetye-alpeme

Story Goes Out and Comes Back Home

Altyerrenge-arle ayeye aneke, lyete-arle alakenhe aneneheme, Story was there in the Beginning Time, and it's still living today. My mum passed her Stories on to me. But my mum, she didn't have that Story just by herself, she had that Story from Grandmother. And Grandmother had that Story from her mum. And our Stories just go from up, down. From down, Stories come upwards. So that's why I learned many Stories with a lot of aunt. Our grandfather-Ancestors and grandmother-Ancestors are the ones that was the beginning of the language of our *apmere* and of the Stories. They're at the bottom of us, of our Land, and that's why the Stories come up, from them.

Everybody's Stories are like that. The people that owns the Story and its language, their Story comes up, goes out and comes back again, like that. That's how Story is. Whoever from that Land's gonna hear the Story, they have to really listen to that person that owns the Story, and they must understand it. Understand it from the person who owns the Story, the Story that comes up from deep inside their country. And a person has to learn how to tell that Story. They might be instructed, "I'm telling you this Story that belongs to me. I want you to tell it on really well, so that it can be truly heard and understood. Then it has to be brought back here and told again, so that I know that you truly heard and understood. In the same way, after you've retold the Story to me, I can tell it on as our Story to other people around this country. I then have to bring my version of the Story back to you in the same way that you told your version of the Story to me. But it's my telling of it that you'll hear".

I made this painting with the boomerangs in it. I mean, the boomerang belongs to men, but Story is like a boomerang, it goes out like it has been thrown, and then the woman you told brings the Story back to you, she throws her Story back. And then she's

Ayeye-arle Alheme, Ayeye-arle Apetye-alpeme   Story Goes Out and Comes Back Home

wanting to tell that Story to someone else, and that other one then has to throw *their* version back. "Throw that Story back over my way to me, like I toss my Story over to you". But she must teach about the Story as well as tell it or sing it. Like the elders, you can only tell Story like the elders do. It's the only proper way to tell the Story to people, to tell it like an elder so that people hear and truly understand, and can then tell it like that back to you. Now you can give back that Story or throw that Story back to another one so that *she* can listen to it and understand what you're really talking about. She and I might both have understood it well and remembered how to tell it. And then, after I've told her that Story, I might tell her another Story, and then I might throw the next Story over to another one again. So that *that one* can remember it really well. "And now you throw it over to another her or him". And so on it goes.

All this Story can only be told by elder women to begin with. And while the Story might really belong to one certain person, that Story connects them *all* together. That person inherits that Story from the *arrwekelenye mape*, the ones who went in front, but it's just as if it's been given to them all, like it's handed up or handed around to each and every one, *antherre-antherre-alpeme*, or *anthirtne-anthirtne-alpeme*.

Ayeye-arle Alheme, Ayeye-arle Apetyalpeme, A Story of Going and Coming Back, 2006, acrylic on canvas, photographer Barry McDonald
"*Lyete-arle alakenhe anenheme*. And it's still living today. *Altyerrenge-arle ayeye aneke*. The Story was started by the Ancestors. The background streams are the Stories coming out *apmerenge* and crossing over each other (the spirit of the Land coming out, the messages of the Land). The boomerangs indicate the action of the Story going out and returning again, like a spiral. The Stories have been forever and will be forever".

73

Like my grandfather's Story is handed up to my brothers, then it's handed up to me, and then my grandfather's Story I can tell my younger sisters and brothers. Then these might tell their male cousins, and the cousins might tell their younger sisters and brothers, and then *they* might tell their older sisters. If they all arose up from the one country – brothers-in-law, father's father and mother's father, father's mothers, mother's mothers, all from the one patch of homelands, *apmereyanhe anyente-arenye* – then that Story joins them all, and weaves in and out through that country all the time. That Story will go in and through all those families, because those families are all in there together, whatever skin name they are – *Perrurle, Kemarre, Angale, Ampetyane, Pengarte, Penangke, Peltharre, Kngwarraye*. They'll be all in there, so this Story is handed up over the generations to all those people who are in that kinship network, the *anpernirrentye* of that country, *apmereyanhe*. Because they all arose originally from that country.

As more people come out from that country, Story goes further and gets stronger. Story starts in the centre with one person, then it goes out wider and wider. Then when another person's gonna be born, the Story returns to the centre, it comes back in. Then that one takes it out further and further. Then another one is born, and *they* take it out. Like that, *alakenhe. Angkweye-angkweye-angkweye-arteke*, like that little ant lion, that's how the Story keeps going back in. *Alakenhe athewe.*

Anpernirrentye, Kinship

"Our kinship *shows us the way*, the Rule of the Law.
It has come from our Traditional Land,
and also from the Beginning
to know who we are."

Angkerrentye Anpernirrentye-akerte

A Dialogue Concerning the Sacredness of Kinship

Anpernirrentye-akerte. Anpernirrentye-arle apmere kantreyenge-arle apetyeme, apmere aknganentyenge-ntyele. Arelhe tyerrtye mape kwenengenenge, urrperle mape anwerne anpernirrentye-akerte akwete-arle amangkintyeke, ane intintyeke.

Kinship comes out of the country itself,
it comes from the Ancestor Beings.
Aboriginal people have grown up
deep inside this from Creation,
and they live within it always and forever.

Anpernirrentyele-arle akwele tyerrtye mape lterrke anthurre antirrkwerle-aneme. Anpernirrentyele-arle lterrke anthurre atnyeneme ingkerreke. Anpernirrentyele-arle anemele-arle menhengenhenge anyenhengenhenge aneme ante ahelhe arntarnte-areme, anpernirrentyele. Alakenhakweye Altyerrenge-arle arrwekele anintye-alpeke. Anpernirretyakenhe anerle, kele unte iwenhe apeke rarle unte aneme, you're just somebody else.

Kinship holds Aboriginal people really close and strong, it holds everyone tightly together. *Anpernirrentye* guides and cares for the all the generations of people that have lived within the cradle of their Land. It's been like that always, stretching from the Creation, and it endures forever. It's in the Histories. If you don't relate to each other like this, nobody can know who you are.

Anpernirrentye is about our relationship. Where we were from, about where we begun, begin, began or whatever, something like that. And also 'we've lived our life' – like *anintyeke* – eternally, from our own country, *apmerenge-ntyele*. It's our recognition, just with that name. If you don't have *anpernirrentye* as a person for Aboriginal people, you're just nobody, you know? You might have relationship cousins, aunties, but that

Angkerrentye Anpernirrentye-akerte   A Dialogue Concerning the Sacredness of Kinship

anpernirrentye, it tells what skin are you, and what skin names are those people, and what skin are the Lands – everything that connects is *anpernirrentye* in that Land, to everyone. *Anpernirrentye* comes out of that country itself, the place where you arose. And we as Aboriginal people, we were born and grew up with it, even from before the time we were born. *Alakenhe*. Do you want to say anything about that *alere atyinhe*, my niece?

Veronica *Perrurle*: *Ye*, I want to point out that the country *is* our Ancestors, *alakenhe. Anwerneke artweye rarle apmere-arle ane renhe arrwekeleneyele ilerrirretyarte, utnenge-inpe-arle anintyeke re*. The country really is our Ancestors, our family, part of us. That's how people have told the Story over the generations. Our spirit's still with our Ancestors, always. And Ancestor spirits are still with us on the

---

Left: **Margaret Kemarre,** photographer Barry McDonald

Right: **Veronica Perrurle,** photographer Barry McDonald

77

Land, *alakenhe*. And our Ancestor Spirits, living in the country, they're really pure – the country, the Ancestor Spirits, and the people that live within the actual country. That's if they don't go desecrating sacred sites, and they don't go digging up trees and things, and breaking down things wherever they please. They have to respect all that, because without all that we wouldn't be here, our Ancestors would not have lived here. The trees, the plants, whatever that's on the Land it belongs to all of us, because of our Ancestors. Spirit *itnekenhe-arle ane utnenge itnekenhe anwernekenge akwete aneme*; their spirit is still with us always. When you go out to a sacred site you've gotta *ilerle*. *Ipenye apeke-arle akngeme itelaraye.* "*Ipenye mape ware akngetyenhe* or *apmere ware aretyeke. Rlkerte-iletyale kwenhe*". *Alakenhe apeke.* Maybe you're taking along some strangers, well, you've got to talk to the country: "I've brought some people along that you don't know, just to have a look at the country. Please don't make them sick". In the early days they never used to walk just anywhere to collect water and that. They used to *ingkatyele-werrerle*, walk in one another's footsteps. Always. Anywhere. That's respect.

What our Aunty was saying before is that you've got to carry *anpernirrentye* and practise it. Not just have the skin name, you've got to *be* that person, in practice. Believe what the old people say and listen to them, because the old people are the ones that have the knowledge that they want to give and pass on before anything happens to them. Otherwise the old people take the knowledge with them. *Arrernte* people have to be strong and say "this is our country, and this is our heritage from our own people, and from our Dreaming" – or whatever white people call it, we call it *aknganentye*. They got to make sure they believe in who they are. *Alakenhe*.

Apmere nhenge, apmere urlerte-arenye mapeke-arle, anpernirrentye lterrke anthurre anemaye tyerrtye Arrernte-arlkeke itelaraye. Apmerenge-ntyele re aneme anpernirrentye yanhe renhe nhenge apmere-arlke anperneme anwernenhenge apmere nhenhe atyenge arrenge, apmere nhenhe atyenge ipmenhe, alakenhe-arle, apmere nhenhe atyenge artweye, alakenhe. Apmere anpernirrentyeke arrangkwe akenhe nhenge apmere alakenhe-arlke anpernetyeke arrangkwe-arle. Anpernirrentye nhenhe rarle lterrke anthurre ileme anwernenhe, nhenge nthakenhe-akenhe anwerne anpernirreme

Angkerrentye Anpernirrentye-akerte   A Dialogue Concerning the Sacredness of Kinship

nthenhakweye anwerneke aperle nthenhe anwerneke matye-areye-arlke, alakenhe. Apmere nthenhe-arenye itne anpernirrentye nhenhe impene anthurre anwernekenhe. Alakenhe akwete-arle anwerneke artweye arrwekelenye anintyeke anwerne aneme nhenhe aneme. Ingkernenye mape apeke nhenge-arle aperlpe-apateye ulkere-arle kenhe, anwerne akwete-arle itelareme lterrke anthurre anpernirrentye-akerte nhenhe renhe. Nthakenhe-akenhe-arle nhenge Altyerre apenteme anpernirrentye nthenhele iwenhe apeke renhe. Layake Irretye apeke, Ayepe-arenye apeke, Kere Aherre apeke, iwenhe apeke renhe tyerrtye-kenhe totem-*arle itne akeme nhenge Altyerre-arle aneke itelare apmere nthenhe-arenye apeke re. Kwatye Aknganentye apekawe, alakenhe. Anpernirrentyele-arle renhe-arle alakenhe imerneme nthakenhe-akenhe nhenge apmere-arlke anpernetyeke. Arratyentye ilemele. Apale-apale-arlke nhenge arrpenhe mape inerreme lyete-ulkere. Apmere-arlke aneme nhenge itne nhenge ampe itnekenheke ulpertelhe-arle-ileme nhenge anpernirrentye yanhe apentetyakenhe-arle, alakenhe.*

    Anpernirrentye combines Land, people and totems. A certain country can only be related to by those people who rightfully belong to it, the relationship network amongst those people for that Land is so very strong. This goes for all *Arrernte* people. The *anpernirrentye* that's there, the one that comes out of that place, originates there, it tells how you relate to country. For us, a particular country could be grandfather, or it might be our mother's mother, or it could be related to us in other ways. If you're not connected to that certain country, then you can't relate to it in any way like this. The relationship network we were born into is what makes our connection really strong, however it is we might relate to this or that Land, whether as father's mother, or even as mother country, that sort of thing. Whichever country we're connected to, our relationship to it is really precious to us, it is treasured. That's the way that our people have always lived and will continue to live. Even though the younger generation might not be too sure of the relationship system, we're still right here, the older generation who remember and uphold our kinship. Like how we follow whichever Stories are involved in the kinship for this or that place. It might be Eagle, or Caterpillar, or Kangaroo, whatever people relate to as their totem, whatever Dreaming it is for that country; it might be Rain Dreaming or whatever. The kinship network is what shows you just how you relate to your own country. That's the way it truly is, and how it was spoken in the Beginning. People are marrying into the wrong skin groups nowadays, and this means that country is getting muddied up with their children not knowing which place they belong to. They're not following their kinship in the way that the Land requires.

<u>Margaret *Kemarre*</u>: Some younger people don't understand how people are connected to Land. The Rule laid down by *arrwekelenye mape*, the Ancestors, cannot change. *Anpernirrentye kwenhe anwernekenhe artekerre-arle. Artekerre-arteke-arle aneme apmere anwerne-arle Apmere Altyerre akekeke. Arrenge akekenge, atyakekenge, ipmenhe akekenge, artekerre akweke mape anwernekenge arlenge intenheme. Iwenhe-ante-iwenhe-ante re anwerne ane ampe anwernekenhe mape.* 'Cause *ingkernenye mape* mightn't *itelarerle apeke*, that's why *ingkernenye ampe mapele awetyenhenge apeke alakenhe-arle anintyeke kwenhe. Alakenhe-arle anintyeke alakenhe-arle akwete re anenhele. Altyerrenge-arle ileke renhe-arle.* Can't *akngarte-iwerle*.

Kinship is our roots. It's like the roots to the Land that our Country Dreaming connection comes out of. Issuing from our father's father, and our mother's father, and our mother's mother, and our father's mother, those fine branching root threads run onwards from us, through to whatever it might be, animals and plants, through to our children. Because the younger generation may not realise this, it's important that the children of now must hear that's how it was and is still that way. That's how it is, always was, and will continue forever. From the very Beginning it was *told* that this is how it is. Nobody can't turn it 'round, 'cause that's how it was, and it's gotta stay that way today, like it's always been before.

<u>Veronica *Perrurle*</u>: *Apmere nhenhe-arenye awerre kwenhe nhenhe-areye iwenhe alakenhe-arlke ilerlaye. Nhenhe-areye awerre Penangke mape apmere nhenhe-arenye kwenhe. Kenhe Angale mape nhakwe-arenye, alakenhe-arlke ilerle. Apmere-arle itne alakenhe renhe nhenge anpernetyarte. Arelhe tyerrtye itneke artweye-arteke antime. Iwenhe-apatherre arelhe apmereke artweye aneme, apmere yanhe renhe-arle itne alakenhe renhe anperneme nhenge. Nhenhe awerre Kemarre mape-kenhe apmere*

kwenhe. Apmere yanhe atyenge awenhe-awenhe or *atyenge artweye kwenhe, alakenhe apeke.*

These are the people of *this* country, that's what's been told from Creation. These are the *Penangke* mob from this country; the *Angale*s are from another area, so our Ancestors decreed. That's how Aboriginal people always related to country, just like their family did before them. Whichever area you are belonging to, the country also has that same skin name, and people relate to that particular country in the same way as they do to other people of that name. So, if this is the *Kemarre* group's country, it's also called *Kemarre*; then I can call that country my father's sister, or even call it my father, that sort of thing.

<u>Margaret *Kemarre*</u>: *Tharle awenhe akeke mape-kenhe akwele apmere yanhe. Or akngeye atyinheke-areye nhenhe kwenhe. Or tharle ipmenhe akeke akenhe kwenhe apmere yanhe tharle ipmenhe-arle akeme kwenhe*, even though *apmere arrpenhe-kenhe-arle apeke*, you can still *apmere anpernerle* by just skin group *arrirtne ware.*

And *apmere Kemarre*, that's the country I can call father's sister, or my grandfather. Or I can call another country mother's mother. I can call it mother's mother, even though it might not belong to my direct family, because you can still relate to distant country, even just by skin name.

<u>Veronica *Perrurle*</u>: *Nhenge arlenge-ulkere apeke anpernirrentye-arle itne mwantyele kine alakenhe ileme. Nhenhe awerre ipmenhatye-areye-kenhe kwenhe. Apmere nhakwe-ulkere-arenye mape-kenhe kwenhe, alakenhe. Apmere arerrentye mape-arle akenhe itweke-itweke-arle aneke, anpernirrentye mape. Itne aneme alakenhe re nhenge anpernirreme, nhenhe awerre nhareye-kenhe apmere, anwerneke artweye mape-kenhe kine kwenhe, alakenhe. Anpernirrentyele-mpele.*

So even if it's a distant relative to you by skin grouping, we were told to take care in relating to that Land and those people just as we do to close relatives. Like, this country is where my mother's mother's people belong to, while that country and those people may be a bit further away down the track. Neighbours in your own *anpernirrentye* boundary, they were the closest to each other, and that's where kinship has always worked most strongly: "These are the countries belonging to these skin groups, so they are our own families too". That's how kinship works its way through country and people.

Margaret *Kemarre*: A lot of our young people still don't know about relating to people, like even how you have to sit when you're with your families. There are words in *Arrernte*, lots of words that describe just how you should sit when you're with this one or that one, like where the legs are. That's another sort of language of respect. *Layake*, if you *ilerle tyurrempetyurre apeke anetyarte*, if you mentioned about how we sat in following *anpernirrentye*, sitting with our legs stretched out in front, they don't know *arrirtne alakenhe-arlke*, they wouldn't even know what that word was, or what you were talking about. *Arrkwinyere-arlke anetyeke apeke nhenge ilerle*, same as if you said something about sitting with both legs folded to the side, or cross-legged, or sitting sideways. Some of those names are really different. These are things that people seem to be forgetting, *alkngwirrerle*.

Veronica *Perrurle*: In relationship, it's definitely the way you sit towards people as well, not only the way you talk to people. You've gotta respect the way you sit; you don't just come and squat down, you have to sit down respectfully. All that was in respect as well. The relationship wasn't only Land ownership and relationship with the Land, it was how you respected people in the way you sat down, in the way you spoke, and in the way you approach people too, when you're coming towards a camp. All that was in respect towards relationship. When you related to people, you actually had to do those things, all the time. Even ceremonies. You had to respect how you walked into even minor ceremonies. You can't go in there ten or twenty minutes later. Even if you're family for those people, you can't go in there late. You have to be all there together getting painted up and ready for the ceremony, you can't do it on your own and then come in. You have to be with the group, you have to be there with the rest of the people. And it's ruled by how you're related to people by skin name too. It might be ceremony for all the *Kemarre*s and *Peltharre*s. Us *Perrurle*s can't just walk in, because that's out of bounds and it's disrespectful. That's all in respect in relationship, how you relate to

Angkerrentye Anpernirrentye-akerte   A Dialogue Concerning the Sacredness of Kinship

people and how you respect *their* relationships. It's all to do with everything to uphold the *Arrernte* society. Our mob have a lot of respect for people. *Alakenhe*.

My brother here has mentioned that some white people he knows, some *alherntere mape* think that our kinship 'imprisons' people in this way. On the contrary, it was the missionaries that enslaved *Arrernte* people to the *new* culture. We lived our traditional lives, and we had our culture, and we had our beliefs, and everything else. And then white men came. Not being mean or anything by saying this. White men came. And they got us all together and put us on a mission. Not that they were nasty or anything, they were trying to do good for us, as we knew. But the thing was, they took us from a different culture, and they taught us *their* culture and *their* beliefs. It's actually that we were slaves to that other culture, not to *anpernirrentye*.

Margaret *Kemarre*: In our *anpernirrentye*, we have strong rules. And Rule *anwernekenhe aneke antirrkwerrentye akwete*, it's still hand in hand with us. We didn't feel 'prisoned in our Law society – our Law is very strong, our Law is the way that it has come from our Traditional Land, and also from the Beginning to know who we are, and how we can do things. Our *anpernirrentye* didn't 'prison us. It couldn't 'prison us. Our kinship *shows us the way*, the Rule of the Law. That's *anpernirrentyele-arle anwernenhe iwerre anwerneke imerneke*. And our Rule has never been broken. The ones who have broken and might be breaking the Law now are just individual persons. They have crossed over just in their own personal way. But the Rule itself has never been broken, it's still alive. No matter whether you've married in the wrong way, that child is still that skin name person from those grandparents and those Lands. From their own Rule. That can never be changed. *Anpernirrentye* continues to hold and be held very

---

Barry McDonald, photographer G. & T. McLittle

strongly in yourself, your group, in your family. It still lays in a straight line in those *menhengenhenge ane anyenhengenhenge*, grandfather to father, father to his children. And also in the mother's line, from uncles to their nephews. That Land calls you by its own name. Name and relationship from that Land. Still strong. *Alakenhe.*

That's another thing in *anpernirrentye* for us. For me and *atyenge artweye mape-arle anintyeke arrwekelenge, anwernekenhe anpernirrentyele* never *anwernenhe antirrkwerle* 'prison-*eme-arteke-ilemele*. For me and my families ever since Creation, never did kinship *ever* hold us in chains.

Anpernirrentye anwernekenhele-arle anwernenhe tyerrtye urrperle ingkerreke anthurre renhe nhenhe-arle anintyekwenge akangketyeke, alhengke-aretyeke, tnaketyeke, ante antirrkwerretyeke. Alakenhele-arle anwerne iwenhakweye ileke, mekikwe akangketyeke, apmarleye akangketyeke, atyekikwe, ipmenhekikwe, ampeke, arrenge-arle akeke, ane apmere anwerne-arle antirrkwenheke. Alakenhakweye anpernirrentye yanhe anwernekenhe aneme.

Instead, our kinship has given happiness and great joy in living to all of us Aboriginal people who have been travelling this path from our Creation and onwards. It has given us recognition and identity, and has allowed us to really nurture one another. That's how it is from the Creation, and that's how we perceive it now. Kinship creates and inspires joyful love for your mothers, love for your uncles, love and happiness for your mother's fathers, for your children, for your father's fathers, and abiding love for the country we hold now, and have always held, and will hold forever.

Alakenhe, that's how *Arrernte* describes it. Maybe my niece Veronica can talk about *anpernirrentye* a little bit more like this in English.

<u>Veronica *Perrurle*</u>: The country is what kept us together always, and the relationship come from the country, because our Ancestors lived on the country and they handed down the skin system from generation to generation. And Land ownership was handed down like that because of the skin system that overruled the life of all the *Arrernte* people, of those people that got kin and skin and relate to the kin and skin. And it was always real strong. And that's what ties us to the Land, to our relationship to

Angkerrentye Anpernirrentye-akerte   A Dialogue Concerning the Sacredness of Kinship

people, to the plants, animals, whatever lives on the Land. We're all related because of that. Because our Ancestors has taught us and they worked out this system. It's a real good system to show people that don't know about how Aboriginal people relate to country and relate to each other. Everybody's related to each other in that sense. Distant relatives, distant-distant relatives as well. We still recognise our relationship because we know what our skin name is, and that's how we relate to people. Son-in-law, mother-in-law, father-in-law, and daughter-in-law, all that's all intertwined with the Land ownership. All our stories, songs, all our *awelye*s, our women's ceremonies, everything come from the Land. As we believe. *Alakenhe*.

Margaret *Kemarre*: And it's a *loving* way.

Veronica *Perrurle*: And it was always strong, and we hope our younger generation keep it strong like we have for all this time. We'd like to see our younger generation do the same – look after the Land that give 'em life, water, food, and everything else to survive, you know. They need to make sure that they keep the skin system and carry it on, teach younger generations, and make sure that it's carried on, and people like us are remembered by it, because the knowledge that we give may be the only knowledge that these people'll get. You know that a lot of the older people are dying off with the language, and the young people are not learning the language, or their beliefs and that. *Alakenhe*.

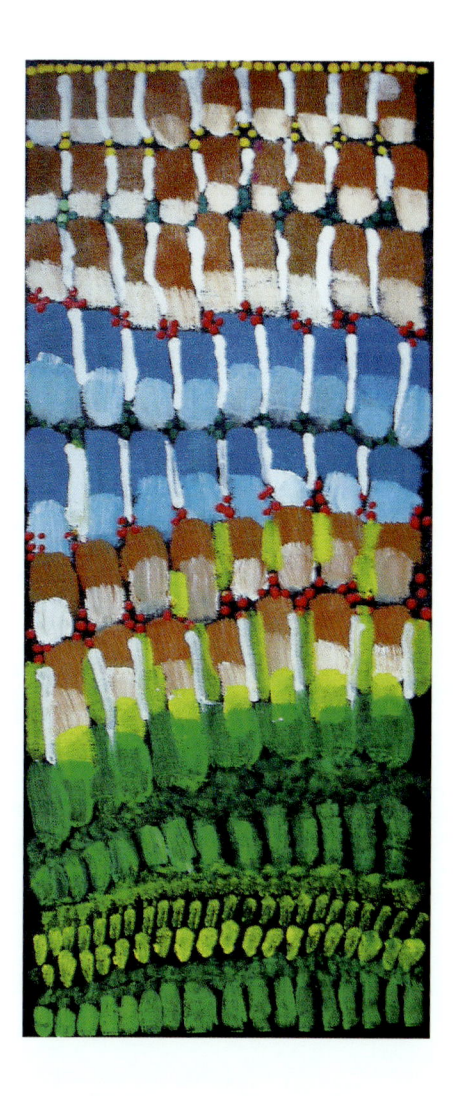

Anthepe, 2005, acrylic on canvas, photographer *Irrkerlantye* Arts
Anthepe is the *Arrernte* name for the dance women perform at initiation ceremonies. The lines represent the patterns left in the sand by the dancers' feet. This dance has been handed down from generation to generation. These are the things we paint to teach our children and to keep our culture strong.

Ikirrentye and *Nyurrpe*

We've got eight skin names in our society, *tyerrtye urrperle-kenhe*. Those eight skin groups lays in the ground, in each Aboriginal people's Land. And that holds the people and the ground, the Land itself, together. And to hold it properly you've got to do everything in the right way.

Ikirrentye is a word meaning respect. And also shame. Not shame because you don't want to do it because it's a shame thing, it's a shame thing because you're not the right skin name person, you haven't got the right to talk about it. Might be your uncle's the right person to talk about something, because he's on the right skin line to do it. That's why shame is not being shy, it's because you're not on the right side of that word for it to be said and to be done. Shame and respect go together, they work together. If you ever do that shameful thing towards other people, that's not respecting. And that goes together, because that relates to who you are, what you are to those people, and what those people are to us. That's how it is, that's how it goes. Shame means that she or he is not the one to put that word out to those skin groups, not the right person. He might be the right family, but he might not be the right person to say that word. The right person to say that word might be from the opposite-side people. And the right person doesn't only have to say that word, but they have to say it in an understanding way that fits into what the conversation's all about, and what the relationships are all about.

Ikirrentye covers all the ways people behave to each other. What you *can* do as well as what you can't do. Because of *ikirrentye*, you can't say the wrong things to your *nyurrpe* side. You must know what you can do and what you can't do, *ikirrentye ane ikirrentye-kwenye*. That is the way of Aboriginal people. I was always known by how I keep respectful distance and also by my close relating. It's the same thing. And that's who I am.

That skin name is really important to us because it draws a line, every individual's line. To what to do, to how to behave, and how to carry on. It outlines where people can stand, what is their right. Which one you've gotta move before you move this one. You can't jump over and do that whatsiname, you've gotta know where are the right movements, *alakenhe*. That's *anpernirrentye, antirrkwerrentye alanhe, aneme-arle alakenhe*. It's a real holding together in that way.

Nyurrpe

Our skin name system is half-and-half, it's got two sides. But this one here, it's a different two sides to the country-relating that I talked about with *ilakakeye*. *Anpernirrentye atherreke-atherre. Arrpenhe mape "nyurrpe", ane itne anwernenhe ileme "nyurrpe"*. So in this system, we call them *"nyurrpe"*, and they also call us *"nyurrpe"*.

Nyurrpe, the Alternate-generation moieties

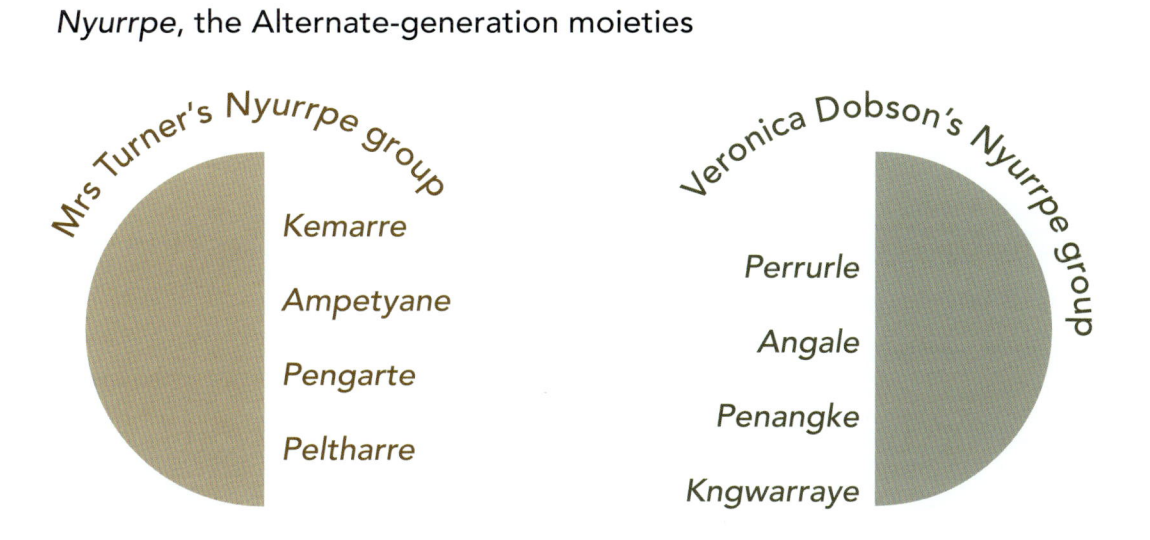

Mrs Turner's *Nyurrpe* group
- Kemarre
- Ampetyane
- Pengarte
- Peltharre

Veronica Dobson's *Nyurrpe* group
- Perrurle
- Angale
- Penangke
- Kngwarraye

Nyurrpe's just that 'generation moiety', that's the name that *alherntere mape* gave it. 'Us' means all my grandmothers, and grandfathers, and my grandchildren, and my husband, my sisters and brothers, my sister-in-law, and my cousin, and myself, like *Peltharre*, and *Ampetyane*, and *Pengarte*, and *Kemarre*. That's the four on our side. On the other side, *nyurrpe* for us, is *Kngwarraye, Angale, Perrurle*, and *Penangke*. My *ampatye-ampatye*'s on that other side, and my *anherre*, and my *alere*, and *ampe atyinhe-areye*; my parents, my kids, all my in-laws, aunts and uncles, and my nieces and nephews. And they've got the same relationships again on their side; like grandparents and cousins, *itneke ipmenhe, itneke arrenge, itneke altyele*, same again, like what I've got on my side.

Ikirrentye is the most respectable name and word that lives in the ground. And also *ikirrentye* is sacredness. You know, you can't confront, look directly at your father; you can't confront your mother, that's really, really wrong. Because you're not the right person. You can't go putting your arm around your sister, or your niece. Turning your niece around and kissing her and poking her on the ribs and all that. That's very wrong, whether for a woman or a man that's wrong. Because that's really shameful, you're not the right skin-name person to do that. And you can't talk face-to-face with your uncle, *ularreke-ularre tnerle*. You're not being rude, but you can't look at him in the eye, you have to talk sideways. *Ikirrentye* is really sacred for us. Every individual *urrperle* person has sacred things. Sacredness in ourselves, that's how we see it. Even an old man sitting down there, he's a sacred person, even though he's not our relation. Because he's an elder, and he's got the knowledge, and he's got the detail of every young people, and he can see what's in us. Also he's got a special skin name. Or sometimes people might say about someone else – he might be a drinker – "oh, he's not worth anything". But that person must be special to us through our Land. And also through our children, our families, and through our country. That's how we see every individual person, like elders and grown-ups. Even from the tiniest kid, you know? Even when you've got a tiny little baby, you must respect him or her. Because every Aboriginal person has *Altyerre*.

All the different family relationships have a different *ikirrentye* for them. You can (i.e. must) act in one way for your *mwere*, your son-in-law, and in a different way towards your father. And for your brother it's a different-acting way again. Even with your daughters you can act in a different way. And with your nieces, *arelhe alere mape*, your brother's kids, you can act in a different way too. In a skin way. And also you can act in a different way with you grandmothers, your 'grannies' – *ipmenhe* you call it – in a granny-way of relating.

Ikirrentye and *Nyurrpe*   Nyurrpe

There's different ways of using rough or joking words. You can't talk dirty jokes to your nieces and your daughters. Because they've got their own way of joking with their cousins. We've gotta joke that way with our own cousins. There's four skin groups in our side, we can only joke with those ones there, unless they're your brothers. Like *Ampetyane* and *Pengarte*, and *Kemarre* and *Peltharre*, 'cause they're on all our side. We can joke for all of them except our brothers. You can joke to your cousins, maybe your brother-in-law might be a jokey sort of person. We can't have jokes with the people on the other *nyurrpe* side, because they're connected to my sons, to my daughters, to my nieces, to my father-in-law, and to my mother-in-law, and to my uncles and aunts, they're all on that other side. Except sometimes you might have an *alere*, a nephew, who's a jokey one too, a playful person who jokes all the time, some people are like that. Well you can have a joke with that sort of *alere*, even though he's on that other side. They call them *arrkene-akngerre*, meaning a playful person who likes to joke all the time.

Cousins talk to each other, *altyelenhenge, marle altyelenhenge*, oh, *ilterrerle arrkene prape* rudest way-*nge*! But it doesn't mean anything, it's just a fun sort of a rude swearing. And the bloke cousins, they can talk that way to each other too. Old grandmothers can have a joke – grandparents can have a joke with grandkids. *Aperle* can have a joke, *aperle-aperle* and *ipmenhe*. They can joke *atnyenerle*. Just a friendly joke, like *ipmenhe-arle arrkene-angkeme*. That's how *ipmenhe* feels to her grandchildren. *Aperleke, arrengeke, ipmenheke*, those grandparent relationships. Like you can have an *ipmenhe* joke, an *arrenge* sort of joke, especially all the women. I think the men have their own joke as well. And sometimes they talk in a special *arrenge* or *ipmenhe* way in telling grandkids about living their lives.

But to follow *ikirrentye* is 'specially important with my uncles, and aunts, and my parents. That's how that respectful distance is always there, and it's really sacred, distancing is one of the *most* sacred things. And also respecting. Respecting your mums and dads, and also to your uncle. Uncle might be the Leadership in your mother's family. Her brother might be the important person, he might be the last person. And you want to really treasure that person, so you really respect your uncle and your mother. Well, they might be the last two that holds the Land or holds the Story; who knows the detail of what's in that Land of ours.

The sacredness of *ikirrentye* comes from the Land. Because of that it's a really strict relationship – son-in-law and mother-in-law can't sit next to, or do anything with each other. But father and daughter is another strict relationship, and also brother and sister. All those distance relationships are sacred. Sacred to everyone – mothers, fathers, brothers, daughters, niece, and also your *mwere*s. They're all sacred to us. And respect in the proper way for all of us, not only your son-in-law or daughter-in-law, but for every one. I can't talk about my daughters in the way that my nieces can talk about them, or how their grandmother can talk about them or to them. I can't talk about any details about them when they go in for birth rites. It's a distancing-sacredness, just the same thing as for your son-in-law. Like if there's an antenatal clinic *kwerre arletye alakenhenge*, then *ipmenhe*, the mother's mother is the only one who can talk to those young girls. And maybe *aperle*, father's mother, or father's father's sister, their *arrengeye*. *Aperleke, arrengeke, ane ipmenhe.* 'Cause *anwerne angkeme nyurrpe anwernekenheke-areye. Nyurrpe arrpenheke-areye anwerne angketyakenhe*, because we can only talk in that way for the people who are on our side of the skin line, not to the other-side people.

As we know, there's four of each side of the skin system, so we talk by relating, and feeling. In the way that we want to talk to people when they're pregnant, and when they're going into labour, and also who's the right people to sit with them. Now today, just anybody sits. And before it used to be really *ikirrentye*. And that's really sacred to us women, *marle mape, nyurrpeke-nyurrpe. Alakenhe.* And you cannot *ilterle* in a bad way for your mother. Now today you see people where all those little kids are learning really bad swearwords to say to anyone, *angkentye akurne aneme ampe akweke mape-arle akaltye-irretyeke ilterretyeke*. They see it on the television. But we want our kids to understand how to talk and relate in a really good way for their families.

If there's somebody sick, well only the right people can talk about it with them or for them, about their body, 'in the body' side. They might have sickness, and might be we wouldn't be able to tell about that sickness, in which part of the body. Maybe

Ikirrentye and *Nyurrpe   Nyurrpe*

it's inside the body and our side can't talk about it – maybe it's a bit shame for us to describe it, about where she's got that sore. If a nurse said to me "oh, your daughter's got this and that", I'll say straight out, "no, you can't say that to me, I want you to say that to my brother's daughters". So my brother's kid, she might be a health worker, she can tell about what that sickness inside of that person's body is. 'Cause I can't say it, and my sister-in-law can't say it, because we are on the other side of the chart, we're *nyurrpe*s to them. That's really sacred to us, we can't talk about those sort of things. Not only women, men have that on their side as well.

But at sorry time, every skin group does special things, the families in sadness really rely on those other-side skin groups. And that's a shame part, that's how like if there's a death in the family, we can't talk about anything for my cousin's side, or my sister's side. We can't talk about it, we've gotta tell our kids to talk about those sort of things. And that runs through our skin line. The opposite-side people have always gotta do that work for us at sorry time. It is shame and it is wrong if the same side does that work. But in actually mourning that person, we can only talk about all the ones on *our* side – sisters, sister-in-laws, our grannies, our *arrengeye*s and *atyemeye*s.

The same feelings that one has for people, one also has for Land. We've got eight skin names, and in that eight skin names half are the 'wrong' people from the other side. Everything's sacred to us in the Land, and also the people in that Land. So you have *ikirrentye* for Land, which always has a skin name, in just exactly the same way as you do for people. And all things that live in that Land are sacred to us. So we can't go down and chop, chop trees, and we can't burn down grass, because that grass's grown from our own Sacred Land. And those trees are grown out from our Sacred Ground. And it's a curse, *imatyewennge*. It's a curse-related. If you don't respect Land in the proper way, you attract a curse to yourself. You might get sick or have an accident *apeke*.

Like my son-in-law's country. I'll respect that Land in the same way that I respect him. And *ikirrerle* you know, there's sacred trees and sacred things that belong to my son-in-law, and I'll respect those things like him, and also his Land. If I eat *kere* with his family on his Land, I've gotta do it with a certain respect. I can't just throw a bone in the fire, because that's not right. It's bad for some sort of reaction. If I'm going to respect that person, I must respect how I live there, and how I fit in with all those people, and with all the things that I do. I've gotta respect his father too, and his children. I can't go to their country by myself, but I can go with my grandchildren, his children. And I can't wander around on my own, climb up a hill or go down there and get anything, because I've got a respectful-distance relationship with that country belongs to my daughter's children.

Kwantheme, Nyurrpe-Teasing

Kwanthemele angkeme means teasing and joking for your *nyurrpe*s. *Kwanthemele angkerreme* was when the two *nyurrpe*-sides used to tease each other in a fun way. *Kwanthemele* or *kwenthemele*, it means the same thing. Those days were really fun. One way they used to always do it was when they played card games against each other, *nyurrpeke-nyurrpe*. My cousin and my brother were playing cards one time, and me and R.D. and my niece was sitting to the side a bit, watching them play against these two old people. These two old people, two brothers-in-law, were *nyurrpe* to the two younger ones. Well, they were playing away, and those two young ones were always putting down the right cards and winning all the money. They'd throw the cards down real hard and fast in that game they call 'Trumps' or 'Rubber' or whatever it is. Every card these two threw down was the right card to win the hand. And this one old lady had been watching closely, and she said to one of my other relations "hey, tell those two brothers-in-law to take off their eyeglass, because the reflection of the cards in their glasses is telling the other two what number cards they have". She just whispered it in his ear, "you see them laughing? Those two young blokes are having a good old joke against their *nyurrpe*s. Like 'throw it down some more, whatever you do we'll beat you!'" Those old people couldn't do anything right, every card they played, those *nyurrpe*s would have another card drawn ready to better it. They were having a good old joke, even playing for money, playing for dollar notes. So my other relation got up and said to them "you poor buggers, those two are beating you through and through, and I'll tell you why. Take off those eyeglass". "Why?" they asked. "Well, when you bring up the cards close to your eye, the reflection

Ikirrentye and *Nyurrpe*   Kwantheme, *Nyurrpe*-Teasing

in your glasses shows your *nyurrpe*s what cards you've got". Well, one of those old men just took off his glasses and threw them down, and he was swearing at those *nyurrpe*s, "oh, so that's how you were beating us!" And us mob watching were just killing ourselves laughing. It was a fun sort of a thing you know, how *nyurrpe*s tease each other sometimes.

Every now and again we used to play another one, 'Bulladeen' they used to call this game. You have to throw down the colour. If they chuck a spade, you chuck a spade again. And we used to play *nyurrpeke-nyurrpe*. And we'd play and joke against our *nyurrpe*s for hours and hours and hours. And people'd pay somebody to cook and feed them while they were playing. And when the money ran out, then some people'd start playing for clothes, and also blankets. Some other *nyurrpe*s used to say "okay I'll put my trousers in, chuck it in the ring!" Or "I'll put my dress in". Sometimes someone'd take off their blouse and chuck it in and just sit there with their bare breasts. And everybody'll have a good laugh, "look, they're even stripping clothes off their body!" That's the *nyurrpe* women, "take it off!" And used to make them take their clothes off and put them in the game. It was great fun. And 'Log Cabin' tobacco they used to gamble for, and money you know, one pound, two pounds.

And out on the stock camps, they'd *really* gamble, you know? Or so I've been told. People'd get desperate if they lost all their money, 'cause they wanted to keep playing. So they'd chuck everything they owned into the game – swag, blankets, saddle, bridle and bit, all his clothes. Sometimes a bloke'd be playing there without any clothes on at all and then he'd lose again! So the *nyurrpe*s would make him go outside and do all their chores for them – clean up the camp, chop firewood, fetch water, those sort of things. And they'd stand there watching him do it naked, making jokes and laughing their heads off. Then they'd give him back all his clothes and blankets after he'd finished and the fun was over.

Touch-feelings

Apmere ahelhe kwenhe anwerne rarle, the Land is us. *Utnenge anwernekenhe apetyeme apmerenge-ntyele*, our spirit comes from the Land. Our names come from the Land, *arrirtne anwernekenhe apmerenge-ntyele apetyeme. Anwerne alpemele aherrkele anwerne arintyeme apmere anwernekenheke kele ingweleme akangkeme.* When we come back and the sun sets in the morning to us, you feel so happy to be there, *anetye-intyemele*.

Utnerelhemele is a special word we can use for that. *Utnerelhemele* is like feeling comfortable in your own country. *Utnerelheme.* Like real relaxing, real comfortable, where you are. And if you go back to your country, you say "ah, *ayenge utnerelhemele anetye-alpeme, apmere atyinhe alpeme.* I'm very comfortable in my own country". *Angkwe-intemele, kwerralye aremele.* When you sleep, you're looking at the stars. *Akeme-irremele ingweleme uterne pwarrtyintyeme*, when you get up in the morning the sun shoots, the shooting of the sunrise. *Alakenhe.* That's how it is.

And also *ilkelhemele aneme*, 'liking it'. Liking where you're at, where you are now. That's another word. *Ilkelhemele anetye-alpeme atyemeye-kenhe apmerele* – maybe in a grandfather's country, or you're liking it because you're with the family, like *ampe anwernekenhe mapenge*, or aunty, uncle-*nge apeke, apmarlenge apekawe awenhenge apeke*, maybe with your kids, your uncle, or maybe with aunties, *alakenhe*. That's a wanting word, a liking word, *ilkelhemele aneme*.

And another word is *ahentye-arle-aneme*. Like, 'wanting', again. "*Ayenge ahentye-aneme apmere nhenhele anetyeke*, I'm really wanting to live here, or stay here". But you really gotta know that place where you wanting to be, you gotta know where your really country is, where your place is. What is so important about this, you gotta use all these words in your own place where you at. Where you wanting it, where you liking it. If I go to my mum's country, or my dad's country, "*oh, ayenge ilkelhemele-aneme apmere nhenhele tharle altyerre akeke-arle*, that's my mother's Traditional Stories Land". And when I'm there I think about my mother, and how her mother was, and how my *atyemeye*, her father was. That's if I go to my *atyemeye*'s country, or my mother's country. And all those families there I see as related to my mum. Which is all the *Alyawarr* people. *Arrengeye ikwerenhe mape*. And all the *arrenge*'s children'll be their dads, like her dads, from generation, *angkweye-angkweye-angkweye-arteke*. And we see them and you feel really pleased. And wanting. And that word, like *utnerelheme*, you feel so comfortable about it, and feel comfortable there, when you go. So that's another word you can use. But you gotta use it in your own area, like in your own country. You can't say that when you're staying in another people's place. You might feel happy, but it's happy to be there in that place where maybe you was there as a child, you were just born there as a child. Sometimes those sort of happiness is not, doesn't really fit into your own Land, like your mum's country, or your grandfather's, your *arrenge*'s, your *aperle*'s. Might be happiness with your friends, those sort of happiness you might have when you stay in that other community. *Alakenhe*.

And then there's *alwharrpe*, which is sadness. It can be very sad when you're not on your own Land. Like, now that I live in town, and knowing that I have my Land out on the eastern side, when I'm not on my own Land, I feel sad because that Land is really my own grandfather's Land. And sad about the people living around it, the ones that still know that's our Land.

Even though the Land can't talk to us, we can talk to the Land, and we know how that Land relates to us. Because we can *feel* what it is to us. And what is every people that's connected into those Lands. If you're sad or something, the Land just urges you, and brings you back and encourages you to go back. Because it's got a sort of *touching*, but only *apmereke artweye mape* can know, only those Landowners. What area you're from is important. And it just like brings you back. Wants you to settle. That sort of touch we get from the Land. Not only Land, but for people too, you really urge for people. Especially that person from that Land. You really want to be there in that country, or want to be with those people. It's a special love-touch and relation-touch.

The Land has all those feelings, and it gives those feelings to people. And also how you feel about the country itself. Like what that feeling to me is like my grandfather's-feeling. And you get that touch. Sometimes people really cry with that feeling, and that touch of feeling always comes. It's in the Land, it's in us, it's in our *ikirrentye*, and it's in our *anpernirrentye*. Touch-feeling, *ye*.

Our name for 'touching' is *anpeme*. And *anperneme* is another word that means like, well, "*the ngenhe anperneme apmarle*, I relate to you as *apmarle*, because you've got the same skin name as my mother". It goes out just one way if you say it like that. *Anpernirreme* is like two people, how they relate to one another. "*Ilerne anpernirreme altyele*" means "we two relate to each other as cousins". Going both ways. *Anperneme* and *anpernirreme*. And that's where *anpernirrentye* comes from, it's a name meaning 'each-way relating'. *Anperneme* is sort of a *living* word and a *living* relation. That's what it means to us. We see it as really important, and it's a close sort of a thing, and also it's an energy thing in people. Gives energy, and also life. Life relationship. That's what relationships *we are*.

It's a beautiful touching thing when you relate to somebody. You feel that person as your own, and he or she feels close. And somebody who has the same skin name as your children is also related in a special way to you. But in a sacred way.

It's a touching way of how you can feel for that person, which is the sacredness of that person to yourself, and of yours to him. There's a big line in between that person and yourself. And it's a sacred thing. To keep it alive is one of the things we must do. We mustn't run over ourselves, we mustn't go across, we mustn't twist it around. To be who we are, you can't tangle up those lines.

Anpernirrentye, *ikirrentye*, and touch-feelings are all strongly knitted together. And that all runs in them skin groups. That's the way you feel for all the people with skin names. That's the most important thing Aboriginal people can have, that's a strong Law in us. How we respect, how we've got a different way of feeling for husband's-feeling, uncle's-feeling, mother's-feeling, nephew's-feeling, it's all a different way. And feeling for your friends, for your *atyewe*. Just a friend's-feeling, it's different. Every *anpernirrentye* has different relationships of feeling to that person. *Anpernirrentye*, well there's four lots, *nyurrpeke-nyurrpe*. Four names on each skin line, *alakenhe*. They have different feelings and also different relationship. Like *mwere* is different feeling, a son-in-law-feeling, and *akngeye*, father, is different feelings from your daughter, and mother, *meye*'s different from father.

That runs in that *anpernirrentye*, our relationship, our skin group, how we feel. How we feel for our mother is different. Because you're *from* a mum, and you're from a dad, and you're part of your brother, and your feelings for your husband is a different way of feeling. Where you can hold a person, where you can love a person. That's a different way of feeling, being together. And every Aboriginal people knows that, about feelings. Brother's-feeling is one of the best relationships with yourself and how you are connected to your brothers, a brothers to sisters-feeling. And cousins-feeling, and friends-feeling is also different, probably it's like a close person, you feel close to your friends. Sometimes you're close to friends, sometimes you're close to your friends' friends. To their families, but still according to their skin names. As long as they're in that skin group-feeling. We have eight groups. Well, as I said, we have a different feeling for all those four groups on each side. That's real respect. That's how we respect ourselves, and also respect the people's Lands and the people's ways. Shame, and respect, and feelings. When and as we're growing up we're always told that.

I might meet a person I didn't know before, and when I find out their skin name, maybe they're the same name as my dad, then that skin name will tell me what respect I have in relating to that person, and what sort of feeling-touch I'll have for them. Because he's as important as my dad is. And if I met somebody with the same skin name as my children, it'll be the same for that. And it goes on and on. And if that *Kngwarraye* got hurt, then I'd really feel for that person like it's my own child. Look, I'll tell you a story. There was one *Warlpiri* girl who was very sick and got taken to Adelaide. I just really felt in my heart for her, just like she was my own child. I felt that way because she had a name like my children, and that mother had the same skin name as myself, *arelhe Kemarre-kenhe ampe Kngwarraye atyenge-arle ileke*. Some people take it really strong, you know, and they'll have really strong touch. And people might say "hey, she's not the real mother to cry like that". But it's just how they feel for the skin names.

Spouse-feeling

There's a special touch-feeling for the right person that can be your husband or your wife. That feeling will just come up between them two, especially when you tell those grandkids "you're the right skin for them, and you're this skin and he's this skin, and your parents and grandparents are these skins. And you two both come from the same Land".

Husband and wife got to really respect one another. Because he might be a really important person. And wife might be really important too, both ways. I still really respect my husband, even though we left one another. I really respect him as the father of my children, and also he had a strong relationship to my parents. I really respect him through our relationship in the country, and through what his skin name is. That's how I feel – not to get him back – but that's how I feel for him in a traditional way. In traditional husband and wife-feelings. And also how he related to my parents, and how his parents related to my parents and also to us. That's how Aboriginal people really respect themselves.

Having a good strong tie to himself means that person feels he has authority, that he holds their way of relationship. That's what's really important to us, and that's why I really respect my husband, because he holds that. He's the father of my children, and he's got the sadness for me, for my parents. Because he's the husband of mine, and the father of those really special old people's great-granddaughters and great-grandsons. And he relates himself in sadness in a special way through *anpernirrentye*. And we share that sadness with him, and it can never be lost. An old husband will always have a feeling for an old wife through his old father-in-law and his old mother-in-law.

That's how we see a husband or a wife, through their relationships. We don't see a person as just one person, we see them through their relationships. You can *see* that relationship tie, what it is. And that's that lovely feeling we have for people. If you're brought up in a traditional way, you *have* those feelings.

Parent and child-feeling

Meyeke akangkentye, akngeyeke akangkentye ane ampeke akangkentye, love for your mother, your father, and your children. Our mother and father, *ratherre*, they're the ones now, who brought the daylight for us. And they protected us from ants and prickles when we were tiny. That's just a saying in *Arrernte*. That's what they say, "*yerreketye, ane anthelke-ketye, ane intwerrkere-ketyele-arle arntarnte-arentye kwenhe*. They protected us from ants, from the rubbish and grass lying at the bottom of trees, and from prickles". *Intwerrkere* is like a little three-corner jack, just from a grass.

The feeling for your parents is that lovable feeling of relation. Loving your mum and your dad, that's a special way of feeling, that's a relations-feeling. And your feeling for that sweetheart person, like *unte apeke anewakeme*, it's a different feeling of wanting. You want her and she wants you, and you both have that feeling. But that feeling for your parents, that's a loving and a nurturing feeling. *Alhirreme* belongs to *anewenhenge*. That's the sweetheart-feeling, you might call it fancying someone very strongly, like you're burning to be in with that person. It's in the holding feeling when you hold that person towards your heart. With your wife and with your sweetheart, and her holding-feeling, it's different to your mother-feeling. The hugs are different.

The relations loving-feeling for your parents is *utnengele-arle antirrkweme*, your spirit holds. With a touch, you know? And this other feeling you have for your sweetheart, that's *alhirrentye*, and *ahentye-aneme*. This feeling that you've got for your parents, it's an inside feeling. The other one is an outside feeling, except that it's inside for you two lovers, *alakenhe*. Like you can't go along and say "oh *Mame, ngkwenge ayenge ahentye-anthurre-aneme*, Mummy, I really love you". You can't say that. Not loving in that way of use of words. Because that mother, that you-really-like mother, that's your relations-feeling. And a real motherly feeling is different from the outside feeling.

Crossover-feeling

Sometimes people can feel wrongly for people. Sometimes when somebody's falling in love with the wrong person, they think that it's the right way because of the strength of feelings they have. But it's not. It's like breaking the Law. According to the Law you cannot relate to that person because you're not that relationship. Bad relationship occurs because of that, and the children they have will get bad feelings about that. But today people just get married anywhere. When people wasn't living in the old community way any more, but still lived in the proper way of the missions, and still kept their old community styles, they used to just get married proper way. Maybe because the Law was very strong, and our families was still in a close group on the mission, and there wasn't any other activities. Now today there's a lot of activities amongst all of our children, but still people have got really strong laws to support our children. But we don't have much teaching for them, you know, instruction. We should think that instruction is really taught at home for our kids, *anpernirrentyeke akaltye-irreme*. And sometimes kids don't listen, and sometimes even parents don't listen and tell them the right way.

In the old community style of living, before *alherntere mape* came here, if people married wrong way, they used to go away, they were made to go. But on the mission they never went away because there was no any other places they knew. When they grew up in that place, the place they knew, they just had to stay and fight. They gotta just keep up with the things people say to them, and it'll wear out. When they have children, it wears out. And the people get to know them, recognise them because of those children, *alakenhe*. And they live in harmony after. And everyone relates to those children in a special way then.

How can the wrong feeling come into somebody's heart? Well, sometimes if a person has accidentally switched over, that goes all wrong. There might be a wrong feeling, might be a crossover-feeling, that's when you get that funny feeling for the wrong one. Crossover-feeling always happens. Like it might be somebody *makes* it happen to you, people sometimes joke about how they sing that sort of *ilpentye* magic. Or sometimes you'll *alhirrerle* when there's no anybody in your own place that you can relate to in that special sweetheart way. You can *alhirrerle* for that too. Like there might be families there, and then there might be another family came in from another place. Because you can't get that sweetheart-feeling from your own neighbours, you'll have a feeling for that visiting person there. But it mightn't be the right person. It happens to a lot of people, for people just visiting, you know? That right feeling of somebody's might cross over into another, wrong feeling. *Ye*, those sort of things. And when you have that feeling you gotta stop. *Ye*, it's not s'posed to happen that way. And also you can talk about it, people *gotta* talk about it, "hey, I feel something, really something for that person there. But he's not the right person for me". A lot of people can stop that for them then.

People know when they're getting the wrong feelings. And they've gotta make sure that the strong feeling they have for any person on the other *nyurrpe* side is a proper way of feeling for them. For that relationship. Might be a sad, or might be a loving feeling. Either way, when it's a right one, it's a lovely traditional feeling for that person on the other side *apeke*. That's why if you're gonna feel so happy about your uncle or your aunt or your nephew, you've gotta make sure that you like that person in a *different* liking way. Not in a way that you're gonna be really attached to it, wanting in the wrong way. You've gotta have a feeling for that person in an other-side sort of a way – a really *ikirrentye* way. *Ikirrentye* way, distance way. And for the right-side person, you've gotta have a feeling-way in your right way, like for your cousins or something. You've gotta have different ways of feeling for everybody, but distance-way feeling you must *always* have for the people on the opposite side. *Ikirrentye*-way feeling, because they are on the other side.

Body-feeling

From me to my children, I can only relate in a motherly sort of way; like, who I am to them. *Kemarre-arle ampe atyinhe-areye the anperneme atnerte-iperre* way. I can translate this by saying "as a *Kemarre*, I relate to my kids in a stomach-connected way". And this tells about a link from you to the child, from your own body-feeling. That's a love feeling, but it's a special sort of love for your kids. The love feeling for husbands, it's also a close love but in a different way.

Feelings between children and parents come from the liver, *aleme*. Then there's *urtakwertenge-ntyele* for anybody *aneweke*, boyfriend or girlfriend. That means the feeling comes from your heart. *Itirrentye* makes a feeling with your mind, and *alkngenge alhirrerle*, that's from the eyes, when you're looking at people. *Urtakwerte-inpe-arle ahentye-aneme*, that means your heart is really willing for that sweetheart person, but *urtakwerte*-feeling can also be a different feeling for your kids too. It's come from the same part of the body, but it's different again. All over your body it's got different feelings. And you can talk about your different families in finger talk by touching different parts of your body.

To mean your little brothers you make a hand sign by touching the top of your shoulder. And for nephews you touch your chin with your hand folded into a fist. And you touch on the middle of your stomach when you mean your kids. There, *aleme*, *aleme-iperre*, from the liver. *Aleme-iperre* means where your kids come from. Because *aleme* is connected to *atnerte*, your stomach. And you cannot swear at your *aleme-iperre*, it's very wrong. And when you do *this*, nephew, when you touch the back of the shoulder this way – well, you're the elder one, and when you touch your shoulder behind, that means your *atyeye*, your little sister. You can say about her, "*yanhe ayenge-arle alkngarelheke*, that's my little sister". Because you've turned around for her with your eyes, looking behind you, *alkngarelheke*. There's a hand sign to mean every one of your relationships, and you touch some part of your body for each one. Like this is *aperle-aperle*, your father's mother or your son's kids, when you pat yourself on the knee. And there's a lot more of them too.

Nephew and niece-feeling

I relate to my nephew in the way that *Kemarre* is to *Perrurle*, *Kemarre-arle alere atyinhe-areye the anperneme alhwe anwernekenhenge-ntyele*. Because your nephews and nieces are from your own flesh and blood, while your own children are from *aleme*. Sometimes Aboriginal people see that the closest relationship you can have is for your *alere mape*, your nieces and nephews. And your own children are very close to your brothers, or their father's sisters. I really like my kids, *ampe atyinhe mape*, and also I love my brother's children, because they are very close to me, they're part of me, my own flesh and blood. A really close group in relationship is yourself, and your children, and your brothers, and their children. And their children's children, it goes on and on.

Akangkeme

Akangkeme is a word that a lot of people just translate as 'getting happy', but it's more than that. It really means full of happiness, feeling very lovely, in a soul way, for your family, your friends, especially when they're joined together with the Land. *Akangkeme*. Like your parents are here, and your children are here, and *akangkeme* that a child, a grandchild is getting better. It's just like a really relief then. *Akangkeme-arle*, even like *apmere mwerre*, a good feeling for your Land, and also *akangkeme merne mwerre arlkwetyeke*, for food, and *akangkeme itenge-arle aneme*. Not *ite* like a throat, 'sitting to the throat', but *itenge-arle anerrirreme*, people together, joined together, sitting around talking. That's *akangkeme* as well, when you feel really lovely for that.

Akangkeme is not only being happy, it's a lot of things. And people can see when that *akangkentye*'s in you, and they become happy too. Because nearly all the time touch-feeling is going the same both ways. They can see it, and your *akangkentye* shoots into that person, and they'll get the same feeling. Love goes out and comes back in again always. *Akangkentye-kwenye* is when there's no happiness, no love. When there's a lot of badness, you can see that also. Because the body tells you, and also the reflection. And some people say "hey, he wasn't really happy, that was just a make-up happy". You can see that, and you can feel that. These are things that Aboriginal people can see, *arelhe urrperle mape*, they can *arerle*. Somebody might be nice to you, with a lovely smile and saying nice things, but their reflection might be telling you a different thing. Aboriginal people, *urrperle mape* can read that straightaway. We've seen a lot of people coming to us and being real happy for us, promising us things. But it hasn't turned out that way. And we as Aboriginal people can really see now, by the way people talk to us, whether things are going to turn out that way or not.

Mourning

When Sad People's Fires are Burning

Sadness is an illness. People who had sadness in the past, it's like a disease, *ye*. Sadness is not a thing you just have and it goes away. Sadness forever is. Sadness lives deep within you, it doesn't go away very quickly, it's like a disease. I mean you can't see it, but you can feel it coming into you. The reason why it comes into you is because, if you have a sadness, it breaks open your sadness from the past. Even just hearing or seeing people weeping in sorrow, *akayele artnelhe-ilerrerlenge awerle*, it brings that all back to you. I still have grief inside me, no matter how long my people's been gone. I still have that grief, and tear, and rip in my heart like it happened yesterday. I still have that grief. *Alakenhe*.

And it will always be there, and in all those journeys in your life, *alethe akwete alakenhe rarle aneme*. You must always know that it will come back to you, that it is part of Aboriginal people's ways, my way and our way. It's like a journey itself. Even *alherntere*, non-Indigenous people can feel it. Kids can feel it. Some kids don't, and some kids do. When they hear weeping, some kids get very emotional. *Alakenhe akwete-arle mape akngerre-kenhe anintyeke*, that's how it is for a lot of us. Sometimes we only weep strongly when we first go to sorry camp; sometimes it happens all the way through. But most important thing is, we've gotta let children know when we're grieving. Otherwise kids might think that Mummy's really sick. Kids have gotta know that this is part of us, it's gotta be part of our teaching, so that when they grow up they can tell *their* children. Also important in our sadness is that we use white pipeclay, so that people will know that we're mourning, and also to teach our children.

In the past, in my mothers' time, my mothers used to have weeping-sadness at morning daybreak, and in the evening, and that's the things that I witnessed in my life. And now today, I have that. We call it the daybreak, and also the sunset, seeing the sun go down, and also watching the day beginning. The sadness of watching the sun go down and watching the sun come up is the Law. Not many people do that

Mourning   When Sad People's Fires are Burning

nowadays. Grandmothers did it in the past, and I've still got it in my heart, that's part of my life, and I can't forget. That's how much sadness I have in my life. Maybe some other people don't do it because they didn't have that experience with their parents, *alakenhe apeke-arle arrpenhe mape itelaretyakenhe ane aretyakenhe itnenheke. Lyete-ulkere arrwekelenye-arle aneke-arteke kwenye aneme.*

    And later on my children will have that sadness, and then their children will have that sadness too. And when my children read about what I've been through, they'll know that experience, and they can know what it is to have those sort of feelings, and they can be strong. Today there are a lot of things we can do when we're in these sort of situations. You can go to somebody who can talk to you, elder Aboriginal people who can help make you feel better. Or they might come to you. And that's very important for traditional women especially, so that they can go on with their life. And if they don't do that, they'll always get sick. The sickness you never had will come into you. When you're in sadness, the sickness will come into you, and so you must let *arelhe akngerrepate*, Aboriginal elders talk to you. In the old days, getting together to mourn as one people performed the healing. It's most important to meet all the families, and after the sorry business you can wait for other people to come to you, to sit with you, and to talk to you. People will always acknowledge you

Itelaretyeke, Looking at memories and being sad, 2002, acrylic on canvas, photographer Barry McDonald
"This painting is about keeping in mind someone who has passed away. That person who has passed on is not lost. Her spirit comes through and lives on in another person. The colours used here stand for different things. Black represents *ingkwe-irremele*, darkness falling on someone. White indicates sadness, and green stands for the next person being born from out of that one who has gone away".

105

in that way, that's part of the illness-healing. That's sacred, sacredness is part of that. Sacredness comes in to keep people alive and well and also strong. So your life can go on. So you can do whatever it is you want to do. I like to let people know when they're reading this that this is really important to Aboriginal women, *arelhe urrperle mapeke*. And to our culture.

Sorry time

When it comes to sadness, the first ones to have that real sadness for those families that have lost somebody, is people who live by themselves. And that's a great honour for the sadness people, who are now also on their own. It's a big feeling that that person will bring to them. That's a part of our culture, that's a part of us.

Sorry time is really important to every one of us. And it's a really silence time for each one of us. You can't go in there with tape recorder, you can't be listening to a tape recorder on the other side when there's sadness there. You can't yell when somebody's being sad and you go and see them to comfort our families. And you can't talk about any names connected with it, nothing. Or yell at your kids. You can't walk in front of old people sitting down if they have sadness. And you can't pull up in the car or smoke a cigarette and put it in the fire when there's sad people's fires burning there. If you're driving up in a car you can't park the car in front of where people who are sad, or even people who have *had* sadness. Even they might have had it about three or four weeks ago, you still can't do that. 'Cause those people still see it like it's today.

You have to spread that sadness out long and wide so it can wear out. And it does wear out. You've got to go and hug or shake hands, and there's a lot of people you've gotta see so that it *can* wear out. It's just like it's giving it to someone, and that one gives it to someone else, it's just like that. And sometimes people forget then.

Before, people never used to *arrwekele iltye irrkwerrerle*, this shake-hand business just came *apmwerrkenge ware*, just lately. People-*le-arle tyikante-irretyakenhe anyente-ante ware irremele*. To finish up-*irretyeke*. They used to just come together and hug one other, hugging in a sad way to finish up. *Artnelhe-ilerle atware-artnelhe-ilerle.*

Crying with the person who's mourning a loved one while they're hugging them. *Arelhe atherre artnelhe-ilerrerle.* Might be two women hugging each other and crying, *ante ampe mape artnelhe-ilerle, lhampwe mape,* and the kids, those orphans, they get cried over too. And the children who may have lost a brother or a sister, well the aunties, and uncles, and grandmother will cry over them too. The shaking of hands is just a nowadays thing, saying that you're sorry for the loss of someone. That's not the way it used to be. Just shaking hands *yanhe*, that's a common way of doing it now, but even just shaking hands can still make a lot of difference to people too.

But it's better if you hug this one, and well, it comes into you and it takes it away, and then you hug somebody else. That's a real touch-feeling, and you feel good about it. Your friends might have a bad luck or anything, and you've always been with them, and when you don't go to them you really feel it, feel out of place, like you're holding the problems with you, like holding the sadness there with you. To break it out you gotta go and see them. They gotta see you to break that out, that's how it is. It's just like they're calling you, and it makes you go. "Oh I gotta go, I can't stay here. I gotta go and see these mob. I gotta go and see my brother, I gotta go and see my cousin, I gotta go and see my friends". That's the way that Aboriginal people feel. We've got those sort of feelings in us. Probably non-Aboriginal people have that too as well, I don't know. But that's our Traditional Law. We must do that. We must *participate* that. We must be in it, we gotta be there. *Alakenhe.*

Anpernirrentye and Mourning

You've gotta have special feelings for that sorry time. You're related in your aunty way, you're related in your mother way. Related into those people; they've got the same skin name as your children, as your family. I once went to these families, but they were on the other, the *alturle-thayate*, western side. But I related to them as my own uncles, and my own nieces, that's how I felt for her, I had that same feeling as I had for my own nieces, like *Napurrula*, and *Napanangka*. I related to them like that, even though I'm an *Ikngerrekwiperre* person and they're *Alturlenye*. Had real touch-feelings for them, like my own families, because they've got the same skin names as my dads and my mothers. For my *atyemeye*s, I felt really sad for them. That is the proper way for us mob. That's how skin names relate people. That lays in our culture.

You don't say anything wrong to other people, unless you're angry, but *never* when you have those feelings of sadness, or relate-feelings to those people. Sometimes with those people there, you put your feelings into like if you're an aunty. Because of that *anpernirrentye*. Or like if you're *aperle*, you feel for them like your own grandchildren. And those people can have touch-feelings about it too, you know? A lot of people talk to me, "Aunty, you relate to us really in an *anpernirrentye* way". That's why a lot of people respect me, and I also respect them as well. Sometimes I say to them, *angkerle itneke* "*ye, tyerrtye anpernemele warte* feeling *atnyeneme*, of course I follow a person's skin name when I relate". Because I really do relate to people in a real feeling way that follows their skin names. Sometimes people who are not really a grandmother to someone, they'll still class themselves into a real grandmother-feeling for them because of that skin name. Sometimes outside people have even more feelings for someone than their own grandmothers or uncles or aunties do, because sometimes they're very close, like a close friends you know, those sort of things.

When I relate to people in a real *anpernirrentye* way they feel really close, and I feel really close to them too. They treat me really in the same way as my own family group. A lot of *Warlpiri* people and a lot of *Alturlenye*, Western *Arrarnta* people, they really relate to me, and I really relate to them as well, as their parents, like their uncles or aunts, whatever they are. That's one of the good feelings, and when you have those sort of good feelings, people always protect you. You have good protection, you don't get names said about you, those sort of things. They say that, "here's a person that knows who we are, and what our relationships are". That's one of the best things. When anybody relates in a *prape anpernirrentye* way to people in sadness, it really gives them strength and support. It makes them feel good inside. Sometimes it breaks away, dissolves the sadness in them, because of those people's relating.

If there's a sadness moment, well you can have that sadness moment with your husband or wife. And you will always have sadness if you're a true Aboriginal person. Other people always see you, and if you don't have that sadness, then you're not that person, according to your skin relationship. People can see if you're not sad to that person, and they'll notice you straight out. Sadness to anybody who's in mourning – your husband or wife, your nephews. People'll recognise you straightaway if you don't have that real sadness and they'll always be bitter. They can tell from the way you sit, and the way you touch, the way you cry. They can see you, even when they come to you. And if you're talking in a manner that is not the proper way, then they know that it is not a good relationship. If you are not the right person talking in that sadness, then you are not the right sad. You've got to have that proper genuine sadness for your skin name.

Some people today, if they weren't brought up in a traditional way, they mightn't want to go and see one of their old people who's sad. They might say "oh, I don't want to make that person more sad, because they're sad already". But that's *your* thinking, not that sadness people's thinking. Because you haven't been brought up in a traditional way. That is not the right way, to feel like that. For people who are brought up in a traditional way, it's different. Traditional people's mourning goes longer and wider, because the sadness they've got in the community is different, it's there all around. It's got to go through a lot of relating things before it's past. Young people in town today, they might not understand properly, understand how to hold that sadness in them. Sometimes in town they might say that if you hold sadness all the time, it's not good for you. That's really understanding in a sort of way, but you gotta have respect for the people that hold that sadness – the old grandmothers, the old aunties – you've gotta have respect for what they're going through. The old community sadness is longer.

Iltyeme-iltyeme, Hand talk

As we know, if somebody's in sadness, you can't yell and scream. If you're a parent, you never yell at your kids, or just get up and do things that you've been doing all the time. You've gotta really respect yourself. And old people can only talk by hand. Sometimes people today don't know much about that. But old people know, and it's really sacred. By talking with their hands, only people who really know about hand signs can understand. More people in the communities know about hand signs than town people do, even young mothers out there will know. But it's really important for us all to understand what those old people are saying.

My mum used to really talk with her hand sign through all her sadness; all through her mourning for all my brothers and all my sisters. She had a really long sadness, for maybe nearly two or three months she used to just sit. I mean she used to go hunting, collecting everything, but she used to still be sad, you know? And she would always cry every night, no matter what. After three years she'd still be crying. 'Cause the sadness always comes in at night. Maybe she must've missed seeing them. And also daybreak will always be sadness. And you know, we used to take her away, my sister used to take her away and bring her into town to get her away from that, but she would always be sad. You couldn't change old people's ways. Nothing will change old people's ways in their sadness. Not many people follow that now. The Church came in, and a lot of people are ministers and those sort of things. But these are things that we gotta really know are really important to us. In *tyerrtye-kenhe* way, you know? 'Cause that's how we hold our sadness. And the sadness is part of us, and that's part of our life.

Arelhe ampwe mape, those old people still *iltyeme-iltyemele angkerlte-aneme,* they still talk with their hands. And sometimes they take it for a long time by talking with hands. There's a real, real, real, real gentle feeling in that when you're talking with hands, like that person would be just whispering if they were using their voice. People stop talking out loud in sadness time, because they don't want to make the same words or sound – that same sort of sound to get them words out that they used to when those loved ones were still alive. My mothers used to talk like that all the time.

We know how weak they feel when they ask with their hands for a little water, like as if it was in a tiny little voice, or if they asked "when are we gonna eat? I'm hungry, before I sleep I want to eat". It's really sad, because on that moment when they have that hand language, it's that moment of that real sadness, and people don't talk any louder to them, because they've got no words to come out, to say it back to them. And sometimes family will say to them, just in a whisper, "hang on, *ure-arle itemenge*, I'm building the fire to cook your food, *kere itetyeke ane merne itetyeke*".

I used to just do things without Mum knowing. Cook everything, do the other things, then go to bed early, 'cause that evening was a real sad time. My mum used to have a little cry before she went to bed. And that's a healing thing; after that she'll get healed, and probably maybe another two years' time, she'll be happy then. Sometimes people take it for three or four years; sometimes people like to get it out; sometimes people see it today like, they don't want to upset their children. Because there's a lot of chemicals around, there's a lot of *ngkwarle*s around, grog: "If I cry a long time I'll upset my children. And they might go and do something else, they might get into a car and go somewhere and do something to themselves". But there might be some strong children and grandchildren can understand their old people's mourning. Sometimes they might go away somewhere. Like "Mum'll probably cry tonight, I'll just get away, I don't want to get that feeling from her. So it doesn't hit me, and it'll bring my sadness, and I'll have a sad sleep". So they go away somewhere. There's a lot of change in it. That's why today, people have a shorter sadness. Maybe they go into Church and then they're happy after. But old people out on the community take it for a much longer time. You have to move out of your house, and when you're living in town here it's different. 'Cause you're living amongst town people, and you can't just go somewhere else. If you're living in a community you can swap houses. You can't do that in town. You've just gotta go back to your own community, or stay with another family. Today's sadness is really different to the sadness of before. It seems to be getting more smaller – shallow, *ye*. But other *urrperle mape* still hold it.

Some people, when they feel sad, they make sure that they go back to their homeland, so that they really fit into that Land. And that's the time a lot of people go back and really settle in. The Land gets into them and some of the sadness goes away when they go back. Or sometimes it doesn't. But mourning in another country, on someone else's Land, even here in town, is really, really sad.

Apmere, The Land

"To go back and
smell the smoke and the air of your own country,
hear the birds singing and talking,
watch the stars at night,
see the sun rise and the sun set."

What Land Means

A Place Everywhere

When I talk about Land, as we see it in the eyes of us – our group, all my families – we see it because that Land is really part of us. Our relationship is in everything what's in that Land; hills, creeks, maybe trees, waterholes, animals that we get from it, the wood that we gather to make ourselves well, and also for fire to have for light or to cook. And things that we see; like the moon, the stars, the sunrise, the sunset. And also the rain that comes down on us and gives us good season.

Uternele arrtyernintyeme apmereke, the sun shoots its rays into the Land and the people and brings it all to life.

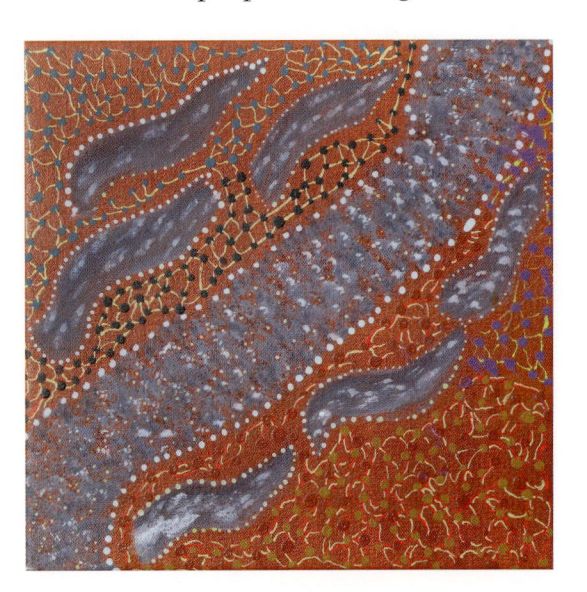

Pwarrtyintyeme apmereke, it reflects back onto the Land, filling everything there with its light.

Alkere inteme apmerele, alkere apmerenge, the sky lies on the Land, the sky is from the Land.

Ingwe atnyele-aneme utnenge, Altyerre utnenge ayeye ingwekenhe arrateme, the night falls on the Land and sleeps there and brings out the spirit of the Creation and its Stories.

And the weather. The wind blows every day, and the stars tell that Story; the flowers of the trees tell their Stories; plants give their Story. We're part of the animals that live there, and birds; we listen to the birds and their Stories. We're part of the water there, we're part of the grasses, the medicines, the fruits. Not only people live on that Land, because the Story is

---

Angkulye Inthwenarre Alhwerrpenge Arrateme, 2006, acrylic on canvas, photographer IAD Press
Winter clouds are coloured reddish-white and they travel really quickly. The shadow from the cloud makes an image on the ground like a river.

come from our own Nature, that's why we really see our Land as so beautiful. And that's how the Land is; it's the same for all Aboriginal people, no matter where they are.

Apmere apanpe is like 'a place everywhere', 'everywhere is a place'. That's *apmere apanpe*. Like a big Land itself, the whole Land, not just one land, the whole country, the living spirit of the Land. I can call that *apmere apanpe nhenhe-arle aneke arrurle urrperle arrwekelenye-kenhe, itne-arle anenheke* – forty thousand years ago, this whole country belonged to the Aboriginal Ancestors. The whole country, the whole Australia, you know? Probably must've been a lot of Aboriginal people. *Aherrke-arle arratemenge, aherrke-arle irrpemenge.* From where the sun rises to where the sun sets. *Alhwerrpe-arle apetyemenge ante aretharre-arle apetyemenge.* From where the cold south winter comes to where the hot northwest wind blows. *Alakenhe*, that's how it is. And that's what we say; "*apmere apanpe*, the places everywhere, *antirrkwerrentye aneke*, was joined together, their roots holding each other in relationship".

And still now, there is no piece of land, anywhere in Australia, that doesn't have someone to speak on its behalf. It doesn't matter how built-over it is. There is somebody there everywhere, there are Aboriginal people everywhere, no matter where. If you're an Indigenous person, there is always somebody there to talk about that piece of Land. Even if the buildings are built for miles, you know? There is always an Aboriginal person will know about it, connected to it. And they'll tell you the same Animals are related to them as are related to yourself.

And our Land is as sacred as yourself, as a person like you are. And always, you treat the Land good, the Land treats you the same. The Land and us are all the same. 'Cause the goodness of the Land and the goodness of the people are there, you know? We eat from the Land, we live on the Land, the Land teach us, show us. If there's no track or pad, if you don't know where to go, the Land just like tells you. "Oh yeah! This is the way to that place". It'll show you where the hills are. It'll show you where the birds are singing – that's those water birds, they'll tell you where to find water and food. Because it's a message to both sides – we can talk to the Land and who we are, and the Land'll always relate. The Land and people are the same. Same.

Irrerntarenye and *Arremparrenge,* the Little People of the Land

The country itself's really alive, and it relates to us just like a person. It's a live thing in those hills. People might think that hills is not alive. But that hill represents somebody in that country, and we can see it, we as Aboriginal people see it. It's a live thing, even though it's just a hill, or a tree, or might be a creek. It's where the spirit of people lays. You must really respect, and you must really relate to your own Land. Every place, they got that. It sits or stays there – *aneme* – in each person's own place.

Irrerntarenye mape's everywhere on our homeland, *apmere anwernekenhele*. And you have to talk to them, like *apmereke artweye mape* must talk to their country when they bring different people onto it. Otherwise those People of the Land will make those visitors uncomfortable. 'Cause the Land sees you as well, you know? If you say any jokes about it, you don't have good hunting days. If you scream and shout and yahoo yourself as you walk in the country, the Country'll say "ah, you won't hunt these things, you won't hunt these animals, you won't find these animals, you can't see these tracks of these animals". You might just see an old track. They'll cover that new track over with the old one, those sort of things.

Even the trees. You can't just go along and, "oh all right, I'll make a windbreak, I'll cut some of these branches off and make a windbreak". You can't do that. You can't say "oh, I'll just light a fire here". You can't do that either. Because all those People of that Land is watching you, the Little People of the Land that's inside there. Digging the Land is just like making a hole in somebody's body. The Land is a living thing. So digging or pulling trees down is just like killing somebody's body. The Land sees when you're thinking or doing wrong and it tells you, you feel really uncomfortable, and you feel real guilty about it. Maybe you saw a tree and you just wanted to chop it down. You get really upset about it. Unless you talk to the Land why you done that. That's forgiveness-talk. You have to always respect your own country and other people's Land when you visit. And all those families. And how you relate that country to those people. That's how people used to live in harmony with other people in the Land.

You have to talk to the Land. And also, like I said before, the Land's gotta

What Land Means *Irrerntarenye* and *Arremparrenge*, the Little People of the Land

have people to talk on its behalf. As we see it in our own eyes and how we feel, it's just like a living thing when we talk for it. The owners might say *"ay, apmere akenge ilemele angkerretyale"*. That's like "don't destroy our Land by talking rubbish-way to it". And we feel it, it's like the Land feeling that, that's how we see it. Like putting that other Land down. "Oh anyway, we can't talk about that place, it's been destroyed by many other people, and you're no longer living there, other people are on it". You can't say that, that is not the right way for an Aboriginal person to talk. That sort of discrimination, you can't put that across any other Aboriginal people. If someone rubbishes Land, even people who are not connected with that Land can feel it, "hey that place is sacred, it's part of us". If people talk rubbish-way to Land, the Land can feel it and gets very hurt. Whether putting other Land down, or putting down the Land's people, it's against Aboriginal Law and our Aboriginality. It's very important to respect the Land's sacredness. Never to treat it with disrespect, even by talking.

Aboriginal people must never rubbish other people's country. We must always be true and honest. A lot of people get sick, a lot of people have bad injuries, things like that, when you say wrong things about Land and people. *Anwerne-arle anintyeke arratye anthurre ilenhe-ilenhe, arratye anthurre angkenhe-angkenhe. Ane arratye anthurre anpernirrenhe-irrenhe, ane arratye anthurre ilerrenhe-irrenhe*, like Aboriginal people are really honest people, and our relationship is really true and straight. And also we are born with the right way of talking, of telling things. If you tell messages that aren't true, people could get killed. By the words of your message. It's not right to tell lies in the eyes of the Land. You've gotta be honest, *arratye anthurre iletyeke. Unte urrtyirreme ileme, apmere ngkwinhekele-arle akurne-ilerle*. If you say the wrong thing, the Land will punish you. If you say anything wrong through the Land, you will get punished. That's the true way that me and my family have learnt.

Apmereke artweye renhe-arle rarle irrerntarenyele-arle arntarnte-areme, the *irrerntarenye mape* also guide and take care of the people who lives on the Land. *Irrerntarenye*'s just described like dwarves, you know? Maybe a lot of people in Ireland knows about those sort of things. Ireland-*arenye*, people Ireland-*nge-ntyele apetyeke mape-arle*, those who migrate out here, really knows about those sort of things, like exactly the same as we do. About leprechaun *mape, ye. Yanhe rareye-arteke-arle apmere arntarnte-areme*. They must be the same, because they look after the Land over there as well.

I was talking to one man, telling him that our country gets looked after by the Little Spirit People. And I asked him once, after he'd shown me some pictures of Ireland, "hey, how come those hills and ranges have moved all close together? Have they been put together by someone?" "No", he said, "that's how they were created, and that's the Creation Symbol of that country, how those hills are stacked together on top of each other. Our little men seem to look after it". That's the leprechauns that he was talking about and telling me about. They're the ones that put those hills together in the First People Time. And I thought, "oh gee, these mob probably live like we do".

That one man from Ireland told me his story which was just like ours. And once we was watching TV, and I saw, when these white people went to dig up this place in Ireland, they saw these little men coming out, and I wondered, where did these little men come from? And I told this one man that they saw all these little men coming out from under the base of a tree. And he said "yeah, they're our little men from the country". It's just like ours, and I said "but we're the only ones that can see them here, Aboriginal people. It's only the people of that Land see them, and if there's strangers there, they sometimes show themselves to them as well, at night. Even during the day, if you come around towards evening". Well that man said "oh, I think that it's just like that over where we come from".

And I used to think a lot about that you know, and then a lot of people used to tell me about that then, that it was just a story. And the Landowners, the *apmereke artweye mape*, they didn't want to tell everybody I s'pose, like to those who might say that there's no such thing as a Little People *apeke*. So they'd tell only the people that knows it already. Who know it like they do. If you see Little Spirit People of the country, if you tell someone that the Little People has given you this food – we know that these Little Spirit People give us this meat when we ask. When we tell somebody who don't

What Land Means *Irrerntarenye* and *Arremparrenge*, the Little People of the Land

know anything about *irrerntarenye*, they say "I don't think there's any such thing as the Little People, it was just shot there by accident". But we know, as people from the country, as Aboriginal people, we've always known that if we didn't talk to the Spirits when we went hunting, we wouldn't get anything. And that is our Rule. *Anwernekenhe iwerre, anwerne-arle itelareme. Alakenhe.* That's our Path, and that's the way we understand it.

Irrerntarenye's everywhere, all over this country, and overseas as well. Oh yes *alere*, they're in country belonging to people everywhere, everybody's. And some people may not know that there's these Little Spirit People. But you've got to talk to the Little Spirit People, they're waiting for you to talk to them and tell them who you are. And that's how the Little Spirit People see it when you're on country – you gotta be happy and tell them. When you go there you tell them, and if you take strangers there you tell them, and you can tell them you're coming back home. After that you feel real good, because they get real happy for you. They even show you where there's water when you go there, they tell you about the meat for hunting. *Irrerntarenye mape* come from a Sacred Place, because our country's really thing you know, there's a lot of sacredness in our homelands, in our country. Not sacred site everywhere, but sacredness in the Land everywhere, the Land itself is sacred to us.

There's another sort of Little People too, called *arremparrenge*. *Arremparrenge*'s like a double of you, but in a spirit way. Might not be you, it could be like that other person over there. Once I was asleep, and then I woke up. It was fairly dark, and I saw these two little boys standing, and I thought "why are these two little boys standing around at night?" And they wore the same coats as my grandsons were wearing that night. But I didn't think that my grandsons would be standing around next to the fire at three o'clock in the morning! But I seen them, I might have still been half asleep, or I might have dreamt it, but they were there, it really resembled those two closely, they were identical to them. It was *arremparrenge*. And that little girl also who was trying to fit in with our country. 'Cause I got up and seen that little girl, she was wearing a black skirt and a yellow top. I thought, "that might be that little girl's *arremparrenge*".

A lot of people used to see them there on that country; on that particular place the *irrerntarenye* seem to be plainly visible, because it's a Sacred Place for them. And not only that country, everybody's country's like that, everywhere. And people have gotta let them know when they're coming or when they're going. And when you're dropping off to sleep you talk to them, asking for a good night's rest. And if you're going hunting in the morning, you ask them to provide the animals. That's the way we see it, that's our understanding, that's Aboriginal people's way. We know that those things are going to happen – good things, bad things – those sort of rules we hold.

Ye, alhengke-arle itne areme, iwenhe-apatherre itnenhe, apmerele. The *irrerntarenye mape* watch you all the time, and they can recognise people by their skin names, because they're from that *apmere. Ye,* that's the main way they recognise them, *alhengke-arerle itnenhe. Apmere-arenye-arle itneke,* because they belong to that *apmere,* that country. But if you come along from another country, *apmere arrpenhe-arenye,* and even if you're the same skin name as them, and you start doing anything *apeke* shoot-*eme-iletyeke* or *akurne apeke,* anything bad like shooting things, then they'll fire you, *artarrernerle,* fire you with their stingers until you have to get out of the place. It's just like when people say "they'll bone you", *alakenhe.* They'll just put that fire in you. Like one man, he was shooting birds, *thipe mape atyerretyeme,* just as the birds were sitting down towards evening. *Thipe mape anyente-irreke,* the birds had gathered together to roost for the night. And he was shooting away, and then he just felt like that big thing coming like – Whooof! *Irrerntarenye mapele weke,* the Spirits chucked that right at him. And it's *hard,* hard *anthurre,* 'cause he shot many birds. And the People of the Land said "*iwenheke-ame anhelheme*? Why are you being cheeky? *Thipe angerange itne-arrpe-irrerle-aneme-arle kwenhe,* 'cause those poor birds aren't doing any harm to you, they're just minding their own business". It was only because he had a weapon, and the weapon wasn't even his own, that gun he was shooting with, *makitele-arle atyerretyeme.*

And so his friends brought him in the ambulance to the hospital, and the doctor wasn't quite sure about his ailment – "heart *ikwerenhe mwerre nthakenhe-arle*? His heart's fine, how come he's like this? Hmm, you probably have a touch of pneumonia".

What Land Means *Irrerntarenye* and *Arremparrenge*, the Little People of the Land

And the man said, "oh, *urtakwerte-arle areke daktele, ayenge mwerre aneme*, oh, the doctor's looked at my heart and seen that it's okay, and I've still got those pains in me, it's really cutting me inside". 'Cause *irrerntarenye mape-kenhe*, that Little-People magic, it's got like *apwerte irrerntarenye-kenhe arrirlpe mape*, razor-sharp stones, it's got that real sharp, *akerle-anetyeke*. That sharp-cutting feeling that just keeps on cutting. But only the *itne-ante* know-*eme-ileme*, only the Little People know just what it is, or how it works. So anyway, the man and his friends seen this one old man going past, and he *alakenhe*, the old man said to them "hey, oh somebody *artarrerneke kwenhe*. Your friend's been punished. *Irrerntarenye-kenhele-arle, irrerntarenyele-arle artarrerneke*, he's been punished by the magic of the Little People of the Land. They fired that into him". And the sick one realised straightaway then. That he'd been shooting all these birds, and he was hit with that – *Doong*! He heard that big knock, and he'd thought "hey, somebody got hit". But it wasn't *somebody*, it was *him*! And he knew straightaway then, and he exclaimed "*yekaye*! Good grief!" And that's why they'd brought him into the hospital, *akngetyeke*. And they said "oh look, he's really sick", they was a bit worried. And later that old man told him directly, "*irrerntarenye-kenhele-arle uthneke*, the magic of the Little People has bitten you, punished you, you must've done something wrong". And his mind told him straightaway then. And next day he went back home; he was all right later. But he stayed really scared, careful not to touch anything on the country. And he loves all the birds now – "hey, hi birds!"

Any country, don't do that sort of thing on any country.

Recovering Our Land

We Had No Title

When they first came – Aboriginal peoples saw these other people coming – Aboriginal people probably thought that, you know, they would look after the Land. But they saw different animals coming in, and because they didn't have any titles for it – only titles in our own traditional ways to hold that Land – we saw, and we thought, "oh, those people are good people coming in". But then again it just says like, we never had any rights for it to stop those people coming in. Because they came in and probably looked after my grandparents, and my great-grandparents before, you know like giving them rations and looking after them. But my family still knew where the Sacred Grounds were. And you know, cattles coming in, they thought it was right for the cattles to come in because we didn't have title rights of saying "they can't come on this Land, it's our Land". Because we just sat, you know? A lot of people just sat, and people got station owners coming in, and station owners going out, and they thought they was just good people coming in and looking after them with rations, and foods. Like when there's *merne ikwemeye*, Christmas came here, and they got rations, free rations, free things. We saw people coming in, but we could still hunt, you know? And we could still go to our hunting spots, and where the waterhole was. They just saw those station owners was part of them, and station owners probably thought *they* was part of *them*. Because a lot of those people worked on those stations in that country itself, but a lot of people knew those Sacred Places and waterholes, and it's still there today.

My mum never used to talk about those sort of things, but other people used to tell stories about it. I just heard, you know, other old people talking about those things. At first they thought it was a spirit people coming in and giving all these food; and these foods was in a something that you can hit with a rock, like jams, you know. And flours. I think my parents didn't want to talk about it because the way they looked at it, maybe in the end they saw those was just people who came in and destroyed things. I don't know what they thought. I just wondered why Mum didn't tell me about this and I used to hear it from other people. I'm telling you the truth, *alere*, my parents never used to talk about them things, because maybe their grandparents or their mum didn't talk about it. Because it wasn't right to talk about those sort of things, it wasn't really *necessary*. Because they got taken over, and the Land got taken over, and that was that. Probably they didn't want to talk about it because they didn't want to offend anybody. Because a lot of Aboriginal people thought, "oh well, non-Aboriginal people are coming in, they got every right". And if the station owners say "chop down all those trees", they *gonna* chop down all those trees. And if the station owners say "shoot all the dogs", well *shoot* all the dogs. Or if the station owners say "you hunt in that area, but you can't hunt in this area", well you know, those sort of things might have been put to them.

The reason they took those notice, because then still they can stay in their own country, in their own Land. Because otherwise they might get moved out from that station, or that area where they're living, which is their own homeland. That's why they used to be really…have good balance. Balance of living. But they were very strong in their culture. And they spoke their own language. Still the same today, their children and their grandchildren. And that's why people hold their Land so strongly, for those sort of reason. And in the end, some of them station people became friends, and some of their children became friends with our kids. And some of those children learned to speak our language. And that's really important for understanding.

But a lot of the country got destroyed because people didn't talk about what was sacred to them. The early-day people were never even asked "is this a sacred area?" Because they didn't have rights. Like *urrperle mape* just thought that only *mperlkere* mob, the whites had right, you know? 'Cause we used to see like *mperlkere mape* could move us any way where they want to move us, you know? *Alakenhe*. And we even thought that *mperlkere mape* wanted our family to survive, *merne-akertele arntarnte-aremele*, because they were always looking after us, making sure we had enough to eat.

That's how a lot of the people who were here before us saw it, *urrperle mape arrwekelenye mapele itelareke*. Those old people knew alright. And now that we got rights, that's how we can talk about all the things in the Land. What's in that Land, and what is right and what is wrong. "You're not to put a road there, not to chop those trees down". But it was only told just lately to all of us. Only the people who knew before was the elders. Like today we don't have very much elders in our people, like 'specially in our mob. Not many elder people on the eastern side, only a few. Like *Ikngerrekwiperre mape aneme*. Only *urrpetye ware-arle arelhe akngerrepate-arle*.

But it would be good if we could take care of things like how the early-day old people looked after the Land. *Ye*, because they really looked after the Land. No trees were chopped down. It was well looked after. People travelled everywhere, all over their country. They used to keep an eye on what's there, clean it out. Go and clean it if the birds went 'round there, maybe the tree fell there. They used to keep it clean all the time, make sure the waters run clean, and make sure that the water is running in the way that it should, rockhole-*nge-ntyele apeke*. *Alakenhe*. They knew when the seasons will come; "well, season this time's gonna be rain season. Well, we might go and pick the bush banana, *alangkwe*s, and *atwakeye*s, the wild orange". They never used to store it away, they used to pick it to share it out. They might, "all right, *alangkwe* season, well those people over there, family *arrpenhe mape* on the other side, they mightn't have enough *alangkwe*, we'll take them over some". There was a lot of sharing and guiding of *apmere*, you know? *Alakenhe-arle aneke, arrwekelenye mape*. All the women going in a group, and all the men going in another group. Like *arrwekelenye mape*, "all right, *arelhe mapele-arle alhelte-iwerle ntangeke-arlke apekawe*, okay let's all the ladies go and collect *ntange*s"; maybe not *ntangeke* really, like *awele-aweleke-arlke apekawe*, or might be

Rockhole, photographer Mitch Jones

tyape ingwenengeke or *tyape atnyematyeke, ngkwarle yerrampeke*. Collecting seeds, grubs, and nectar. *Alakenheke arelhe mape alhetyarte, ane artwe mape-kenhe alhelenge kereke-arle*. While the women went off looking for those type of things, the men went off looking for *kere*. Any meat. And then they'd bring that back, and then they'd share-*eme-ilerrerle. Marle mapele-arle anthele ane urreye mapele-arle anthele. Alakenhe*. Even the young girls and boys would share what they'd got. Or they might fetch it back home and the women would give the old ladies their portion, *akngetye-alpeme* like *anthele arelhe ampwe akngerrepate mape. Ane artwe mapele-arle,* and the men might come back and give the male elders *kere mape*, those cuts of meat which are really important to them. *Alakenhe-arle aneke*, that's how it happened. But *arrwekelenye mape aneke*, like the one I was just telling you *arrwekele nhenge yanhe ayeye, arntarnte-aremele, apmere arntarnte-arintye-akerte-arle aneke,* that's a story about how the country was always looked after and guided from the Beginning Time.

We Who See the Beautiness

When we talk about 'our place', Aboriginal people see our place as really important, they see what's inside, what is the most valuable things in that country. When they're talking to anthropologists or somebody, you know, sometimes it's really hard to explain to them why they really want that place back, why they want the country back. And like how we saw this country of ours. Even though the station man took this Land away from us, we see the sacredness of that country to us. It has really strong meaning of us, also a part of us. And what those, like, the water – how we relate to water, how we relate to where the hill lays, where the creek runs – how we relate to those sort of things. That's how we see it, but I don't know how we translated that to people when we talked about Land. Like, some of our mob, like old people, they just used say, "that tree is sacred. And that creek". But not really telling what that *really* means, but they can only see themselves what that tree meant to them. What it is. That's how we know it. And it's really hard for…you've gotta sit down and talk for a long time to get people to understand.

It's not the way that anthropologists, how they talk. Sometimes they talk in a really professional way. And sometimes we as interpreters gotta ask twice what they really mean. 'Cause sometimes they don't explain, "this is how I see it as a non-Aboriginal person, that's a word that I use"; and it doesn't fit into the way of the words we use to describe it, and how we see it, what it is to us. If you ask that old person why that tree is sacred, he won't give an answer straightaway. 'Cause sometime it might be really hard about it, and also maybe that sacred tree must've come from somewhere else, and just stood there. Because if he says that that's a sacred tree, the person who's asking probably mightn't ask where that tree came from, where that sacred tree was marked. But that old man can only see it in his mind. Sometimes it's really, really hard to put words to it, unless it's spoken very clearly to that person. They'll say "that tree just came, and became, and stood there". But only the people that started from where that tree came, how it follows, only they can tell that Story. That's how it is.

Old people can see the Story inside them, but might not be able to put it into words. The Story lives inside them. Also the people from where that tree originated really hold the Story about that tree. In the eyes of Aboriginal people, and in their ways of thinking, you never tell somebody else's Story. You gotta tell only your own true Story. And how we picture our country. What *arelhe urrperle*'s country is, what it means. I can't start talking about these other people's country, or those people's country. The way I like to tell the story is how I see how *arelhe urrperle*, Aboriginal people, relate to Land. How it is important to us. Because sometimes it's not really listened to properly. That's why I like to *ilerle*, to tell, *nthakenhe-arle anwerne apmere areme*, just how we see the Land. What it is to us.

And if you're seeing the Land without the Story, then there's nothing there. We see our country, even though it might be destroyed by another species, we see how the beautiness is still in the country. *Anwerne-arle areme apmere nhenhe nanthe-arle pweleke-arlke-arle akenge alhintyeke, apmere anwerne-kenhe-arle arrelyemelyeme apmere utnenge anwernekenhe-arle.* It doesn't matter that horses and bullocks have caused such destruction, we still see the spirit of that Land glistening. 'Cause *apmere anwekakerrenhe-arle, apmere anwernekenhe anwerne areme iwenhe-arle aneme*, we see what's in the Land, and how we fit into it, *nthakenhe-arle anwerne antirrkweme.* 'Fitting in' means how we hold, and how we relate to it. *Ane iwenhe-arle apmere yanhe ikwere-arle aneme. Apmere yanhele aneme anwernekenhe kwatye aneme, kere aneme, anwernenhe apmere anwernekenhele-arle arntarnte-arerle-aneme, rlkerte mwerre-ileme.* We get water and meat from our countries, the Land guides us and looks after us, and it heals us. But the most important thing is to understand that we are part of our Land, and that the Land is part of us. *Akngerre anthurre kenhe anwerne itelareme apmere anwernekenhe, anwerne renhe-arle, alakenhe.*

Well, it doesn't matter if they dug something out in that Land you know, that special thing is still there – *alherntere mape* mightn't see it, but Aboriginal people see it, and it still lays there. Even that dug-out thing got thrown away, the special nature is still there and remains in that area. There might be one patch they dug, and there's still whole patches all around it. Only eyes of Aboriginal people can see it, not in the eyes of non-Aboriginal people. But we know it, we can see it, we can feel it, 'cause it's part of us. I mean it's very sad when you see it when it got dug down and it made a hole in, it's just like making a hole in somebody's body; that's how we see it, you know. Because the Land, it's a really strong thing, a living thing to us. And that's how we try to stop people from digging anywhere, or pulling down trees, 'cause where the plant or tree's pulled down is just like killing somebody's body. Because it's in that area of our Land, whose own Landmark is there. We who see the beautiness of the Land.

When we used to talk to people in Land Council, there was not much…it wasn't really translated properly; what it is and what it really meant for us. And also transferred and explained to the people who don't want to give us back the Land. It wasn't really translated to them, and they'll have false words, messages. We should go up and talk to a station man ourselves about how we look at the Land, and also how he looks at his station, and also how we'll fit in with him. Those sort of things hasn't been dealt with before, there was not many consultation between the *apmereke artweye* and the station owner.

We didn't have a chance *nhenge* station owner-*ke angketyeke*, you know, to speak to the station man ourselves. The Aboriginal people who lived there were the only ones that the station owner knew. Maybe some of the people who lived there, maybe they wasn't the real owners of that place, that country *apeke*. Maybe they just moved in by work, they brought them there from somewhere else to do stockwork, teaching them to be workers, to be cleaning people. And these workers might've just come to visit those people in that country who *did* own it. Maybe they got attracted to that place, they must've just saw them as, "there are young people there. In that place where those other people's country is".

I know some people, station owner *kwenhe*, people station-*arenye*, *apmere arrpenhenge-ntyele mape-arle ikwerenge warrke-irretyarte*. Workers who just came in from another place. They used to work there, and the people who used to work there before them, *apmereke artweye mape*, the real Landowners, well, they'd moved on earlier, and these other people came in. So in the end, those people, the new people they had, was entitled to get a piece of living area where they could stay, and work, and make it like their own. And then when those other people, the real *apmereke artweye* came back, "hey, *yanhe mape apmereke artweye kwenye. Anwerne-arle apmereke artweye arrwekelenye anwerne warrke-irreke akngeye ngkwinhenge*, or *arrenge ngkwinhenge*. Hey, we're the real traditional owners of this country, not those mob who's working here now. Our fathers worked with your grandfather, then maybe with your father". Like, sometimes the station owner might not know that the new mob with the living area are not really the Landowners to have that title. And that the real ones worked with his father and his father's father, but he didn't know them because he was too young. 'Cause sometimes in those days they didn't have a record of those people who worked there. Might be they were called other names.

Never did a station owner and *apmereke artweye* talk in a very understanding way. Never an understanding conversation with the *apmereke artweye*, the people who were trying to get their Land back. They're not getting the Land back to take the whole cattle off them or take the whole bore off them. They just want to get back and live on the Land, and eat anything, and hunt in their Sacred Ground, as they see it as an Aboriginal person. There's sacredness in that Land. But, as the station people see it, for them, it's a 'wealth', or whatever they like to call it. It's a grazing land for cattle, or where they can put bores for raising animals and beef stock. *Urrperle mapele-arle areme* – Aboriginal people see it as a Sacred Land, and on that Sacred Land they can hunt, and drink water from the Land, and live on the Land. They ask for just a little piece of that Land which is in the eyes of themselves laying all around that big station, where the station owns it. But still the Aboriginal people sees it as, "well, he owns the topsoil of that Land, but that big solid Land inside under there, *utnenge*, that Land's flesh, it's really ours, it's really *us*". That's how people see it. But it's very hard to say this to a station man, unless he really wants to sit down and talk in an understanding manner. 'Cause sometimes people are very frightened. And sometimes the Aboriginal people are very frightened too, "hey, he might get his gun out and shoot the lot of us!"

And there's other people who come in and talk in a certain manner that Aboriginal people don't see as real consultation. This might be between a Land Council lawyer and a station owner. It's like an anger thing, and Aboriginal people don't like those sort of anger things. And it divides that station owner to be bitter for those people that are *apmereke artweye*. And Aboriginal people don't want that, they want to let the station owner to understand more. Even he mightn't *want* some of that Land there – the bore's been broken down, and the water still lays there – and it's still on the same Land, and they might ask for that. They don't see that Land as rubbish, they still see that goodness that's part of them, and that part of that Land is still alive, as we see it. I don't want to say, if somebody might be a lawyer, that they're wrong. But if somebody might want to listen, it's just the way that Aboriginal people see it. Sometimes a lot of Aboriginals feels that way. They think lawyer *arrwekele ahele angkemele* station owner-*ke angkeme*: "*Apmere yanhe intintye-alpeme, apmere itnekenhe.* You gotta *itnenhe anthele itne apmerele anetyeke rawerne*". That the lawyer says in a demanding way to the station owner, "that's their Land and you must give that Land back to them! You gotta give that place so the poor people can live on it!" Maybe those sort of things were talked by the two non-Aboriginal people together. But

Aboriginal people can talk for themselves, because some station owners and Aboriginal people grew up together, and that's a really healthy way of lifestyle in them. They can know, "well, your father used to work there, and you grew up, and we grew up together. I think it's better for you guys to live on this Land, because you know the station rules and we know your living rules in the station". Those sort of things. But if you come out, like if you were taken away, taken to another community and grew up in another community, then you didn't grow up with those station people. Only those other people who came in later grew up with the station people. Sometimes mistakes happen because of that too. And sometimes the station man might say "hey, how come you reckon you own this Land? I never seen you before". But he didn't see how they were moved away. *Apmereke artweye mape* got moved away like to missions and other communities, those sort of ways. Sometimes they rely on those other people living on the Land now to tell for them: "Tell that station person that you're just working and living here, that the Land is really ours, and that your Land is on the other side, and maybe you're just joined to this Land".

Sometimes when people do get some Land back, it's by telling that station owner "that is where my father's land is". And if that station owner knows that person, the Aboriginal person might say "okay? I'll stay there, I'll look after that place". And if that station owner says "yes", they feel so proud, they really, really do. Sometimes they cry if they can stay, it's so emotional. And it's just like getting gold back, or striking gold. So rich, the richness for them. If they get that piece of Land to live on, they'll be so happy, whatever that Land's like. He might say "okay you can build a house there, but that station's gonna be still mine, and I still own it". They might ask to build something on it, make a road, put something up. They feel so proud, it's a real happiness to all those families, especially to the elders. That's one of the most important things that could happen to those people, if they could have a house built there. Not only just to get the Land back. The family itself *survives*. How those children'll grow, how those families can live and have their own strong Law for that life. For themselves and their future generations, the living style. The living style, and the Rule of that country – how they hold the Rule, how they see it, what it is for them, what message they can have for one another growing up there.

Grandfather's-Stories Land

We went back there one time, and we sat down and we talked about it with the station owner. And we was asking him, "oh, we just want a bit of this Land". And our Landmark was really twice as much, you know, as where his station area was, like the boundary of his station nearly, and our Land really covered moreover of what he had his landmark there. And some of our family, because the station owner owns these Land, they said "the station owner he owns just the soil part, where his cattle grazes, where his bore is, where the station is. But underneath, it's really our own Aboriginal Land". And we were sitting down and we sat down there and we saw this, and we sat beside this creek where these old people used to drink water, and now today those children, my sister's children, drank water in that old soak there where they still got water. And I sat down and I thought, "eh, I bet my grandfather's Stories on this Land is watching all of us here, fighting to get back something that we really own". In the eyes of Aboriginal people. But then again, that station owner knew some of our families, the ones who worked there before.

And I was just sitting there looking out, and I felt really peace. And they gave us a bit of Land there, but it's not in the title, hasn't got a title yet. You gotta go through the white law, you gotta wait years and years; some people have died waiting for law to come, some of the old people have passed on now. But still some people's got the Stories. But oh, to see that soak where my mum and my great-great-grandparents drank that water, and my brothers and sisters and the kids today still drinking that water! It's a place called *Akerte*, that's where all my family come from; my grandfather, my father's father come from. And to see that soakage, it was really great that we could see it today. And it was still there! But at least we've got somewhere to stay and live, and make it our own, call it our own, always been our own. And you couldn't call any other people's place your home but your own. Where your grandfather is, you gotta know which is your grandfather's country, or your mother's country. That is one of the bestest tie, in yourself, as an Aboriginal person. What is your skin name, and how you relate and how those children will relate to that place.

Healing

Healing comes from the Land itself. When we're sick or in mourning we go back to the Land to feel better, and to really relax deeply. We go back so that we can eat things from the Land. Like we might want to go back and eat kangaroo, or we might want to go back and eat goanna, might want to drink the water of the Land, and also get healed by the fire from the Land. That is all healing. And living amongst our own families, seeing the children play, our own children, our grandchildren. Or staying there with your sons and your daughters, and the rest of the family. That's a really healing thing. To go back and smell the smoke and the air of your own country, hear the birds singing and talking, watching the stars at night, and seeing the sun rise and seeing the sun set. And also talking about things at night when you're looking at the stars. Seeing what the stars tell you. All that just gets into you and heals you.

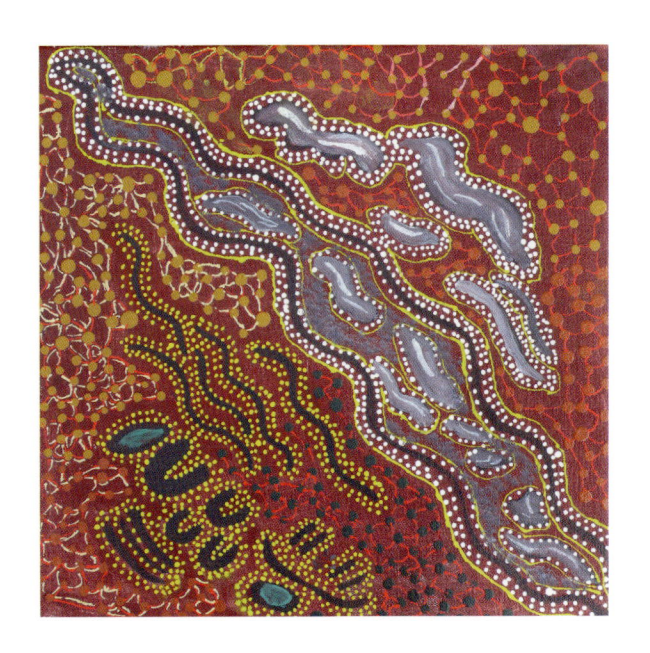

Plants Grow With the Power of the Land

Arne ulye ane arne rlkerte-kenhe. Whether it's for their shade or their healing properties, we look at plants and trees really highly. *Nthakenhe-akenhe arne nthakenhe-akenhe-kenhe arne ulye-kenhe, ulye-arle aneke-ipenhe imernte ure anteme irremele*, also *arne atherrke apmerenge-ntyele amangkeme*, and also *rlkerte-kenhe anteme-arle*

Arelhe Ipmenhele Ayeye Amiwarre-akerte Ampe Akaltyele-anthemele Ileme, 2006, acrylic on canvas, photographer IAD Press
Grandmothers explaining the story of the Milky Way to kids.

arne. Different plants are used for different things. Some are used for shade, some are used for firewood, and some, especially the ones that grow on your own country, are used for medicine as well. *Rlkerte-kenhe arne* people-*le itelareme apmere kantreyenge-ntyele.* People know the plants from their country that are used for healing. They reckon *kantreyenge arne arrwengkelthe-kenhe apeke amangkeme apmere-arle kantreye yanhe-arle aneme-arle renhe-anteye-arle, renhe angkwerre-arteke-iwirtneme,* they say that all medicine plants grow with the healing power of the country in them. That plants cure you because they come from the same country that you do, they have the same healing power as your Land has. *Layake tyerrtye ingkerreke interrentye ilirtnerle, layake mpwarirtnerle, alakenhe-arle,* people *arentye-akngerre.* And they heal the body back to its natural state of health. That's the way people see it, it happens all the time. Some people, if they don't have any *arne yanhe-arteke, arrpenhenge kine alhele apmere-kenhe-werne aketyeke* you know, if they don't have any medicine plants growing on their own country to pick, they'll *alhele apmereke artweyenge ware arne aketyeke,* they'll go with owners of another country to pick medicines there. Because those *arne* belongs to those other people, *rlkerte-kenhe mape,* you know? *Alakenhe.*

Plants grow with the power of the spirit of country in them, *ahelhe utnenge-arenyenge lyapeke.* That spirit shows itself when they grow up and become strong plants. Sometimes people really rave on about it, and sometimes they really *see* that plant, because it's a plant that really comes from their own country. Like praise-*eme-ileme-arteke,* like *tnakeme.* They praise the plants up, almost like skiting about them, "that plant grows in our country, and it makes people well – kids, grown women, men, everyone". *Ye, apmere utnenge-arenye, utnenge-arenye, utnenge-arenye ahelhe, ahelhe utnenge-arenyenge-arle layake lyapeke.* Oh yes, those plants grow out of the Land, ripe with the spirit of their own soil – the spirit of the Land that's always there, even though the plants themselves come and go.

So when they *alhewelhele apeke,* it's just like *itnenhenhe lyaperle-ilirtneme-arteke.* When people wash themselves it's like it makes them grow back to their natural state of original wellbeing. *Mwerre-ilirtneme,* the plant medicine makes you complete, just like when they themselves grow up and come to be strong plants. People-*le atnerle-arerle*, you know *renhe-areye*, they really skite about those plants. *Atnerle-arerle* is like *tnakerle-arteke*, praising-up, skiting because you know you've got backup behind you. Because *ahelhe itnekenhenge-ntyele*, it comes from their Land. They really rave on about it because they can see that plant really comes from their own country. Praise-*eme-ilemele-arteke, tnakerle*. They really praise it up like, "*kantreye anwernekenge-arle arne nhenhe lyapeke* – this plant grows in our country – *anwerne itelareme arne nhenhele tyerrtye mwerre-ilenhele*, and we know that this plant always heals and cleanses the body. *Iwenhe apeke-arle ampe apeke, arelhe akngerre apeke, artwe apeke, nhenge rlkerte. Alakenhe.* It doesn't matter whether it's a child, a woman, or a man that's sick, it heals them all!" Like that they talk.

Arne-arle awelye-arteke kine, the medicine from the plants can act just like the healing that's sung, it can *angkwerre-iwerle*, heal you in a really physical way. You can *arrerneme*, put that bush medicine on, and it must be something like *alyemele-arteke*, you know? Like if it sings you. It must be probably sings that, when it gets in the body it probably like sings it and gets it away, hunts it away, *ye*. And kills it down, even though it might be *anwernekenhe* body-*arle areme*, it *sees* the body and heals exactly where it's sick. Like when you break out in sores, *utyene-apeke-irrerle*. When you put something from the Land on a sore, there might be lots and lots of little like, radiate-*arteke aneme*, waveling rays being sent through your body, and medicine goes in and fills in all that whatsiname. When it fills it, that *rlkerte-ame arratintyele*, the sickness leaves from your body, it gets hunted out. *Kenhe arrwengkelthe atwenhe rante-arle irrpenheme*, only the right medicine for that particular sickness will enter into your body like that. *Awelye-arlke apeke*, it's just the same as with the healing from songs. *Irrpenhele kwene-werne merrethene*, only the specific medicine goes in, whatever that medicine might be. It's like it draws it out, and when it get draws out, all the goodness starts growing back from *kwenenge-ntyele*, from deep inside you. And *mwerre-arle-ilerle*, this goodness restores you to your original and proper state of wellbeing. *Alakenhe-arle tyerrtye anwerne*, you know, *arelhe mapele arentye-akngerre*, that's how Aboriginal people really see and understand it. Even though people are not even *angangkere* or anything, they're not traditional healers themselves, that's still how they see it. And that's how they describe it, describe-*eme-ileme*, you know.

Powerful Little Medicines

Anwernekenhe-thayate-le some people-*kenhe-thayate nhenhe alakenhe*, over this side, the healing plants that belong to our *Arrernte* mob here are like *arrethe* (rock fuchsia), *utnerrenge* (emu bush), *aherre-intenhe* (harlequin fuchsia bush), and *pintye-pintye* (apple bush). And people used to use *apere artekerre* (river red gum roots) and *athenge artekerre* (ironwood roots) *alknge alhewelhetyeke*, for washing their eyes, and *apere arntape* (river red gum bark), and also *apere utnenge* the solid wood from the trunk of the red gum. *Arntape nhenge yanhe ulkere*, they used to boil-*eme-iletyarte*, *itelhetyeke, alhwe-arle-arteke alhewelhetyeke*, and wash with it. That bark, they used to boil it, to warm yourself up and wash in it, it's like you were washing in blood. And also they used the *apere akwerrke* (red gum leaf shoots), you know, *akantye-ipenhe nhenge ulkere-ame*, the young gumleaf tips. *Renhe ulkere-arlke-arle inetyarte mapele, itemele alhewelhetyarte*, they used to collect them, boil them up and wash themselves in the water, and it smells eucalyptusy. There's a lot of things people used to use.

Ilpengke means, *anwerne-arle ileme*, when our-side mob says it, "*kwatye ilpengke*", that slow misty rain, you know? It can also mean a swamp. Also when the water just lays in the creek, and there's grass growing around it; still, cool water that just lies around. When you get the medicine from the bush called *ilpengke*, needle bush, then it's a bit like *irlweke*, the white cypress pine. If people are hot, they can rub that on and it cools them down, just like the cooling rain.

If you're sick you can burn *arrethe*, the rock fuchsia, and the fragrant smoke of that makes you well. People around Arltunga used to collect bags full of it for the old people. People grab little old clumps of that *arrethe* for firewood, you know? That's one of the powerful little medicine *ure*, that one. The old women used to tell us that, if we felt sick, "go and get the fuchsia firewood". Lots of young kids and teenage women used to go along on the collecting trips. We used to go along the side of the hills out there at Arltunga and collect the little dead trees, pull them out of the ground, and put them in chaff bags. We used to fill the bags up and bring them home, and give some to this old lady, some to that one, give some to another. The bit of wood we'd collected, they used to only burn it a small amount at a time. They used to make a low fire, a real smoky one at first, then later they'd make the fire bigger. Sometimes they'd do it before they went to bed, so that when they slept, there'd be coals from the fire that people would put bits of fuchsia wood on, little by little, so they were breathing it in just before they dropped off to sleep. It puts them to sleep really. That's one of the healing things that never got forgotten; like having a fire at night, and having the fuchsia smoke last thing to put them to sleep. It's got that healing smoke. If Daddy was sick or had the 'flu, we used to go with Mum and collect fuchsia firewood, bring it back, and then it was burned. Little clumps of fuchsia they'd burn, just as they were going off to sleep.

    You can use *arrethe* in other ways too. You cut the branches of the *arrethe*, and then you break off just the tips of the growing shoots, 'cause they're the really fresh part, the tips. You get that and grind it up into a paste. I seem to remember that the old people ground the *arrethe*, covered the paste in emu feathers, then mixed it with emu fat when they wanted to rub it on sick people. They massaged them with the ointment, and maybe sometimes they gave it to sick people to use on themselves. If someone had a bad head, they might smear the medicine on something and wrap that around their head. Nowadays people get it and mix it with butcher's fat. And when you break it up and grind it, and then cook it a little bit in a small fire, then it *lyelyelye-irremele*, makes a sizzly noise as it heats up. You know, all that bubbly sound comes out as it simmers.

    You can make rubbing medicine, you can make washing medicine, you can boil *arrethe* up in a big bucket and put a few cakes of soap in with it. 'Velvet' *thupe mape*, maybe 'Velvet' soap, or something nice like scented soaps, *thanteye-thupe apeke*, so it can smell nice. They used to put carbolic soap in it, that *irlkngerre-irlkngerre* one, the nice shiny green one. Station owners used to use a lot of it, they'd strain the liquid through a hessian bag. Later on they started draining it through a nylon dress, you know the see-through sort, and then they went on to netting, insect screens. After it was strained they'd leave it to set, and then they cut it up into blocks, just like a bought soap for washing yourself, *alhewelhetyeke*. They did that all the time, keeping healthy by keeping clean. And sometimes they'd do it for sick people too, so they can wash themselves.

Utnerrenge, the emu bush, is used for a lot of things too. Like, *utnerrenge* you can *iterle*, people *nhenge iwenhakweye urrparelhentyele kwertele-ilelhetyeke*, you can burn the wood for cleansing yourself in the smoke. And also *ampe akweke kwertele-iletyeke*, you smoke the child as well, and *mikwe kwertele-ilelhetyeke*, and the mother does it to herself, and anybody who's sick can warm and cleanse themselves in the smoke of the emu bush, *rlkerte apeke kwertele-ilelhetyeke alakenhe-arle utnerrenge*. You can wash yourself with it, make it into a soap as well. And it's really good if you wash with it, all that itchiness goes away. But you can't get it near your eyes. You can wash your whole body with it, and it makes you proper clean and really shiny. When you boil it, it comes really yellowy and really…what do you call it? *Urrknge*, slimy sort of – nice, and really thick. You can put that out and put it in a bowl or dish or anything – a tray or a jam tin, 'cause some little soaps were round shapes – the Arltunga mob washed themselves with it after making soap like that. *Utnerrenge*, they use it in traditional ways, but also *rlkerteke*, for sick people, and *ampeke*, for kids, and *ampe menhengeke*, for mother and child, and *kwertele-ware-ilelhetyeke*, for self-cleansing in the smoke, and *apmere kwertele-iletyeke*, to smoke out the camp after someone has passed away.

Kwertele layake apmere kwerte arrerneme utnerrenge-iperre ile it will *aywepwenhele iwenhe apeke ikwe-arle aneme renhe*, you know? If you smoke out a house it'll get rid of whatever essence may be lingering there. That *ikwe* means that *unpe*, some people call it. It's a smell. Smell is a thing, and that thing like goes away. So it can then smell like *utnerrenge*, and also later on you'll feel happy about it when you do that. When you don't *kwertele-iletyakenhe apmereke irrperle*, if you don't smoke out the camp, you feel really fear when you go into it. That's why people like *anwerne* people who *akngerrepate*…we *kwertele-ilerle*, we smoke it out then, especially if it's an elder. When people depart the house, that's when we smoke it out, and then everybody who'd lived in the house has to go through the smoke. Because that smoke is what heals people, holding them together after their loss. And it comes from *apmere ahelhe anwernekenhenge-ntyele*, from our Sacred Land. And all Aboriginal people know and understand that. That's why we want to teach our young people about the *utnerrenge*. That's *utnerrenge ayeye*, the *utnerrenge* story.

Aherre-intenhe alhewelhentye-akngerre kine, harlequin fuchsia bush is a washing medicine as well. Nowadays people grind it and put it in that oil, 'extra virgin'. They get that and put it in a big bottle or plastic jar. They rub it on or sometimes they wash in it. After washing in it – if you have a bath with that – you sleep really well, *mwerre anthurre ankwe-interle*. You sleep well because *aherre-ime yanhe-ulkerele-arlenge interle*, because the kangaroo he will sleep under that bush all day, and he just lazes away; everywhere you can see where they've been laying underneath, under the shade of the harlequin fuchsia bush.

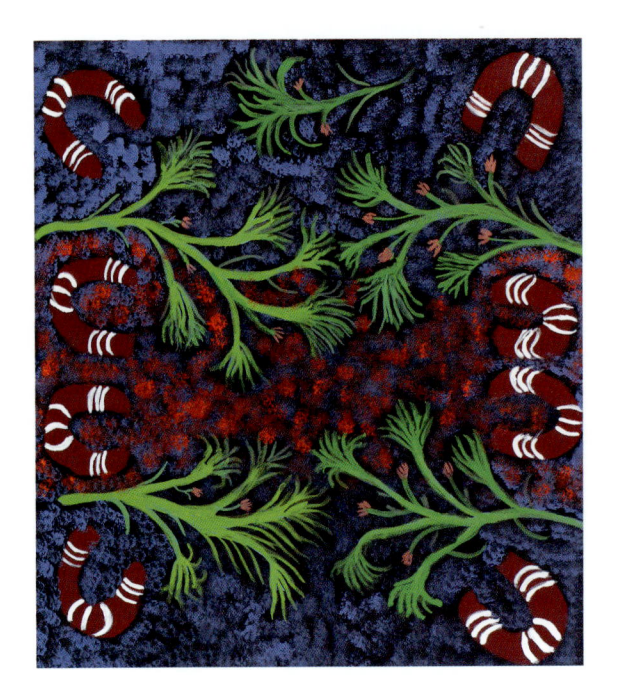

Also another one is *arrkernke*, the bloodwood tree. *Irrkipere. Ye, arrkernkenge-ntyele irrkipere*, the bloodwood sap or gum. People washed with it if they had sores, *utyene*. But they used to use that *irrkipere* on camel sores too, you know, they used to collect it and put it on their camels' sores. They used to put a

---

Watchful Eyes See the Bush Medicine Grow, 2007, acrylic on canvas, photographer *Irrkerlantye* Arts
Watchful eyes can see the bush medicine plants grow. This is *aherre-intenhe*. *Aherre-intenhe* is one of the best medicines people collect all the time. It grows in many places, all around this area. You pick the leaf, and then you grind it. You put it in hot water and boil it to bathe anybody who is sick. Or you can grind it and put it in a dripping or make it like an oil so you can rub it on when you've got aches and pains. You come out of the bath, put some of that oil on, have a good sleep. It is also called 'kangaroo shade' because it makes shade for kangaroo.

tar, might be a tar *uthene* oil *angkweye uthene*, mix-*eme-iletyarte*. Tar and old motor oil were mixed together, and then put it on them camels. They used to put a little bit *irrkipere* in, that's sap from the bloodwood, *ye*. And people put it on their own sores as well, in the early days.

That's how all the *merrethene-arle anetyarte utyene-kenhe putye arne alakenhe mape*, that's what medicines were like, those bush medicines like that, for sores. *Apere artekerre-iperre-arlke*, from red river gum roots *arlketyerre iwenhakweye-arlke*, and from the dead finish roots, *ante arlketyerre-iperre*; dead finish-*iperre*, *artekerre*, and also *athenge-iperre*, *artekerre athenge-iperre*, from the roots of the ironwood. Used to dig it *ante alhewelhetyeke alknge-arlke*, you know? For washing their eyes. *Ye, alknge-arlke alhewelhetyeke*, to wash eyes as well.

Apwertele-arle tnentye-akngerre unpe akngerre akwerrke mape. There's a plant growing in the hills that has a really strong aroma, especially the new growth. A big bush really, growing in the hills, *pwetheyekate artarre akwele*, 'pussycat tail' they call it. But it's really a mustard, it's a curry tree. When you *ulpe-ilerle, ntyernerle mmmmm*! When you crush it up, it smells really beautiful. When you grind that into like a petroleum jelly, or an ordinary dripping *apeke*, oh it smells so good! You can *yanhe-ulkere-arlke apernelhele*, rub it on yourself, you can rub it on when you're sick or anything and it goes in. When your chest *apernelhele, alhenge-arlke arratenhele*, when you rub it on your chest, it clears your nose you know. It's been like a, maybe, *altywere-ilenheme apeke*, an opening medicine. And *utyene apernelhele*, you can rub it on any sores, when you got ordinary sores. *Alakenhe*.

Oh, *yanhe* people *prape atningke-arle akemele iterle*, people used to pick and prepare lots and lots of *arrwe-atnurlke*, the striped mint bush. *Atherle*, and they grind it. It's like burning *arrethe*, but this has got a really nice smell. *Atnurlke* is that *antere atnurlke*, it's the fat from the bottom of the *arrwe*, the rock wallaby, and also kangaroo. That smell, and *yanhe-iperre atnurlke* means *alakenhe*, that's the name of that fat from those animals. Those *atneperrke*, the guts of the animals, that's what makes people's hair go grey, and then white. The *atnurlke* was only eaten by the elders, because they already had white hair, they were already classed as senior. So it really fitted them to eat that fat, they were the only people who could eat that. The hair is supposed to turn white, but people still seem to eat it, because they really like that *antere*, that fat, it's got a nice taste in it. *Ikwemeye anthurre*, really tasty. And it's because of that smell that the mint bush gets its name in *Arrernte*.

Angkweleye, the bush plum's really good too. Another name for it is *arrankweye*. You can boil the *angkweleye* leaves, strain off the water, and drink it with apple juice. *Angkweleye* cures blood pressure problems. People up on the *Alyawarr*-side told me that once they started drinking the *angkweleye* juice, they stopped having blood pressure, even though they'd been suffering from it for a long time. *Warlperle mape* should test-*eme-ilerle*, the scientists should test that juice and see what's in it, and what it's good for.

And *ingkwerlpe* is the wild tobacco. Another name we call that plant is *arrirrkenhe*, which means 'itchy mouth'. *Ingkwerlpe apwerte antherrtye-arenye* is one sort of *ingkwerlpe* from the high cliffs. *Kenhe ahelhe urlternte-arenye ingkwerlpe-kenhe* different idea, that's *pitwerre nhenge yanhe-arle*. *Pitwerre*'s another sort of tobacco, and it's got real shiny leaves. *Ane akngerrepenhe anthurre*, and it's pretty big. *Ahelhe urlterntele*, it grows on the limestone, and the best place to get it's at *Ltyentye Apurte*, Santa Teresa. People used to collect heaps of it and take it home by the bag. *Pitwerre*'s real cheeky, and people used to use sometimes *pitwerre* mixed with *ingkwerlpe atnwengke*. 'Cause *atnwengke* hasn't got that real kick in it, so they used to chuck it in with that. One old lady from the west, she asked me, "hey, get me some *pitwerre*, but hey *pitwerre*'s really strong, too strong by itself. I want some so I can mix it with this other *ingkwerlpe*". *Athetyeke*, for grinding. *Atnwengke*. 'Cause *atnwengke*'s sandhill-*le lyapeme*, it grows in sandhill country and it's not as strong. Sandhill, *ye, ahelhe arlpe-arenye*.

The sandhill *ingkwerlpe, arlpe-arenye atnwengke*, the leaves are thin, *utnenge utyewe arlpentye ware*, the stems are tall and thin, not as thick as real *ingkwerlpe apwerte antherrtye-arenye, apwerte atewarte-arenye*. Sandhill people used to fetch the sandhill *ingkwerlpe* because they got used to it. Like the people from the plains, *ahelhe urrkale-arenye mape*, mulga country, where they've got sandhills, they actually like that one 'cause they got used to it. And people who lived around near the hills, they liked *ingkwerlpe apwerte antherrtye-arenye*. When the people came to Santa Teresa, well, they used to get *ingkwerlpe* from Arltunga-side before that, and then they found *pitwerre* growing everywhere around Santa Teresa. Growing wild everywhere on that limestone, growing about *that* high. *Irlpelhe imparrkeye-imparrkeye*, it has shiny, glittery leaves. It was no good for the cattle. It still grows there, in the gullies.

Sometimes they used to fetch the herb from the high cliffs, *apwerte antherrtye-arenye inerle*. That's the mountain *ingkwerlpe*, *apwerte antherrtye* and *apwerte atewarte*. *Atewarte*'s a little hill, standing on its own. Hills, might be standing by themselves, got that big slabby rock, it's just built-up in a big slabby rock. The water runs quicker off those *athirnte*, the rockplates, and gets into the soil, and grows whatever things. Because the rocks on either side seem to channel the water to certain areas, it blocks it from both sides, the ways, the channels. That's why the *ingkwerlpe* from *apwerte atewarte*'s really good. And when the plants grow between the large slabs, they're really protected from the sun, and that's how it keeps itself real bitter, really hot. Now *that*'s a flavour! It's got that nice flavour in it. Like if you have a tobacco, it's got that nice kick in it, *ikwemeye anthurre*, you know?

And sometime there's *ingkwerlpe-ingkwerlpe*. Down the creek you see 'em *ingkwerlpe-ingkwerlpe*. Not really *ingkwerlpe*, that's just a copycat one, *ingkwerlpe anhelhentye*, real fake *ingkwerlpe*. *Ingkwerlpe arremparrenge*, you know, just *ingkwerlpe*'s double-double. No kick, no taste, it's got a watery taste and smell in it. But it relates in a way to the real *ingkwerlpe*. When the *ingkwerlpe-ingkwerlpe* grows tall, you take notice, because then you know that the real *ingkwerlpe* in the hills grows tall too.

People used *ingkwerlpe* as a medicine, to make their bodies feel well. But if you chew 'Log Cabin' tobacco, your throat itches. Tobacco and ashes, 'cause you're not supposed to do it with the whitefeller's tobacco. That's just for the wild native tobacco, *ingkwerlpe arratye*, the true tobacco, the one that's created to uplift your spirit. And the ashes that you mix with it – *irlpmenye* or *ikwentye* – are from *ankerre* (coolibah), *atnyeme* (witchetty bush), *artetye* (mulga), or *athenge* (ironwood). All that *ingkwerlpe*, it only fits properly into that one there, those ashes.

People used to just chew a little lump of *ingkwerlpe*, chew it for a while then put it behind their ear. You can go anywhere, run around, even lie down to sleep and it doesn't fall out from behind your ear. *Ingkwerlpe* is good for the body when you chew it, it's like medicine again for Aboriginal people. It relaxes the body and gives you a good sleep. But little kids can't chew it 'cause it can kill little kids. Only big people can chew it. If little kids chew it, they can get a real head-spin. Only kids that have been taught how to chew it can do it without getting giddy and sick.

And talk about addictive! You think people worry for cigarette, *ingkwerlpe* is more worse! When you run out of it, you look around even for the *ingkwerlpe* that you've spat out already! People are always asking, "hey give us a bit of your *ingkwerlpe* will you? Have you got a bit to spare, just a little bit?" Sometimes then people might be given the lump from behind someone's ear that's already been chewed!

Healing With Song

Sometimes I put things about healing in my paintings, and I tell my grandchildren about it. They might say, "Nanna, what's all these little stripes?", and I'll tell them something about healing then. Like, sometimes people would *antere alyele*, sing the fat, sometimes they'd put it on their tongue. From special people they used to get it. A lot of them like my mum used to do a lot of things, 'cause she used to be really healthy.

A grandfather might teach his grandsons to be singers of a special healing song. But the healing itself comes from our nature, you know, from the Land. That 'electrolight' is just from that nature. Also they're born with it too, and the person who's got that electrolight nature, he can touch the people around him. When that child is born, "hey, that kid's gonna be this!" They know it straightaway, 'cause he's got that light, that electrolight of nature inside him. So *alkngenthe angangkere-arteke-arle anperle, angangkere anetyenhe-le kwenhe*. Even though we don't see it, people knows he's got that power when they touch him, and he knows it as well, because he's gonna be one of them, one of the *angangkere*s, the Sacred Doctors. Sometimes he's born with it, and sometimes they become that later. Later on, sometimes the senior ones might say, "okay I'm getting old, I'm gonna put all this spiritual healing nature thing into this one here, so that he can carry that on". And straightaway they get it and put it into that kid, and he can only see it himself. It must be a gift, *Ngkartele antheke*, that God gave to the Land. And also to protect – protection *anetyeke*, that is. It protects yourself, and it also protects other people when they're sick. They can protect-*eme-iletyenhenge*. Like *anwernekenhe utnenge*, you know? Protect our spirits. There's *utnenge*, our spirit or soul. Only *angangkere* can see it, but sometimes people get sick or sometimes somebody might get a fright and that thing gets out. Or jumps away, sometimes he might hide under the table, but only the person who's got that traditional healing can see the soul and put it back into that person, *alakenhe*.

And songs, some ladies have healing songs too. Their own songs for like when a mum might get sick, they'll sing that. When they smoke them out they might sing. Or sometimes when they've lost weight they'll sing, but it's only all the women I'm talking about. And the men just know about and teach their own male songs. And women teach female songs. When we teach songs to young girls, they've gotta get into the musical sound of that song, and the rhythms of the song. They've gotta know the rhythms of the song. And also to sing it loud and sing it soft. And when they get soft, they blow that air into that person, to become what they want to be, back to their wellbeing. Like for healing, if the sore's gonna heal, well you sing that song – you sing it not too loud, but you sing it in a good rhythm. *Alakenhe*. You've gotta learn that, they don't just know it without learning, *ware akaltye nhenhe*. And also the humming, *arnwere*. *Arnwere*, you've gotta know what *arnwere* is, that's the rhythm, *arnwere* song *ikwerenhe*. The sick person's got to hear the rhythms of that *arnwere*, and the words gotta go into that rhythm. And the meanings, you've gotta have the rhythm and the meanings for that song. You could sing just the tune, but it doesn't mean anything, that person mightn't get better. You've gotta know the tunes, and also that humming, that humming sound so that he can feel good too when you're singing it. The sick person can feel that humming inside him, and it keeps it inside, the tune stays in there. And that sick thing gets out, gets hunted out, and next day, or in a few days he feels good again. *Alakenhe*, it's really important for people.

That song comes from the Land, and it's given by the Traditional Healers from there. And what it means from that Land, what the Species, what sort of Animal they come from, what *this* Animal does for *this* person to become healed, *alakenhe*. There's lots of songs – for appetite, for walking, and they also sing for fight, you know? To be a strong fighter, to show people that, you know, somebody comes to fight you and he sees you and, "hey, I can't fight him". There's some sort of power is put in that person to block the fight, things like that. Block the fight of that temper-person, *alakenhe*. They can also sing when there's a fire going, to let that fire do its own healing, old people used to sing that too.

Only families used to teach their kids about healing, and young people only used to ask their own families when they wanted to learn. Not many people *alakenhe angkeme*, can sing like that. Not many at all. But there are a few, and when they go and take these kids so somebody can sing them, *alyetyeke*, they know that person is a good singer. Like *akaperte alyenhe-alyenhe-arle*, good for singing heads, or just for singing any sickness, *rlkerte alyenhe-alyenhe-arle apeke*. Lots of people go to those singers 'cause they see other people getting better from them, *mwerre-irrerlenge*. They don't even know what the song really means, people *akngemele mape-arle*, they just know he's got good healing songs. Mummy *atyinhe anetyarte*, my mum, oh she used to *alyele*, sing everything and make all sorts of sick people well, *rlkerte alyele, mwerre-irretyeke apeke* people *mpwarerle. Alakenhe-arle rarle alyetyarte. Utyene-kenhe*, sore-*kenhe-arlke apeke*, headache-*kenhe apeke*, she used to sing cuts, headaches, and she'd sing things like the sickness that sets in when the north-west wind springs up, *aretharre-kenhe apeke*. She used to *alyele alakenhe*, sing all that. There used to be a real pile of songs she sang *itelaretyarte*. And my brothers used to sing songs they learned from my dad.

And people can sing for the Land and Ancestors to heal themselves. The Stories and songs, after they're performed, they come true. They're singing to make their spirit strong. "Oh well, she probably might be singing for healing, to heal herself, you know. And also those People from the Land to listen for her". And sometime when people sing like that, like when they're sick, years later them kids might have that Story for *them*. She might want to sing it and tell that Story for those kids who'll come along, in years to come, when she's gone. Sometimes they can come true, and when you go on the spiritual country, like on your own country, they'll tell you, the *apmere-altye*, those Spirit People from the country: "Hey, *ipmenhe ngkwinhe alakenhe-arle ilyelhetyarte, akunye kwenhe. Apmereke utnenge ikwerenhe mwerre-irrerlemele*. Hey, your old grandmother used to sing her song like this, to sing for her country and also to make her spirit strong". They'll give you that song like that, probably in a dream. And only you can know who that woman is to you from her background, how important she is, what was her role in that special place in her own community.

Sacred Punishment gives Peace

If we do wrong things to other people, we have healing then, we gotta go through our punishment. Sometimes we are bitter because now we are taught to be bitter. Aboriginal people never been bitter to any other person unless there's something very, very wrong. But that bitterness can be dealt through our own ways. As punishment, it is dealt with by that. And that gives people peace, for every Aboriginal people. Some people have bitterness by there's so much alcohol, as we know, *ngkwarle-arle akngerre antyweme. Itelaretyakenhe irremele*, but you don't really know, we don't know just why they're so bitter from that, from grog. Those people out there would understand why they're bitter. *Anwerne tyerrtye urrperle-areye*, we must say "*antirrkwerrerle*". Us Aboriginal mob, we have to hold each other. Not hold one another all the time, but just to be strongly related. Because each other person is important to their family as you are to your family. And that is the proper way. *Tyerrtye urrperle mape antirrkwerrerle*, Aboriginal people holding each other in kinship.

We *gotta* go through that punishment, which is if you done a really, really bad thing. To heal that you gotta go through a punishment. And that punishment of healing is getting people together, going through a real punishment, real bad ways. And that healing punishment, when we go through, we say "oh we've gotta take these people to finish up, they've gotta go through this traditional punishment, we've gotta take them". And that's one of the best things for our culture. It's not happening just today, it's been happening in the past, about forty thousand years ago. If you don't really go through that punishment, you will never, never be able to be free. And walk freely and be happy. You'll always be in fear, your families will always be in fear of payback for life.

That punishment joins into our Land as well. That comes from the Land and that comes from the people of the Land. It's one of the best things. It heals the people, the deceased's people, and it heals our side as well. So we can live in harmony. You wouldn't have fear to hunt, and when you went through that you can feel free. That really connects to every Aboriginal people, every family's got similar stories to what I've got here today. I've participated in many sacred healing punishments and it really heals, that's one of the best things that Aboriginal people should know.

The punishment ceremony must take place on the Land. It might happen on your Land, or it might happen on that other person's Land. It's part of living with the Land, and it's a sacred thing. It's not an angry thing, it's a sacred thing. Death is sacred, it's sacred to everybody, sacred to every Aboriginal people. To anybody I s'pose it's sacred. So that's why we've gotta have that punishment. It's a sacred punishment, a sacred event. It gives peace. It gives peace, it's a great peace between those two families.

Let Homeland Heal You

Anwerneke artweye mape re yanhe aneke, not *anwerneke artweye arrwekelenye, anwerneke artweyeke artweye mape, apeke yanhe itelaraye. Prape arrirlpe anthurre itne aneke.* Our old people, the ones that we remember as the leaders of our families, they were real straight-up-and-down people, very sharp. Not *arrirlpe* a sharp point, not *arrirlpe* like a knife, but body *prape tyerrtye anperre, ane prape arrirlpe anthurre, ane utnenge mwerre anthurre.* Their bodies were sharp and flat, and they had a really solid spirit.

Unthenhe-unthenhe, alethe alhenhe. Kereke irrwerntere-irrenhe irrtyartele atanthemele. Arlte anyentele apmere arrpenhe-werle alhele merne-arlke arlkwetyakenhe, kwatye antywerle akweke ware. Merne akweke arlkwenhele, alakenhe-arle aneke. Ane ngkwarle arwengalkere-arlke arlkwemele ngkwarle untyeyampe apeke, athenge-arlperle apeke. Atwakeye apeke, merne atwakeye apeke, merne arrutnenge apeke, merne alangkwe akweke alakenhe arlkweme ware mape-arle unthetyarte. Kere arlewatyerre atwenhele, kere ulkerte atwenhele, kere aherre atwenhele. They never *atwenhele kere aherre apeke, arrwekelenye mapele,* but they *itne apeke,* like *atherre apeke atwerle.* That's all *nhenge atherrame-arle itne akngetyenhe.* They never *atwerle layake* three or four like *lyete aneme makitele atyerremele, irretyeke-arle imperle. Alakenhe-arle akenhe mape arrwekelenye mape aneheke.*

Ane also *lyete ulkere anwerne aneme, layake anwerne anetyarte lyete ulkere aneme, layake merne aname-kenhe aneme arlkwemele. Layake merne* bread-*arle paye-eme-ileme, merne tampe-arle anwerneke, merne plawe-arle anwerneke imerneke. Layake arrwekelenye-kenhe anwerne tyerrtye mwerre anthurre. Merne yanhe mape-arle apele-artintyetyakenhe.* And that's how *merne yanheke-areye anwerne akaltye-irrepe-irreme. Tyerrtye-arlke anwernekenhe akurne-irreke. Putyele anemele aneme merne anwernekenhe arlkwetyarte anwerne* anything-*arlke anetyakenhe. Ntange-arlke apeke,* even *merne layake* station days we used to *arlkwerle merne akweke ware.* You know, station-*ke-arle inerretyarte* ration *akweke ware.* Because most of the time *kenhe* people-*arle alhetyarte kereke alhele, kwatye thuketyeke antywetyeke alhele, kere rapite apeke-arle itne* most-*ulkere atwetyarte. Rapite apeke, kere ulkerte apeke, arlewatyerre apeke, kele unthetyeke alhele.* Or *merne yalke* season-*nge merne yalke arlkwerle. Atherrkenyenge apeke merne atwakeyeke alhele. Atwakeyeke alhele, alangkweke,* or might be *kere alhilperre apeke teke-anemeke* season-*ke alhele, alakenhe-arle mapele. Teke-arle-anemeke aretyeke alhele, apwerte akertne-werne. Kele imernte akngetye-alpemele itetyeke, layake mapele arlkwetyeke.*

Kere iwenhakweye anwernekenhe, kere anwernekenhe anwerne share-*eme-ilemele arlkwetyarte.* Share-*eme-ilerremele ware arlkwerle.* We never *kere arrernerle* "oh fridge-*ke kere yanhe arrernaye ingwenthe arlkwetyenhenge*", 'cause that *kere* wasn't kept in the fridge *arrwekele*. Like *kere* kangaroo fridge-*ke arrernerle*, if you put it in the fridge it'll just go off in there straightaway. *Kere putye-arenye akwele kere warlperle-kenhe* you *arrernele kere* longtime *anthurre anerle-aneme*, 'cause they're made to be put in that fridge-*irrerle. Urreke anetyeke. Kere anwernekenhe akenhe lyete-arle arlkwerlenge ingkerreke-anteye. Alhwe-inpe-anteye arlkwerle.* 'Cause *alhwe-inpe-anteye arlkwemele kere anwernekenhe.* You don't *kere inerle kere tyipe-ilemele uterneke impemele* or somewhere-*ke arrernerle.* You straightaway eat it, *arlkwerle*, 'cause that's against the Law otherwise. *Kere arlkweme, atweme-arle, ingkerrekele anthurre arlkwetyeke.* And when that *arlkweke-arle*, and only when that's eaten, can you go and get another one, *ingwenthe arrpenhe apeke alhele, arlte arrpenhe-arle.*

People used to *ware*, they never used to *kereke-ante unthetyeke alhele*, they used to *ware-arlke alhele*. They walked for energy-*ke* or just for *tyerrtye mwerre awelhetyeke*, or *utnenge mwerre awelhetyeke, apmere kantreye-arle unthetyeke* or *kantreyenge intetyeke alhele. Tyerrtye apeke angkwerre-iwetyenhenge. Alakenhe-arle mape anetyarte.* Now today we don't *alhele* walk anywhere now, you know? *Mutekayenge nhakwe alhele, pathekelenge nhakwe alhele, alakenhe ware aneme.* Like the energy's gone out, not like the old people, *arrwekelenye mape*. Some of those healthy routines *anwerne arrwekele unthetyarte*, are gone out you know. *Alhele arrwekele layake* mother and father-*nge alhele. Mame-le apeke rapite tnyele*, then you can *rapite tnyele nhakwe-thayateke. Mame-le rapite iwenhakweye, atwerle akenhe anwernekenhe ure-arle itetyarte. Iperte-arle tnyele kereke. Alakenhe.* Homeland *anwernekenhe-werle alperle-iwaye anetyeke.* Homeland-*le anetyeke.* Homeland-*le angkwerre-iwetyenhe-arle-ke, apmerele-arle arntarnte-aretyenhe-arle-ke, kere putye-arenye arlkwetyenhe-arle-ke. Alakenhe-arle.*

They always walked around everywhere, those early-day people, they were real fit travellers, and they used to prance-step sideways when spearing kangaroos, in that really athletic, traditional way. They'd often take a whole day to get from one place to the next, without the benefit of much food, and only drinking a bit of water. They might eat only a small amount while travelling, that's just the way they were. They might sip on some wild sugarbag, or on corkwood flower honey, or maybe they'd just chew the sap from the ironwood tree. Sometimes they'd eat some wild oranges or wild passionfruit, or maybe a small bush banana now and then. That's the type of foods that kept them going while on the travel. They could now and again hunt some game on the way too, might be goanna, perentie, or kangaroo. But they never killed more than they needed, those early-day people. They might kill two animals, one to eat and one to take along with them. They never killed three or four – like nowadays people shoot with a gun, and sometimes waste and leave behind – they never did that. That's how they lived back then.

But today we eat food without really having done anything to get it. Like we buy bread now, that's the damper and the flour that's been introduced to us. In the early days we were healthy people. But that early-day food has all been taken over now by introduced foods. *Apele-artintyetyakenhe* means 'and that's covered over all the food what we have ate before'. That's what it means. And *alhernterele-arle apele-artintyeke*, we use that same word for 'the white men have come and taken over'. We're still just learning about how to eat these new foods, and our bodies are getting no good. When we lived out bush eating our own foods, there wasn't anything in them that would affect us. We still ate bush foods mainly, even when we lived on the stations. We only ever got a bit of rations from the station mob. When we lived on the stations, still we hunted meat and drank water from soakages, and most of the time it was rabbit we hunted. That's after the rabbit was introduced to us. So we walked around, hunting for rabbits, goannas, and perenties. Or we dug wild onions when their season came on. And in springtime we gathered the fruit of the wild orange. Wild orange and bush banana, or we'd get carpet snakes when it was carpet-snake-sunning-itself season, you know? We'd look for the carpet snake up on the top of the hills, then bring it back home to cook for everyone to eat. We always shared our food around. We always used to share food amongst our people, eating it then and there.

We never put meat in the fridge or freezer, 'cause that *kere* wouldn't keep in the fridge in the old days. Like kangaroo meat, if you put it in the fridge it'll just go off in there straightaway. But if you put whitefeller's meat in the fridge it'll keep for a long time, 'cause they're made to be put in that fridge, made to keep it for longer. But with our meat you have to eat all of it straightaway. You eat it blood and all. It gives us energy when it's fresh, and also you have to treat the meat in a respectful way. You don't get it, strip it up, and put it out in the sun to dry. You straightaway eat it, 'cause that's against the Law otherwise. When you kill a kangaroo, you've gotta share it around with everybody, and only when that's eaten can you go and get another one, maybe the next day or the day after that.

People never used to go just hunting especially, they used to go walking around and see what might happen. They walked for their energy, or to make their body feel good, or to brighten their spirit, just by walking around on country. Or by going to camp out on country, maybe for the country to cleanse and heal their bodies. That's how they were. Now today we don't walk anywhere. We go places by car, or on a bike, that's how we are nowadays. It's like the energy's gone out, not like the old people. Our lifestyle's really changed. Some of those healthy routines are gone out, you know. Like how we used to walk around as kids. We used to go out hunting with Mum and Dad, and we'd dig out rabbits, Mum at one end of the burrow, and us kids digging on the other. Mum'd kill the bunny when it came out, and we'll get the fire ready, and we'd dig a hole for cooking the meat. And that was part of our work when they'd take us hunting. Some of those things are not really passed on to our kids now. We should be going back to our homelands to show our kids what is really the life of us mob, our Aboriginal way.

And what about that kidney disease? More and more sweets, more change. Heart disease, more and more people being destroyed, destroyed by town life. To live a good lifestyle is people to go back and stay on the homeland, to go back there to live. So that homeland can heal you, so it can guide you, so you can eat the natural foods from your own country. *Alakenhe-arle*, that's gotta be the way.

Our Nature

"In the early days the people
used to drink water from rockholes and soaks.
They used to drink the same water
as the wild bush animals, where the waters always were,
Sacred Waters,
those that belonged to that Land."

Plants and Trees

Ancestor Trees

Anwernekenhe-arle aneme apere arlkaye, layake arne anwernekenhe ulye arlkaye. Apmere kantreye-arle arne but *yanhe-areye-arle anwerne-arteke kine-arle arne yanhe-areye ulye yanhe-areye.* Might be *Arrwekelenye apeke.* People *anwernekenhe mape-arle arrwekele untheke,* and became those *arne.* So that's why we *arntarnte-arerle arne yanhe lyapemele apmerenge.*

Lots of trees, especially the river red gums, are prized for their shade. But the real main reason we look after trees growing on our country is because they might be the ones that became People. When those People walked that Land, then those trees became Them.

We treat those trees like, *ureke,* we don't *ampakemele akerle, ure atnyeke-arle mape ware* people*-le inerle-apeme ure ampetyeke.* Sometimes today, people *nhenge ure ultakeme layake ilepele-arlke atwemele* saw*-eme-arlke-ileme arne intyerrke* you know, not *anthenge, arne intyerrke mape ware. Ureke.* People*-le arrwekele arne ware itetyarte arne intyerrke kwutyemele ware. Ure-arle-arlke, arne yanhe-arle* because *ure-arlke arne yanhe-arlke anwernekenhe apmere kantreye-arenye rarle.* Also *arne, arne yanhe layake arne arrpenheme layake artetyenge-ntyele, atnyemenge-ntyele, inerle atneme-arlke* you *mpwarerle.* Sometime *atwerrenherrenhe arne mpwarerle,* sometime *atneme mpwarerle,* sometime *kwetere* they might *mpwarerle,* something just to share*-eme-ilerretyeke. Arrpenhe-arle apetyemeke* exchange*-anetyeke alkwerte mpwaretyeke layake inerntenge-arlke-ntyele. Layake arrkernkenge-ntyele urtne* part of the bloodwood, well *yanhe-areyenge urtne-arle mpwaretyarte mapele.* Sometime *urtne mpwarerle kere akngenhe-akngenhe,* sometime *urtne mpwarerle ampe akngenhe-akngenhe.* Or *kwatyeke angernenhe apeke. Iwenhakweye, arrkernke angkerlenge-ntyele. Pmware akweke mpwarerle, ye.* For *kwetere,* or *atneme,* or *inernte,* for *urtne,* or *urtne* made from *arrkernke. Urtne* or *pmware.*

The only things they used to reason *atwerle arne,* something *atwetyeke ahentye-anerle layake ngkwarle urltampe apeke arwengalkere apeke-arle aneme-arle layake itne intyetyarte, layake atwetyeke*, you know. But they never ever *ultakemele arne atwerle*, only *tetye-arle itne atwetyarte layake arlengeke-arlenge ware. Tetye, ye alakenhe.* Notches-*akweye renhe ulkere apeke? Tetyeke arnpemele itne intyetyarte, ye, atwetyarte urltampe arwengalkere apeke.* They never used to *itentye ultakerle.* 'Cause *apmere akngerre-arenye-arle arne yanhe.* You know like, might be *apmere arrpanenhenge-ntyele apetyemele apeke anpere-irrenheke athewe, arne. Apmere arrpanenhenge-ntyele apekawe! Apmere arrpanenhe mapenge-ntyele apetyeke. Alakenhe.* That's why people never used to *iwenhakweye ilerle* when they go out *ngkwarle arwengalkere atwetyeke alhemele. Untyeyeke apeke*, they used to just *arneke ware atwerle itereke-anteye atwerle nhenge akertnenge-arle arrateke, tetye intyemele atwerle.* Or sometime they used to *mpwarerle* might be *arne arrpenhe arrernemele.* Sometime like *untyeyeke-arlke, alakenhe-arle, arrkernkeke-arlke*, you know, *tetyenge intyenhele, apereke tetye-akerte intyenhele, arlengeke*, you know. *Arwengalkere atwetyeke.* They never used to *apere irntwernerle.*

We don't rip branches off trees, only the wood that's fallen to the ground is picked up to be used for firewood. Nowadays people might chop wood with axes and saw it up for the fire, but only the dead wood is used, not the green timber. The old-days people used to just pick up the dry wood from the ground for burning. The firewood and the trees are part of our country, and must be treated with respect. And not only firewood, but also these trees and others we collect from to make digging sticks; trees like mulga and witchetty bush. Or sometimes the trees became our weapons. Sometimes fighting sticks we'd make out of wood, sometimes we'd make digging sticks, something just to share amongst ourselves. Or sometimes people might make something to exchange with visitors for other things, like shields made from the wood of the bean tree, *arne tyweretye*. They used to make coolamons out of bloodwood timber, coolamons to carry meat in, or to carry babies. Or it might be a scoop to hold water; they'd make that out of the burl on a bloodwood tree. *Angkerle* is one of those little clumps; that's that burl now. You chop that out, and you make a small scoop out of it to dig with.

The only other time people might want to cut into a tree is if wild honey was there that they needed to climb up to collect. They never cut the tree down, just cut steps into it, so far apart, to climb up. *Tetye*, where they can put their feet you know, when they're climbing up. What do you mob call them? 'Notches', *ye*. They used to climb by putting their feet in the notches to collect the wild honey, cutting them as they went. They never used to break off the limbs and branches, because those trees grow out of Sacred Country. That's how we related to trees and things.

Might be the Ancestors came through from other countries and stopped here on their journey. And they became another tree here, left part of his – what do you call it? – *image* there. A plant or a tree became them as they walked past and became who they are. And then they changed into another one. They might have dropped seeds there and other trees came out of those Ancestors before they travelled on. *Alakenhe*. That's why people never used to do wrong things when they go out hunting for wild honey. So in a corkwood tree, or any type of tree really, they'd chop steps into the side to climb to the top. Or sometimes they used to put up a forked stick, might be an old log they used to get, and lean it over onto the tree, then climb on that and chop from that. But they never used to cut into and damage a river red gum tree; not in any way, not anywhere.

But some people nowadays just break up the river red gums, because they've got other tools now. And they break down the branches. When they used to collect wood from around the camp, women went collecting wood in one direction, and men went on their side to collect firewood. Not all over the place. That's how it used to be, but now people just go anywhere to collect wood. Some people still have strong laws, and some people are bringing laws back into their lifestyle. But a lot of them are being tripped up by other languages, and modern music, and by clothes. Everything's really changing.

It wasn't only river red gums we respected highly, we really respect every tree in the country. Like *arne artetye*, the mulga tree. You can make a nulla-nulla, *kwetere*, from *artetye*, or an *alye*, a boomerang, or *atneme*, a digging stick. Sometimes people make it an *irrtyarte*, a spear, they make it from the roots, *artekerrenge-ntyele*. And *athengenge-ntyele* too, you can make *kwetere*, a fighting stick from that ironwood tree, 'cause it's really solid wood. And *inerntenge*, *arne tyweretye*, you can work that one as well, the bean tree. *Aparrtye* we call it in *Akarre* language. It's good for making coolamons and *alkwerte*, shields, and also good for *pmware*, a scoop. And also for *kere-kenhe*, to make a big flattish dish for carrying meat. There's another tree good for that too, it's called *arlkethe*. It's like a mallee tree, and you can see a lot of them 'round towards Tennant Creek, and somewhere 'round near Utopia area, and also might be Stirling-side. And it's from *arlkethe* that they made that big coolamon-carrier that they can fetch things in.

I've even heard about a musical instrument that they used around here and called *ulpere*, but I don't know anything much about it. It was like a pipe. The only instruments I know about are like *alye rlterrpe*, the boomerang music sticks, and *terurre*, those small clapsticks. And also *walye arrkarlpe*, the ceremonial broom. When they're dry, they make a rustle-rustle sound for music. Clapsticks were sometimes made from roots, like from *apere artekerre*, the roots of the young river red gum trees, or sometimes they cut them from young *artetye*, slender mulga branches. But *angkweleye*, the bush plum is the most popular for those sticks, or sometimes *utyerrke*, the bush fig, they can make really good clapsticks from that too.

People nowadays carve animals from wood – goannas, dogs, mice, perentie, all the *arremparrenge mape*, all those double-doubles, but people in the old days never used to do that. They only ever made music sticks, hunting spears, fighting spears – *urrempere* – boomerangs, fighting sticks, digging sticks, scoops and coolamons. These were the only sort of things that were made from plants. Or *inte*, that really long stick we use to look for where rabbits might be.

Arrankweye and *angkweleye* are the same tree, the same bush plum. They use it a lot to make things out of because it's easy to carve. It has a soft, whitish wood and it doesn't crack, even when we burn designs into it with a hot wire. *Aperlape* is what some *Arrernte* people call the conkerberry. We Easterners call it *arnwekwetye*. That conkerberry's a bush. There's also a tree called conkerberry, it's the *ahakeye* tree. It's like a lemon tree. You might see some up near Ti Tree-side, but it doesn't grow much down this side. People don't carve things from the wood of the *ahakeye*, because it's *merne*, a food tree, and it's very, very sacred. *Ahakeye* tree is the one tree that's *always* sacred, really sacred all the time, everywhere. It's related to some people down here, but mainly all the people on the north side. *Arne ahakeye* are nearly always Ancestor Trees.

People know *Arne iwenhe-ante-iwenhe-ante, nhenge itelaraye, Arne Aknganentye Mape. Arne Aknganentye Mape*, they know. They don't touch those *Arne Aknganentye. Arne akngerrepate-arteke, arrwekelenye mape arne arintyeke, itneke ilemele arne yanhe kwenhe aknganentye-arle*. They can young *mape arrpenhe mape atwerle*, but not *Arne Aknganentye Akngerre*. 'Cause *apmere-arenye-arle yanhe. Apmereke artweye. Layake apmerele antirrkweme-arteke-anteye. Alakenhe.*

People know whatever types of trees they might be, the Ancestor Trees, *Arne Aknganentye Mape*, and they don't touch those special trees. Our old people have always seen those trees as the image of the Ancestors, and respected them in that way, and have taught us to also treat them with the greatest respect. Our mob don't touch that. Even when people nowadays might chop into newer trees, still never they touch the Ancestor Trees. Because they belong to that country, and it belongs to them. They hold the country together, those trees. That's how that holds the Land, and it's part of us, and part of skin group. That's how it is.

Food from Plants

Ye, merne gotta *mwerrentye anthurre mpwarerle*, you know. *Layake mpenge-ilemele iterle, ane ure mwerrele atyerrerle*, like anything. *Layake* even *merne yalke*, you gotta *iterle* properly. You gotta *alpmanthele ware atyerremele arlkwerle iwenhakweye ilerle. Layake* yams, not only *arlkwetyeke*, so also it can be share-*eme-ilerle*, you might want *ampe akwekenge* share-*eme-ilerle*, you might want *arelhe ampwe, akngerrepatenge apeke* share-*eme-ileke*. Even like when you *merne tampe apeke iterle*, people *akngerrepateke mwerrentye akwete iterle*. And might *rlkerte-arle apeke mwerre-irretyeke arlkwerle*.

Layake if you go *merne putye-arenye arrpanenhe apeke inetyeke*, you know, *layake* for people-*arle*, must be *arrwekele arrwekelenye mapele apeke-arle inetyarte merne utyerrke-arle apeke, akngirtnerle anthetyeke* people-*ke, nhenge* old people-*le arlkwetyeke*.

You know, *utyerrke-arlke, awele-awele-arlke itne arlwiletyarte inemele akgnirtnerle atyerremele mpenge apeke imernte arrpenheme-arle arlkwetyenhenge. Alakenhe-arle itne arlkwerrirretyarte antherremele akwete.* Everything *antherremele.* 'Specially old people *mape-kenhe, itne imernerle,* you know, *anthetye-alperlenge. Arlkwetyeke. Alakenhe. Merne anwernekenhe anwerne arlkweme,* we gotta *arlkwerle,* we don't *ware altyeye apeke alangkwe apeke,* you know. Even *alangkwe, akwerrke mape-arlke, alangkwe arrwekelenye mapele*, and you cannot *altyeye ampakerle ingkerreke anthurre,* you know, *arnenge.* You gotta *alangkwe ware inerle arnele apeke ampakerle arnele apeke atwerle. Alakenhe.* 'Cause you gotta *arne altyeye ampakerle* because *alangkweke altyeye yanhe* you gotta *imperle merne arrpenhe-le-areye arintyetyenhe-arleke.* Sometime people-*le alangkwe arletye akngirtnerle,* sometime *mpenge-ilemele atyerrerle,* sometime you gotta *arlkwerle arletye-anteye. Arrpenhe mape mpenge arlkweme. Alangkwe arrpenheme arne akertnenge-arle lyapeme arrpenhe ahelhele-arle inteme. Alakenhe. Ane merne ingkwerrpme. Ingkwerrpme* people-*le arneke ware arlkwetyarte,* used to *akngirtnemele antherle,* old people-*ke apeke.* But most of the time *itne arneke ware arlkwetyarte.* Only *yalke ane alangkwe itne akngirtnetyarte arelhe ampwe mapeke ane awele-awele, ane merne utyerrke, layake* mission-*thayate-arle anetyarte arunthe anthurre alakenhe.*

It's not just trees, you gotta respect all plants, and prepare the food you get from them very carefully. You've got to make just the right type of fire so that the food cooks properly. For wild onions, you have to heat them in just the right type of earth for proper taste. It's the same for yams, because you have to share that food out to everybody after you've cooked it, and you want everybody to enjoy it, especially the kids and the old people. Like when you bake a damper in the hot ashes and soil, you treat that damper with respect, so everyone can have some and feel good about eating it. Might be also there are some sick people eating it to become well.

And when you go out into the bush to get food to bring back for your families to eat, you have to do it in a respectful way also, just like all the generations before us gathered food. Like how they collected figs to bring back to the camp to share around with the old people. They used to gather the figs and bush tomatoes only at the right time, and then take them home and show them to the old people to make sure they'd done it right before they gave it to them. It was the same when they collected bush bananas, they never took all the young fruits off the tree. Some of those vines grow right up trees, while others tend to grow along the ground, *ahelhele*. *Tyertetye alangkwe* they call that, the ground banana. And they pulled or snagged the fruits off those high vines with a long, hooked stick. It's against the Law to pull down the vine itself, you have to leave the vine so that it can go on bearing more fruit. Sometimes they took back the bananas to eat raw, and sometimes they'd cook them back at the camp. Mistletoe fruits were generally eaten straight off the tree while you were walking around gathering food. Sometimes it was taken back home to be shared with the old people, but most of the time they ate it straight off the tree. Usually only figs, tomatoes, bush bananas, and wild onions were taken back for the old people. There was lots of that stuff around the mission, around *Ltyentye Apurte* before.

Stories from Plants

If the bloodwood is flowering, then we know straightaway there's going to be a big mob of honey, *ngkwarle arwengalkere akngerre*. 'Cause the bees gonna be there. And we know straightaway whatever honey that's gonna be about. Like *untyeyampenge-ntyele*, honey from the corkwood flowers. Any other flowers too, *artetyenge-ntyele*,

---

Teaching Ceremony for Young Women and Girls, 2006, acrylic on canvas, photographer IAD Press
The body symbols are shown in ochre colours. The brown circles are grinding stones; red represents mistletoe from the mulga tree, and yellow and white represent mistletoe plants from the corkwood and bloodwood trees.

arlepenge-ntyele, like honey from mulga and acacia-bush flowers. But when that *arlepe*'s flowering, we know straightaway that the kangaroos are very healthy. Because we tell by the flower, *antethe, arlepe antethenge-ntyele*. Because that acacia-bush flower represents the colour of the fat. And the healthiness. 'Cause sometimes *arlepe*'s only really short, and the kangaroo feeds on it. And even rabbits can feed on it as well.

And people used to know that when the bloodwoods are flowering, then the possums are healthy. That's as well as them telling about the *urltampe mape*, *arwengalkere*, the sugarbag. Because the possums eat the flower – because it's sweet, it's still got that honey inside – so they eat that, and people used to eat *lyepe-lyepe antenhe-kenhe*, the milk guts from the possum, and it was so sweet because the possums had eaten the honey. *Lyepe-lyepe* from *antenhe-arle*, possum *mapele-arle arlkwetyarte*. Ye, people loved eating the intestines of the possum, those sweet milk guts, but we don't see possums any more. And people even know the kangaroos are getting very healthy by the grass. When the grasses are getting like lemons, you know? *Antyempeye* we call it – *antye ampeme-arle*. *Antye* means grass, like a burnt grass. When it's a light yellowy colour. Not really burnt like *ampeke-arle*, it's just a name you know, *antyempeye*. *Antyempeye alakenhenge*. That's mean the kangaroos are healthy. Every animals are healthy then. When the grass is green, *atherrke anthurre*, that's mean they got too thin, *utyewe anthurre*, because *kwatye ilknge*, that grass is watery, *ilknge*. And they don't put the fat on then. The cattles are like that too. When the tea tree bush *mape aneme*, when there's tea tree flowers, *irlperle antethe*, you gotta really watch out because *apmwe mape-ketye-arle*. That's the time when the snakes get out, when the tea tree's flowering. Sometimes snakes come out when it's other flowers too, like *atnyeme*, the witchetty bush *apeke*, but most of all, the tea tree bush. After that north-west wind blows, *aretharrele werneme*, then *antethe arraterle ilperlenge*, 'cause that's the time the tea tree flowers come out, *arrateme*. And when that north wind blows, those snakes start putting their tails out. I know people who've seen it. Maybe the smell of the tea tree blossoms goes into the nose and wakes them up, I don't know.

Plants tell you stories, *ye*. And also, you can tell when the summer's starting to come, *uterne urle*, that's when the *arlepe*'s *ampere*, you know? When the acacia-bush's got those little clumps, round one *akweke ampere mape*, those little lumps of flowerbuds, like little kneecaps. That's August I think, then it's *antethe*, the flowers follow on in the same month. Then after August, in September, they'll be *alenye*, seedpods just like little tongues then. Then *mpwepele* – in between September and October, at that time they become seeds, *annge*. *Uterne urlenge*. That's when it's becoming really hot, at the beginning of summer, 'summer's forehead' we call it in *Arrernte*. Then in the middle of summer they *lyarrtyele*, they really dry out, the leaf gets dry and the seeds come right out. That's how people used to tell the weather, by season, season time of any plants. Every plant has a proper season, just how I described it for *arne arlepe*. And *ntange*-time, that's when the birds come, at seedtime. That's when the cockies come, when the *arlepe* and the *artetye* became *ntange*, edible seeds, the mulga and acacia-bush. You see them, and they go in every trees and they pluck all the things. Any birds, you know, but especially the cockatoos and the galahs, they eat that seeds. *Arlepe arlkwetyeke. Arlepe* and *arnterre*, they eat the acacia-bush and colony-wattle seeds. So we tell by the seasons, by the flowers and the plants.

There's no plants really come out in winter, *alhwerrpenge*, except for *awele-awele*, the bush tomato. That's *merne alhwerrpe-kenhe*, a winter food. Also that's when the pencil yam comes, *merne arlatyeye*, but they don't have a flower, they just grow then, they don't put flowers on. *Merne alangkwe*, the bush banana, it might flower too, if they

---

Thipe Angkwene, photographer Barry McDonald

have rain in the middle of winter. We used to have seasons we could rely on in the old days. Like the beginning of winter and the middle of winter were separate seasons. And the beginning of summer and the middle of summer were also separate. But that's all changed now, there's a lot of cut in all that now.

There's lots of different stories from plants. If there's heaps of mistletoe, if *ingkwerrpme*'s around, they'll know straightaway there'll be lots of emus somewhere. If there's a lot of grasshoppers around, *inteltye*, then there'll be a lot of turkeys. And also *ayepe-arenyele aneme-arlenge* time, they know there's a lot of emu'll be eating it, those *ayepe-arenye* caterpillars. Emus and turkeys both eat the *inteltye*, and they both eat the *ingkwerrpme*. The turkeys eat the fruits if it's hanging low to the ground, but the emus can eat it up in the tree 'cause they've got their little arms you know, they've got them little hooks on the side of their feathers, and they use that to pull the *ingkwerrpme* down. And we'll know that there'll be a lot of rabbits around when the little green ground plants are springing up, and then we'll know also that the perenties, the *kere ulkerte*'ll be *antere akngerre*, they'll be fat and healthy. That's how we can tell what it is happening.

Some trees have a different sort of message or power. Like *arne atnawerte*. *Arne werltarre* we call it in *Akarre*. It's the *ikirrentye* tree, the 'keep your distance' tree. Young blokes that don't yet have a moustache, and also young teenage women can't go near that tree. If they do, they have to cover their front as they pass by, cover their chests. If they don't do that, their breasts might not develop. And young girls won't grow hair in their armpits. And the boys have to do the same sort of thing. That's *atnawerte* now. It's a grey-looking tree with a small seed, a seedpod that breaks open and shows orange inside. You can recognise it straightaway by that seedpod and its colour. That's the 'stop away' tree, and people show it a lot of respect. Everyone recognises that, and they'll all say the same thing, doesn't matter whether it's in *Warlpiri* or Western *Arrarnta*.

There's also *arne alkemale*, the desert poplar. The young boys used to fetch water for the camp, and their grandmothers used to say to them sometimes, "come here so I can sing you, so that you grow up quickly into a nice, tall young man". Then the water that he got, she'll pour it on her fingers and splash it at him, and say "this is so you can grow to be tall, as tall as this *arne alkemale*, this desert poplar tree. So you can be like the poplar, and stretch upwards to the sky". Sometimes people used to encourage little boys to actually climb the poplar itself, by lifting them up into the lower branches, so that they can grow up quickly. The old people used to tell that story. No one says that sort of thing for kids nowadays. Mum used to sing her *aperlikwe-areye*, her grandsons, in that way.

Animals

Respect For Animals

We're part of everything on the Land, part of the bush foods. Food from the bush, *merne anwernekenhe*, is part of us. That's why we don't waste it. When we go hunting, we don't waste-*eme-ilemele kere atwerle. Anwerne itelareme kere apmere anwernekenhe-arenye*, we got to *ingkerre arlkwerle*. We got to *ingkerreke anthurre antherrerle*. We share it all. We don't kill it for fun. Because *apmere yanhe-arle anwerne anperne-ikwe-irreme-arle*, that country is like a root or a tie to us, and it gives food for all of us, not for just one or two to keep. Meat animals, *kere*, is part of us. That *kere*, it's a sacred meat, 'cause it come from the Sacred Land, *apmere akngerrenge-ntyele*. Important place, important *kantreyenge-ntyele*, and we relate in that same way to all those animals.

We can't kill a small animal, a baby one, we have to leave it until it grows. It doesn't have a meaty sort of a taste, if you kill a tiny little animal. We only kill animals that are the right size to be eaten. We can't, "oh that kangaroo we've just killed, we'll kill the joey too and eat it". We can't do that. Because it's not meant to be eaten by an adult. It might be all right for kids to eat, or sometimes it's just made for dogs and things like that. If those animals come from your country, those animals are sacred. If you're gonna kill it, you eat it, you don't waste it. If you *have* to waste it, you've gotta give it to the dogs. Dogs of that country. Or the birds of that country. And you can't just kill a big kangaroo and "oh, I don't want to eat that, I'll chuck it over there". You've gotta make sure that you cut that meat up properly and leave it where good animals can have a feed. Eagles, and hawks, and dingoes. But that doesn't happen very often, because we've got really strong laws about killing kangaroos and things. Things of our Land. You can't go and "all right, we'll start going and killing all the goannas I think, and then we'll bring them all back and we'll just give them to the birds". You don't do that. Because all those animals that come from that Land are sacred, and we don't kill them to make fun of them, you know? Other people will see you straight out, they'll think that's really wrong.

And everyone'll find out then. Because that message will just go like wildfire.

When you go hunting for game, you've gotta sort 'em out, share whichever animal it is that you've killed. Maybe a dog might've killed it, maybe people have gone hunting and killed it, and they share it around to everyone. Sometimes the old people may have had dogs that were champions that went out hunting with them. They used to look after those dogs really well, and when they got some meat, they made sure that they shared it with the dogs as well as with everyone that lived with them. The hunters, when they came back they did that. Might be the leg of the kangaroo, another one might get the stomach and the *anenye*, part of the hip joint of the animal. And someone else might get the other leg and the other hip joint. Or *urtethe*, the lower backbone, or the back itself, or the head, or the tripes. Or the milk guts, or other parts of the guts. The ones from around the camp would get those parts, like the old men, the senior elders, the people from that country.

The owner of the hunting dogs, the one that skitched them onto the animal, he brings the meat back, splits it up into portions, and shares it out to everyone. Sometimes the liver would be good to bring back for the people at the camp to eat. And the blood, *awerrpe*. The blood from the kangaroo's chest cavity or around the pelvis is good for people to drink, especially if they've been sick. People drink this in different ways. The blood from around the pelvis, it seems almost as though it's still alive, like it's still raw; but from the rib cage it has more of a cooked taste to it. It's more *antyewe*, clotted-up. It's got a real natural Land-taste to it, *ikwe marenye*. A natural salt's in that, that stew or blood from the chest, *alakenhe*. They eat every part of the animal. And the tail, the tail is cooked, then pounded with a rock to make the meat softer, mincing it up almost. Then they pull the tailbone out and smash that up to get the marrow out to eat. They used to break up all the meat, and never used to leave the bones laying about anywhere on the ground. They used to smash up the bones, they never used to burn them in the fire. Nothing was just chucked on the fire to get rid of it, everything was eaten.

People treated every native animals in the same way – goannas, perenties, porcupines, bearded dragons, pythons, the lot of them. They were our meats. And *antyerre* too, the ridge-tailed monitor, lots of those lived in the rocks around Arltunga. People didn't know much about goannas in that area, maybe there were goannas around Garden Station, but not at Arltunga. Maybe goannas around Ambalindum and Clarabelle, but none around Arltunga. The bush meat comes from the Land, and that was our meat, and that *kere* is part of us. And that *kere* is a sacred meat because it comes from a Sacred Land, from important country. And we really relate to all those animals, because they're part of us. *Ye, alakenhe.*

You can't *apmere kantreye atwemele* anywhere *ware iwerle*. You can't *kere inemele* "all right, *kere arletye nhenge tyipe-tyipe-ilemele iwerle*". To *akngwelye mape*, you can't do that. Because it's *kere anwernekenhe apmere kantreye anwernekenhe-arenye*. You cannot *akengaye-akengaye atnyenerle, you know, kere*. Even with anything, perentie *apeke, kere* any animals, you know. *Ane thipe*. Might be *atetherre akwerrke mape, apeke*. You can't any way *iwerle*, people-*le mwantyele kere atetherre arlkweme*. *Athetherre*'s, all the *kere ikwemeye*, is one. *Mapele-arle arlkwetyarte*. Might be *ilentye-arlke apeke*. *Ilentye* people-*le arlkwetyarte*, but only *atetherre ante-arle prape atningkele-arle arlkwetye arunthe-ulkere, you know*. Mission-*le-arle arlkwerrirretyarte*. Billy cans *ane* billy cans full *akngetye-alperle*. They used to *layake arlkwerle layake artengkwelknge-akertele apeke, arrwengkelthe-akertele-apeke*, or maybe people-*le merne arlkwetyeke-arle atnerte untyeme-irreke-arle apeke*. Appetite-*ke-arle, itne arlkwetyarte*, also they used to really like eating it, 'cause *kere itnenhe atnerte mwerre-ilentye akngerre, atnerte mwerre awelhele*. Old people *arlkwetyarte*.

You can't just hunt anywhere, and throw stuff around. Not allowed to. Can't get meat and, "all right, we'll just cut up raw meat into strips and chuck it to the dogs", because it's our animals we're talking about, from our own country. You cannot mistreat our animals. It doesn't matter what animal you're talking about, perentie, any animals at all. And that includes birds. Baby budgerigars for example. You can't just chuck them around any old how, people have to eat them with respect. Budgerigars are nice sweet meat, highly regarded, so you don't treat them badly. People used to eat them all the time, you know. Or it might be galah. Galahs were eaten, but only the budgerigars were eaten by lots and lots of people. Down at the mission they used to eat them. They'd fill up billy can after billy can and bring them back. Baby ones, you know, young ones, either with or without feathers on. They used to eat them if people had the 'flu or were sick in some other way. Maybe you've turned off your food. Well, that budgie helps you get your appetite back. They ate it for appetite. Also they used to really like eating it because the meat makes your stomach feel really good. Especially the old people ate it for that.

The Eaters get Eaten

Our animals always hunt *merne itne-arrpe*, their own special tucker for themselves, they're champions for that. The bush animals, they taste every one of those *atherrke*, every native trees and plant, and the goodness of the country fills them up. That's when they get healthy. And they never used to have a big bowl of *kwatye*, they used to just drink a little bit of water and then travel on to another area to eat a little bit of green plant food, and then they move on again.

Atyelpe, a native cat might dig and eat *kelyawe* and other lizards, or a dingo might dig up lizards to eat, or maybe a perentie. And they knew, the animals knew when the season was of the animals they were going to eat. Like if there's a lot of that red mistletoe, *ingkwerrpme*, well, emus will know, "oh this is the season of *ingkwerrpme*, we'll go and eat it, *ingkwerrpme arlkwetyeke*". And if there's a lot of butterflies around, well *arlewatyerre*, the goanna you know, he'll eat that. And the perentie, *atyunpe*'ll know because the animals – those other animals are getting fat by this food – well they'll go and eat *that* animal, that *arlewatyerre* maybe. They all satisfy themselves in that way. *Arlewatyerre* eats that butterfly or grasshopper, *atyunpe* eats *arlewatyerre*, and people eat that *atyunpe*. So it doesn't matter, we're not fighting with our animals over the same food. 'Cause *itne-arle arlkwerreme mape*, something always eats something else, and people, well it's like *arlkwereyeke-arlkwereye*; this one eats this one, and that one eats this one, and we eat that one. The eaters get eaten. That eats this and you eat that. Same like *arrwe*. The rock wallaby eats the grass, and the carpet snake, *antetherrke*, eats that wallaby *akwerrke*, and we eat that *antetherrke*, you know? Like *kere antetherrke-arle*. Well, *arrwe apwerteke aremele*, you see the wallaby in the hills, and well, *antetherrke* grabs that wallaby. *Akwerrke*, a young one you know? *Alakenhe*. And we eat that *antetherrke*.

We've always cooked and eaten all *kere* with respect. Even introduced animals we cook and eat with respect because that animal, it was *kere apmere akngerre itnekenhe-arenye*, it was meat from those other people's Sacred Land, a traditional food for a traditional people somewhere.

But people like *kartweye mape*, *kereke artweye*, those who have an animal for their totem, well some of them they might not eat that *kere*. *Ankerreke-artweye mape* – Emu Dreamers – well, they don't eat emu. People around here don't eat perentie meat 'cause that's *itnekenhe aknganentye-arle* – that's their totem, some people call it. 'Cause those animals are part of them, that's why they don't eat them, *arlkwerle*. I know there's a lot of people don't eat emu, 'cause emu's part of them, *aknganentye* again, even though emu *kere*'s a really good meat. A lot of people I know don't eat emu, and a lot don't eat perentie. Because they're related too closely to those animals, and also because of their connection – *ye*, 'their connection' is the best way of putting it. *Ye, alakenhe*.

But still a lot of other people do eat emu, and always have. People used to walk in a group, and that emu is a big meat you know, big piece of meat. So after killing it they just used to cook it and cut it up into pieces on the spot – into pieces of flesh and fat and flesh and fat, *antere-ante-tyelke*. And all that bones *ngkwerne*, people never used to just throw them away, they used to crush them up, or put it under the ground. Sometimes the *arrwekelenye mape* used to dance with them bones. Just like that one old man who used to sing the songs about them bones. He told all the stories about all them bones, and they ground them up, just to represent that bag for burial-*ke* in the ceremony.

Help from Animals

Something I learnt about in hunting was how to look after dogs. The dogs were very special to us, because they were the real good hunters. My parents didn't have any guns, because they were olden-day people. But those dogs were just like guns, only better, because they knew how to catch a goanna or a perentie, without ripping anything, without tearing them apart. And I learned *arengke mape-arle kere artarrernerle*, how to sool the dogs onto a kangaroo. Those dogs knew just how to kill a kangaroo; never caught them by the leg, but had to catch them by the head or the neck. The dogs were really protected, kept away from other ordinary dogs in case they fought and got hurt. And we used to just hear them how they'd sing the dogs. My parents used to sing their dogs, *akngwelye alyele*. To be *pwelete anthurre alhetyeke*, to go faster, just like a bullet! And they used to sing that so they could catch kangaroo quicker. That's all they had. I can't say any more about it, because I don't know. Like once I asked,

"*Mameye, iwenheke-ame unte yanhe, iwenheke-ame alyelheme?*"

"*Ne, akngwelye nhakwe-arle the alyeme re, akunye,* energy *anthemele. Re kereke arrengkere irretyeke*".

"Oh".

I asked Mum why she was singing that song, and she told me that it was to give her dear dogs energy, so that they could really fly along after the kangaroos. Maybe all them powerful songs that they had, they never let us learn about it. We didn't even ask them about it either, you know? I mean, to teach us what the song is. Maybe they just thought that that song's just for them, so I didn't ask anymore, I just left it. *Mame atyinhe* used to be a really good hunter, and my Dad, they used to really love one another. Never anything anger *apeke anerle*. Everything used to be really good *ikwere atherrenge*, unless they have a little argument with themselves I s'pose. Like over the dogs maybe. They might tell each other off over the dogs, those sort of little things. Never any fight.

Birds are related to the plants and the animals and they can tell us stories about them, so they help us find food too. They'll sing out and tell people what is the season for plants, what's flowering. Like what fruits are ripe. We can know by the birds telling those stories, by hearing those birds. Also we can know about water by the birds singing or making a crying sound, in a singing cry you know? They see the clouds coming right down on the other side – *kwatye tnarlkweme, kwatye irntwarre anthurre arlenge apetyeme* – and we can hear that, that bird telling that story about that rain coming in the far distance. And like when we see an animal, we might see a bearded dragon sitting on the top branch of a tree, *ankerte apeke, kere amwelye apeke arerle akertnenge antyerlenge*, and they got their heads held really high. That's mean they're looking at the rainclouds. And that's how we tell that the rain is coming you know, what those storm clouds hold, *kwatye akantyerele kele areme, thipe nhenhe mape rarle ileme*. Sometimes when the birds sing out it means there's animals somewhere in the distance, or somewhere nearby, or water might be nearby, and we can also see that by the wasp and things hovering around us. And also bees – there might be bees hanging around – that means there might be sugarbag, *ngkwarle arwengalkere* somewhere there. That's how people used to tell. And they used to look under the trees for the tiny little droppings, so then they'll know – little yellow droppings, 'cause when the bee carries, sometimes he drops it and drops it in the sand. Then they look, and they find that little 'nose', made out of…what do you call it? Like a wax. There might just be a few little bees, *amenge mape* hanging around it. Then they climb up, and chop that down. But you can't eat that straightaway, not when you're walking around, 'cause any sweets can make you thirsty. You have to take that back. So that's how we find out, from birds and bees and flies, and also from other insects, like even with ant. If we see *yerre mape akngerre alheme*, oh you see them ants working everywhere, everywhere, here, there and everywhere. 'Cause that means that *kwatye akngerre-arle apetyeme* – there's gonna be

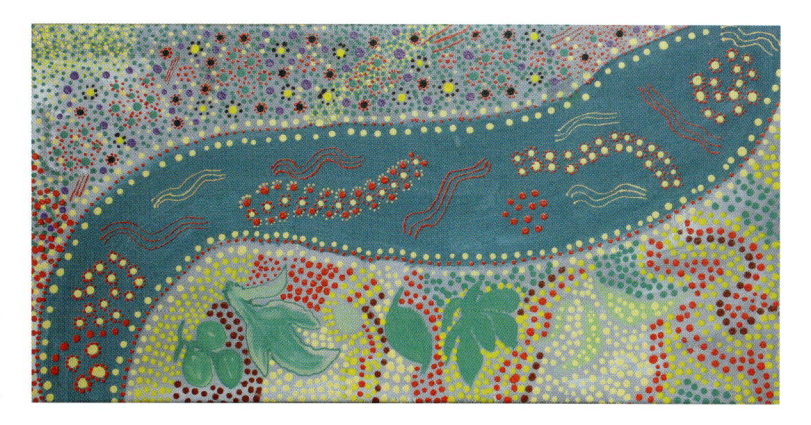

Kwatye Urewele-arle Ayeye Angkeme, Ikwerenge Atherrke Antethe Itwele Lyapeme, 2006, acrylic on canvas, photographer IAD Press
Telling the story of a flood, and of flowers and fruits springing up nearby.

a lotta rain. They're in a hurry, building something, and then we know then. And later on, "see, that ant told us about this rain". *Alakenhe*. So we get our stories from ant and everything, you know.

Thipe-arlke. Well, *thipele apmere kantreye-arle anemele thipele-ame ilerle alethenge-arle apetyeme*. And also *arnenge ngkwarle-akerte, ngkwarle-arle aneme*, you know, season? *Alakenhe-arlke thipele ilerle*. And also *kere apeke imernerle. Layake atanthemele*, you know. Sometime *thipele-arle atantheme kere alhepe-alhelenge*. Or *arlkemele apeke ilerle. Alakenhe thipele ileme*. And you can *thipe awerle ingweleme angkerlenge, thipe akethe-akethe-kenhe. Ane thipe ingwekenhe anwerne itelareme, ingwele angkenhe-angkenhe. Ane thipe arrpenheme layake*, and *itelareme layake thipe imaremele angkenhe-angkenhe, thipe inentyele-arlenge, inentye-le-kenhe. Thipe mape itelareme arrwekelenye mapele itelaretyarte, alakenhe.*

Ane thipe arrpenheme layake kere arlkwenhe-arlkwenhe, ane thipe arrpenheme arrkarlpe inenhe-inenhe, alakenhe. Nhenge arrkarlpe marle mape arrkene-irrenhe, you know. *Layake arrkene* might be *marle-kenhe awelyeke arratetyeke, alakenheke*. And *ampe marle akaltyele-anthetyeke arrkarlpe mpwaretyeke*, you know, *alakenhe. Thipe arrpenheme itne atwenhe-atwenhe. Ane thipe arrpenheme kwatye, kwatye imernenhe-arle kwatye alkngarre-ilenhe thayate mape-arle ileme. Nyingke apeke awemele, thipe nyingke apeke awemele*. Oh, *kwatye-arle yanhe kwenhe, kwatyeke irrperrerle-aneme*. And that's how *yanhe thipe mape-akerte rarle yanhe. Ane thipe arrpenheme*, layake something, maybe he might *arengke apeke-arle ngkwinhe ilwekeke apeke*, or something people-*arle untheme arlenge, apeke imarte arrpenhe mapele itelarerle*. And also *awerle*, you know, *angepe apeke-arle angkeme-arleke, ilemele-arteke*, you know, *nhakwe*. Sometime *thipe arrpenheme alkngarre-ilenhe-ilenhe. Alakenhe*. But *thipe arrpenheme-arle arratye kere arlkwenhe-arlkwenhe mape-arle. Alakenhe. Ayeye nhenhe-arle thipe mape-akerte.*

But especially we get stories from birds. Well, it's the birds living on our country that tell you when strangers are coming. There's even a bird who really says those same words when he calls out "*ipenye apetyeme! Ipenye apetyeme!*" They'll also tell you when the wild honey's in the tree, that's the sort of things that birds tell you. Also they show you where animals might be. They swoop down pecking at them, swoop down and attack the lizards while they're crawling along. Or they'll let you know by singing out. And you hear the birds in the morning telling you that it's daybreak, and we also take notice of the night birds, the ones that call at night. Some other birds that we know about, they can put a curse on you, like the *kwertatye* man's bird. We see the birds as our Ancestors did.

Some birds we eat for meat, and some we collect for their feathers, for headdresses in women's dancing. For when women come out dancing their fun corroborees, or for when they're teaching the young women how to make decorations and ornaments out of the feathers. So some birds are killed just for their feathers. Some birds like the little zebra finch, *thipe nyingke*, they always show you or alert you to where there's water, even if it might be a long way off. And then you know, "oh, there must be water over there, the birds are all crowding around it". Some birds might call out to warn you about things; it might be that your dog's lying dead, or that strangers are walking around – people will know these things are happening from the calling of the birds. And also when you can hear the crow calling over there, you know then that you're being warned about

Top: **Thipe Nyarewe**, photographer Barry McDonald

Lower: **Thipe Nyingke**, photographer Barry McDonald

somebody passing away. A lot of birds tell us a whole pile of stories like this, but some birds are just right for eating, *alakenhe*. And that's a story about birds.

A Tale or Two

Bilbies, *aherte mape*, weren't eaten by the old people as far as I know, they were just killed for their *alpitye*, their furry tails, which were used as a headdress, *arrkarlpe*, for women's dancing. For beautiness-dressing for ceremony. For women's dancing, *anthepe*. I've never seen it myself, I just heard about it. It was like it was really sacred when they were getting the decorations ready to put on, my mum and them. There weren't many bilbies around in the 50s or the 60s, or even in the 45s. They used to talk about it, "oh, all the *tyape* grubs have been eaten out from around here by the bilbies", and people used to spot all the holes where they dug around and they'd say "oh, that's where a good *tyape* place is", because they can see the signs of where the bilbies had been hunting. When people wanted witchetties, they used to follow where the bilbies had been digging for them around the trees. And they found out then where all the witchetties were. They're very smart those bilbies, they can break the roots of the tree open and eat the *tyape* from inside there. They pull them out with their paws to eat.

In wintertime you can go hunting for carpet snakes, *kere antetherrke*. They reckon it's good for diabetes, it's a really nice meat when you cook it. They cook it in a hole. And they cut it down the back, slit down on either side of the spine so that it doesn't bust out when it heats up, and they put it down the hole and cook it. Take the fire out and put the snake in, cover it up with leaves I think. *Kere alhilperre*, 'flat-end nose' they call that snake sometimes. People never used to eat the poisonous snakes. But they used to kill them, then rub the fat all over the kids, and when that kid walks around everywhere with that snake smell on it, then the snakes won't bite him. Maybe they think it's another snake, I don't know much about it myself. People used to tell me about it. I wouldn't tell it as a real true story of my own. I only like to tell stories about what I've really seen and done myself.

If it's a full moon, that's time to go hunting for possums, or *inarlengeke*, for porcupines. *Inarlenge*s can only see at night, because they only got such small eyes; people say that the sun would burn their eyes right out in the day, they're so small. So people would hunt them by moonlight. Husbands and wives would go together. Dad would climb trees and look for possums, and Mum would climb up on the rocks to listen for *inarlenge*s. Because they've got sharp claws, and they move rocks around, you can hear them climbing in the rocks.

Oh, and people also used to eat young cicadas – *tyerraye akwerrke*, or *alknginere. Tyerraye* people *arrwekelenyele-arle arlkwerre-arlke-irretyarte. Akwerrke nhenge arraterlenge*, or sometime they used to go *arnkarre itere-werle tnyemele arlkwetyeke*, and also *nhenge namele teke-anerlenge akwerrke mape*, you know. *Arrateme nhenge-ulkere.* But also *tyerraye yanhe itne uterne arrarlte arrerele-ilenhe*, they make the heat, the summer, they really draws the summer. *Arrerele-ilentye akngerre.* Because they *itne uterneke akwete anthurre arlkerle-anerle, uterneke arlkerle, arlkerle, arlkerle, arlkerle. Arlkemele akwete imernte re arltwe itnyemele, kele arrpenhe-areye anteme arlketyeke nhenge akerte arratye-irrerlenge. Kele arrpenhe-areye anteme arlkemele, arlkemele arlkemele uterne arrerele-ilemele arltwe itnyele. Uterne arrarlte-kenhe-arle yanhe. Layake tyerrayele-arle kwenhe arrarlte-arrarlte-ileme. Arrarlte* means that hot heat, and that stinging heat. *Ane tyerraye-arle arrarlte-arrarlte-ilentye akngerrenge, akenhe mape ingweleme ware iletyarte*, you know, when they want to go hunting they used to just hunt early in the morning, 'cause they know that *tyerraye yanhe rarle uterne ikngwerle-aneme.*

Aherrke akwernelhe-alhele. Aherrke irrperle kele itne nterte-irrerlenge. Kele aherrke arratintyele akenhe itne awethe angketyeke, iwenhakweye. Tyerraye yanhe-areye-arle uterne arrerele-ilenhe rarle, and *uterne akngerre anthurre anerlenge yanhe.* Sometimes gets people *akaperte akenge-irrerle*, "*tyerraye-ante-ame awemele!*"

Sometimes people used to eat the cicadas when they were just coming out of their holes, and other people used to go and collect them on the sides of river banks, when the cicadas had just come from their shells and were clinging to the grass to dry themselves out. Those were the times they were collected and eaten. And the other cicadas, those ones that made it up into the trees, they used to cause the hot weather to come on, hotter and hotter. They're the ones that *make* the heat really, they make the summer by drawing the sun closer and closer. Getting it to come quicker towards them. They keep on singing out – singing, singing, singing. They keep screaming out and screaming out until they keel over; empty, exhausted. One lot die off then another lot line up and come to scream at the sun, keeping on and on without stopping. Then those ones drain themselves, fall dead, and then more come forward to start calling out, taking over from them. They all get into the act, one after the other. They start calling and singing and screaming to make the sun get hotter and hotter, then they drop dead, drained.

    Cicadas really *belong* to the hot heat, belong to the great cycle of summer heat. Cicadas make the heat cycle faster, hotter, closer. Because the cicadas bring on the heat in this way, people used to get up early in the morning and go hunting before the cicadas started their singing and bringing on that stinging heat. Because they know that the cicadas are the ones now, urging the sun to join them, begging it to come close.

    The sun goes down. Then the cicadas all go quiet. When the sun comes up, the cicadas all start squealing again. They're the ones that bring the heat right up close, they really create the heat. When the sun gets too hot, people end up getting bad in the head, and then all they can hear is the cicadas singing inside their ears. It can make people get over the bend a bit, that hot heat, or maybe even from the sound itself.

    People also talk about cicadas when somebody might get hit, and only things they could hear is cicadas, that cicada sound. Like when you get knocked out. It's just like that whistling thing, "oh, *yanhe-arle atweke-arle, tyerraye-ante-arle aweke re tyerraye-ante awetyeke renhe-arle renhe atweke kwenhe*, that person's been hit on the head, and now he can hear only cicadas". Like the sound of that *tyerraye* talking, that whistling sound. When people hear somebody say that, they'll think, "hey, that might be really bad", because the name of that animal's been mentioned, because it's also the heat-drawing thing, a bit like a curse. It's like *arerte-arerte-arteke-arle-ileme*, making somebody crazy. It's mixed in with that heat thing, because they come with that heat, they draw that heat, and they die with that heat. They sing to the sun, asking it to come closer. They scream out 'til they drop down dead. Other people don't worry about it too much and say, "oh well, they can scream all they like, they'll just end up dropping dead".

When it cools down, *tyerraye* don't make much noise, they just talk softly. But when the heat comes, they start. In the wintertime they don't call out, because they don't come out during the winter. They come out in the summer and they leave holes everywhere. Everywhere! All around the place, and they even climb onto the inside of the house walls, all over the place, hanging, even from the ceilings of the houses. There's always lots clinging to the outsides of the houses. And on branches, on grass. When people used to dig them, they used to accidentally burst some, but they'd still eat those ones too. It has the flavour of the soil. So that's a little *tyerraye* story. I mean it's not a nice story, but it's a good thing for you to know.

Once the White People Came

And Here They Still Are

Introduced animals is not *kere* really *anwernekenhe*, it's not really from *anwernekenhe apmerenge-ntyele*. It's not part of the Land, *kere yanhe-areye. Ware anwerneke-arle imernintyeke ware.* They just brought them in and introduced them to us and here they still are. And the meat from these introduced animals, *kere anwerneke-arle imernetye-alheke* is definitely different to our own meats – *kere layake pweleke, yepe-yepe, ane naneyekwerte, ane pike-pike, ane tyweke-tyweke, ane tyweke-tyweke kwarte.* That's mainly bullocks, sheep, goats, pigs, chooks, and chook-eggs I'm talking about, *alakenhe*. The horses were brought in first, and as soon as that happened, all our foods, like the edible seeds, small seeds that birds used to eat, especially the ones that the little birds survive on, they started destroying it. *Ntange akweke mape, thipe mapele arlkwetyarte, ane thipe mapele arlkwerle ntange itnenhe, ane thipe akweke itnenhenhe-arle akenhe arlkwerlenge anwerne.* The birds ate those seeds and we ate the birds. None of those other animals, like bullocks, we didn't recognise them as being really *kere*.

When whites first came to *Arrernte* country, the people of the Land speared their bullocks because they did bad things to the country. Maybe the old people killed the bullocks because they were polluting our Sacred Waters. They used to spear them maybe to eat, or maybe they just wanted to get rid of them. My family never used to tell stories about all that, they probably didn't want to. They used to talk about it, but they never told *us* about it. Maybe they didn't want us to know 'cause they thought it was something wrong that those old people were doing. It's only nowadays that you hear about it, from people who used to live with those old people.

We don't see bullock as really a natural thing, you know? *Pweleke-arlke, iwenhakweye-arlke*, as you know, when that baby bullock's still in the stomach, it's already been doctored, already been tranquilised with some medical sort of a thing. *Kere putye-arenye*, the bush animals doesn't have any of those things. They only eat the green grass. But our animals have gotta go a long way to get that grass today, and the hunters have gotta go a long way to get the animals. Because the right grass today, maybe it only grows in the hills, or under mulgas, or under gidgee trees. On the side of hills, that's where all the bush animals' plants grow, where it's sweet, and where it's got that nourishment. That's what it's like for the bush animals. Whereas with bullocks, they get fed and grown up by someone else. And people grow food for them, like you've got hay or lucerne, and the lucerne's grown up with something, you put chemical on it, or something to grow it. And that's why there are a lot of *arrwengkelthe*, diseases and poisons on the crops. But we still eat it, *yekaye*! Good grief!

Bullocks and pigs, well, it's like that they're *antere ularte-arteke*, like they're all fat. And we never ate real fatty meat before, we used to eat just a little bit of fat, and the fat of our animals is different as well, more healthy. That's why you see those old Aboriginal people in books and photographs; and those mob, they're just straight up and down. And from that time, the more animals that was introduced, you can see how people's figures have changed. In a certain number of years, from the early days when these people were first found by the whitefellers, they've become *this* now – tea, sugar, jam, and all that became them, and their bodies changed then. Nowadays, many *Arrernte* people are eating just those meats that aren't very good for them – chicken, and pork, and chook eggs.

One time people feasted on the ribs of kangaroos, but nowadays people just seem to eat bullock's ribs. I like rib bones now and again, but not all the time. Because all the native animals are disappearing, there's not much *kere* around. Only when you go back out to communities can you eat *kere akngerre* every day of the week. Also, *arrwekelenye mape*, the older mob, well they never really ate all that much meat anyway, *kere akngerre putye-arenye*, and the little they did get was shared out amongst the family. And people never used to get slobby you know, their life was full of energy. Now we don't seem to eat *kere* like that. If we get kangaroo, sometimes we freeze it away you know, and it doesn't taste as good as it was when you've eaten it straightaway. That goodness and smell, it's got different smell in it, it changes the flavour away, *kere ikwe*. Even with any bush meats.

The introduced animals had a different kind of fat. And the bush animals, well they all have *their* different way of fat. They weren't kept you know, they was free. They could hunt every day, they could run every day, their energy and things was really stretched out. But those others, *kwene-arenye mape* – the stay-inside mob like bullocks, sheep and pigs, well they leave them in the paddock, and it's only in the paddock they can stay. Never wild. A lot of people today lives on just these sort of meats, like chops, and also *pweleke-kenhe*, tripes, but it's not as good for them as our original *kere*.

Some of the introduced animals like donkeys and horses have gone wild now, but I'm not sure if that makes them better to eat or not. I don't know whether people eat horses, but I have tasted camel meat. Those ones are recognised as *kere*, but we don't class them as having the same comfortable, ownership quality as our own animals. We recognise them today only because we have to go too far to get our own meat. And people didn't necessarily always respect all of them as being someone else's *aknganentye*. That's the difference between whitefellers' meat and blackfellers' meat.

Pwetheyekate, it also went wild, and it was eaten by a lot of people in the bush. My mum and them used to eat that pussycat, and it's a really tough flesh. Mum used to mix fat in with it to eat it. One time Mum was cooking all the rabbits and pussycats too, cooking them together. And when they gutted the cats, they didn't eat those guts, they gave them to the dogs. It was only the rabbits that us kids ate mainly, but we did eat a little bit of that pussycat, and I remember it had a really tough flesh. And they split it in halves, just like a rabbit, yuk! And I happened to see the cat's head floating in the stew and I said, "oh no, look at that *akaperte* there", you know? I thought my big brother, *akelye atyinhe*, he might give it to the dogs, but he chopped it up. He treated it with respect. Because the pussycat is related to some other people you know, *pwetheyekate aknganentye. Pwetheyekateke artweye*. People from another country. *Apmere arrpenhe-arenye mape*, people in another country who have a sacred relationship with that animal.

But we thought that rabbits, even though they were introduced as well, we thought they were native animals, we recognised them as belonging to us. Because they lived in the bush in burrows. You gotta dig them out and kill them just like any other animals that live in holes, like goannas, even bilbies, those ones that *were* our animals. So when people first ate rabbit, they were sure that it was native, that it was *putye-arenye*. But a few years later, it wasn't a native animal anymore, it was just brought into this *apmere*!

When we hunted rabbits, first we made an *inte*, a long stick for checking where they were in their burrows. It used to be a really long one, to feel for the rabbit. They'd take the stick and wet one end with their mouths, and then touch it in the dirt to get a bit of soil on it. Then they'd put it in the burrow, maybe there'd be rabbits inside, and then they'd pull it out, and they'd see from the amount of fur sticking to the *ahelhe*, to the soil on the end of the stick, if there was a lot of rabbits in there. They'd touch the end of that hole with that stick to see if it's worth digging for them. Also people noticed, when the rabbit gets into the hole, that they used to fill themselves back with soil. *Artelhirtnerle* they call it, where the rabbits would cover themselves back up, it means they'd cover back their little tracks. You could see how they burrowed themselves in that way, backwards. "Oh, there's a rabbit in there", they'd know straightaway. Well, those people'd fill that entrance hole up, and start digging down into the burrow about halfway along. Because that's *arlwekere rarle mpwepe-arle*, that's the rabbits' family camp, right in the centre. *Arlwekere*'s where they all get together, that's where they all are. And that's where those old women dug into, from the top. Into that gathering place, right in the centre. Then they get it out and then *turle-akerle*, they grab them by the feet and the back of the neck and pull to break their neck. They'd 'cruel' them that way, *ye*.

Then we used to gut them, cook them and eat the guts, just like our own animals, but we didn't joint them. We used to just cut them fair down the middle, split them from the tail to the head so that everybody can have half. With the skin on. And *ithwarre* – that word's got something to do with the taste, the flavour, with eating the whole skin and all, like rabbit, or kangaroo tail 'cause it's got all that flavour in. That's why they used to eat it like that, 'cause it's got the flavour of the whole animal in it. *Ithwarre* is really good, it kills all that smell in yourself, like you might have a 'flu smell, you might have a sicky smell, or young women might want to eat *kere ithwarre* when they're lying in hospital.

We ate lots and lots of rabbits, especially out at Arltunga and Ambalindum because there were so many around. People used to *unekele alhele* – go for several nights at a time to hunt for rabbits. They'd kill heaps of them. People would kill them and then travel with it, bringing the meat back home. And from Santa Teresa, people would go hunting out from there for a few nights also. I remember when Mum and all of us went hunting them, right up into the hills around there.

And they used to eat those rabbit guts – *lyepe-lyepe* and *mpurle*, they were real good meat. We used to treat 'em like a real native, *urrperle-kenhe kere*. It always had that real nice taste in it, and people used to eat the head, *akaperte arlkwerle*, and the milk guts, *lyepe-lyepe arlkwerle, ante akurrknge*, and the brains you know, and also *mpurle akweke*, the little intestine they call that. They used to get that and clean it out and eat it. Everything, those things was all eaten. People really used to treat them like a bush animal, *kere putye-arenye-arteke*, cooking them up in the hot soil under the coals. *Ahelhele-arle alpmanthele atyerremele itne arlkwetyarte ahelhe-iperre ikwe*, so that it also had that earthy flavour, that *ikwe*, which is given to it by the Land. You know, people sometimes used to cook *rapite* in the oven – white people used to sell 'em that way, but it didn't taste the same, it didn't taste the same when that rabbit was skinned and put in the shelves. We always singed their fur and gutted them, *atninemele, interlpe arrernemele, atyerrerle alpmanthele atyerrerle*, we pinned their stomach cavity together with a wooden skewer, then cooked them in the coals, no skinning. And it was really nice. But there's not many *kere rapite* around now, because of the disease. Rabbit was really good meat. It really *survived* all the people around Santa Teresa, 'cause there wasn't any much *kere* around. They only used to go for rabbits, and goannas, and a few wild goats, you know, kill every day.

That *kere naneyekwerte atwetyarte*, the nanny-goats used to be eaten a bit like the rabbits, even the heads and the guts and the skin. People used to *inetyarte kere naneyekwerte iterle*, cook the skin and all. And when they used cut-*eme*-up-*ilerle*, then people used to *ntheke-iwerle*, throw the left-over skin on the fire to singe the hair off. *Ntheke-iwerle imernte itemele alpmanthele atyerremele*, they'd singe it, then cook the skin in the hot earth and ash, and sometimes used to leave it for a while to make it nice. They'd roll it up, put two stones or three stones on it, then put that hot soil on. After that, people used to pound the skin to make it soft, and then eat it. We used to have it all the time. They never used to *alhwe inerle antywetyeke arrangkwe*, get the blood to drink out of the nanny-goat though. Because that's *kere iwenhakweye putye-arenye*, that's only for bush animals.

But rabbit we used to treat really good, they used to think it was food that belonged to Aboriginal people, and they used to think it was good medicine meat. They used to get rabbit *mpwe*, the bladder, they used to bladder *tyerrerle*, pull the bladder out, and they'd put it on their sores – sores on their head or maybe on their feet. When they used to gut it, they used to pull the other little guts out, and next minute you go in and you pull that little *mpwe* out from there, it's a tiny little one. They never used to put it in the eyes, but only on the head sores, or sore something, you know? And he used to heal it all the time – they used to wash the sores with that rabbit urine. We never used to do that with our own animals, only with rabbit. I don't know how they found out. It used to sting-*eme-ileme*, sting all those sores and make them real dry. But not in the eyes or ears, just outside sores.

Where Are Our Foods Now?

When the first settlers came in and chopped all those trees down, they not only chopped those trees, they chopped all the people in the process. They destroyed them, and the people got destroyed by everything. By everything that came into us, we are all destroyed by chemicals, anything. Those foods that we eat now, we don't get it from growing out of the spirit of the Land. The vegetables are grown now by people a long way away and brought in here. Grown by industry – potatoes, pumpkins, onions. Not those old onions that we used to get out of the ground, or those potatoes that grew amongst the grasses. And they throw fertilizer on top to make the vegetables grow. And they experiment on food now: "Hey, let's grow this cauliflowers bigger than the old ones used to be!" And the cabbages, they used to be really nice and round; and now, big huge cabbage! And also look at that pumpkin! Miles away it's so big! They have to get a truck to carry it! And watermelon, you can't eat a watermelon that's right up to *there*. Those watermelons are really too big now. And the pumpkin used to be just small ones too; well, you get pumpkin about *that high* now. *Ye alakenhe aneme*. Everything's changing.

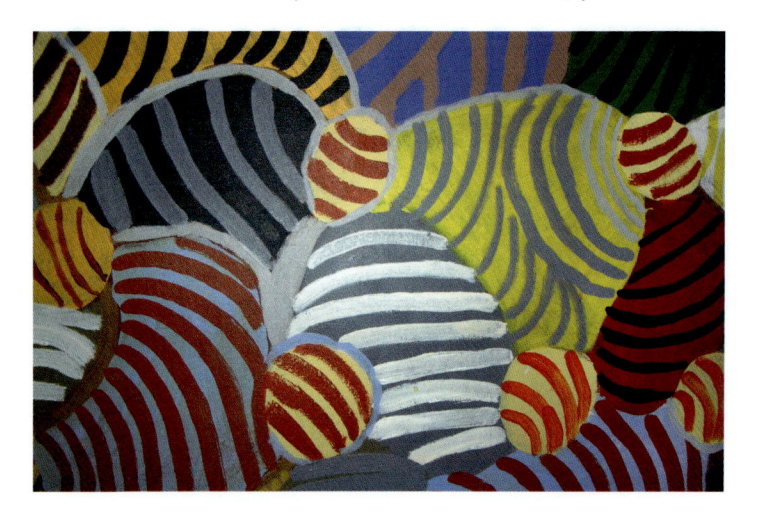

On the Land there used to be lots and lots of seeds to eat. Not only for us, but seeds for the poor birds too, and you don't see much of *them* around now either. There's not much of any seeds around now, even of the pigweed seeds, *ntange ulyawe*. I don't think we'll find *any* pigweed seeds now to grind up. They used to be everywhere, and bigger than they are now, with big flowers that could hold a lot of seeds. And their seedpods grew big and long, and their stems were really red. There were lots of seeds came from the one plant, you could fill a small pannikin with the seeds from just one plant. And they grew thickly, "oh look, there's a big patch of *ulyawe* growing real thick". Or maybe behind the hill there might be lots of it growing. Or on the river bank, lots there maybe, and nowadays there's nothing.

Sometimes you see places like where seeds were ground by the early-day people. You only see the grinding stones laying about now, the ones that the old people have left there, but there are no seed-bearing trees anywhere around there. Once we went looking

---

Three Grandmothers Painting Three Teenage Girls, 2007, detail, acrylic on canvas, photographer *Irrkerlantye* Arts
This painting is a story about three grandmothers painting up three teenage girls for ceremony dances for *ntange ulyawe* (pigweed seed), *ntange arlepe* (acacia-bush seeds) and *ntange atnyeme* (witchetty-bush seeds). The dances are performed during the seasons when the new pods come out, celebrating the new pods. You can eat them raw, put them on a rock and grind them and mix with water and make patties. You put the patty on a rock and hold hot bark over it and toast it.

for those sort of grinding stones on *Ntulye* Plain. We saw a few of the stones, but we couldn't see any seed plants, not even *ulyawe*, or *ntange iltyartwe*, the native millet, or *ntange aywerte*, the spinifex. Those old people must have used to get those seeds from close by there, but when we went, we saw only a few old, sick spinifex plants. Also *ntange arlepe*, the prickly wattle or acacia-bush, we saw a few of them, but they were really spread out, not growing thick like they would've in those old days. We found round grinding stones that was used for the hard seeds like the prickly wattle seeds, but not many of the trees themselves.

Arne arlepe used to be everywhere. And their seeds used to be big ones when they ripened and fell off. They're only little ones now, because the Land has been spoiled. Some sort of a creature has stamped the soil down, and they've got some sort of a chemical on their feet. Take horses for example. What have they got on their feet? Horseshoe! And they're chasing down the cows when mustering's on. And that's how the Land's soil gets powdered up, by chasing bullocks around. It's all that iron they've got on their feet. And it spoiled the ground, powdering it up and poisoning it with chemicals. And when the bullocks get sterilised, maybe stuff could drip down onto where the food plants grow, the seed plants. And after the bullocks have their medicine given to them, well they go away and eat their food

---

Arlepe Atweme, 2008, acrylic on canvas, photographer *Irrkerlantye* Arts
Arlepe atweme means "cracking the acacia seeds" in *Arrernte*. *Arlepe* is also called Prickly Wattle. We can get the seeds when they're green or when they're brown. These ones are brown. We crack them and then we grind them. Sometimes you can just get it in your hand and put it in your mouth. Or you can wet it and make a dough. It's good for everything. Good for your whole body. Gathering seeds was very popular for Aboriginal people. *Arlepe* was always very, very popular for trade and for giving to people like a gift. *Arlepe* flowers are one of the best flowers. We know the animals are healthy when we see these flowers. The kangaroos eat the bush. The flowers makes the leaves sweet. That's a healthy time. We know the animals are healthy. They're fat. They have that inside them.

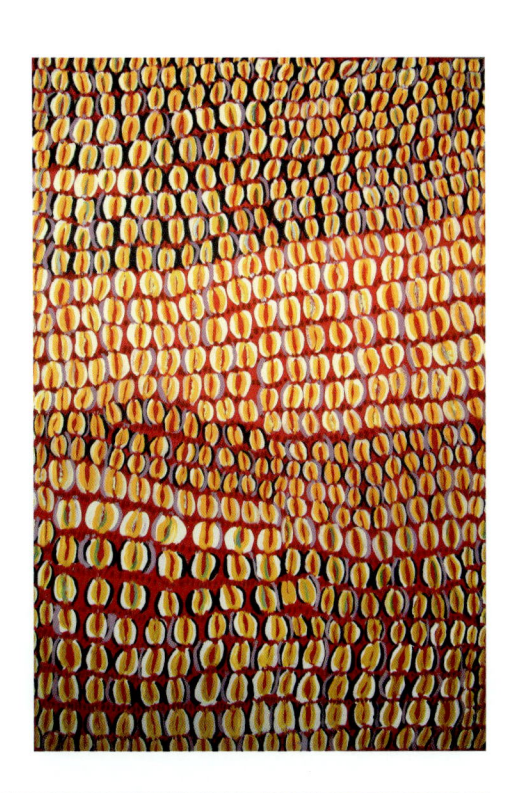

out in the bush, and they drop their dung, and the dung flies away and gets onto the plants all around, poisons those seeds. The manure you know, it dries out and gets to be really fine and powdery around the bores, and then the wind comes and blows it around onto all the plants. And into the rockholes as well. And maybe that's why the rockholes become blocked up, and the springs feeding them stop running. Might be like that, I'm not quite sure.

We don't see much of our *merne*, our fruit plants growing now. The Land has changed for them too. Bringing in bullocks and horses has really changed the country for the worse. It's made the ground softer, and they've killed off a lot of those growing plants. But in the old days there were lots of green food plants and fruits in this country of ours. People used to go hunting in the springtime, hunting all over for bush fruits, like walking around for wild onion, *yalke*. There were lots of *yalke*s on the Land where we lived. You could get them close by, and the old people used to eat heaps of them. My old cousins told me that there used to be a place out on the eastern side, not far from here, where *yalke* grew all over. Now it's just buffel grass.

Not only *yalke*, but also fruit plants like *inmartwe*, the bush pepper. You don't see *inmartwe* now. And *merne mwanyeme*, or *merne arrwarlpe*, some people call it. That's a really yellow plant that grows on the top of small hills. They've got a really nice smell when they ripen up, like a rockmelon smell. But they're pretty rare around the hills now, we don't see them much. Also people used to look for *merne angelthe*, the bush pear it's sometimes called. It's a little plant, and it's got little fruits on them a bit like *alangkwe*, and people used to eat them a lot. I saw one out near Emily's Gap recently. One! I don't know if it'd be any good to eat now, because of all the changes in these foods of ours. *Alangkwe*s themselves are smaller now, and they don't flower as much as they used to. There used to be lots of fruit on one plant, but now you don't get as many. And *ingkwerrpme* is a sort of mistletoe that's getting a lot less common. *Pweralheme* is another mistletoe that grows on the whitewood trees. It's a bit like *ingkwerrpme* but it has a yellow fruit. Where's that one now?

Merne ilkwarte, the bush cucumber, was also eaten. They used to be bigger, but now they grow really small. And it takes a lot longer for their fruits to ripen, because there's introduced plants growing around them everywhere. There used to be lots of *ilkartwe* growing around the rivers, but you only see them here and there now. You sometimes see them under tea tree bushes, and only then if you're lucky. Maybe that's how they've survived at all, in the shade there. You don't see them out on the plains at all any more, *antyere akwekele*, on the waterways, where the water used to lay. That's how much our country's changed for *merne mape*.

Manna, *ngkwarle aperaltye* used to grow really thickly, everywhere. When I first came to Alice Springs, the old women used to collect a lot of *aperaltye* down in the creek just south of the town, it was everywhere around there. They never used to break the limbs, they'd only have to shake them, or rub the leaves and the manna would drop down on their calicos. *Aperaltye* grows on the river red gums, and there were lots of these *apere* trees growing everywhere. All over the place, it was like that. And *ntewale*, the blossom on the bloodwood tree, that used to flower really thick. But not any more. People used to eat the *ntewale* flowers, sucking out the honey. All those things used to flower like anything in their season, along with all the other plants, but you just don't see many now.

And you don't see much *arlkerle* around any more either. That's the rolypoly bush, and it has a grub living in its roots, one that we used to eat. *Arlkerle-arlkerle-arlkerle-arle aneke*, the place used be just covered with rolypoly bush, and now there's not much at all. And also the trees don't have as much *tyape*, not much witchetty grubs in them now. People used to be able to collect lots of witchetties from close by. Maybe the trees and the water is different now. When the rain comes, maybe it brings soil into the roots of those trees that's not so good. They used to collect lots of *tyape* in the *ankerre*, the coolibah trees. And even the red gums, there's not as many *tyape* in them, *tyape ahernenge*, the grubs that live in their roots. It's just here and there now.

Arne apere mape, the red gum trees themselves, they used to grow really thickly. Lots of saplings, and nowadays there's not so many growing, only a few of them are growing together now. And they seem to stay stunted for a long time, growing in a stunted sort of a way. Maybe the trees are more dried out now, and maybe only the gums that are actually growing in the river are getting enough water, enough so that the witchetties can live in them. Even then the grubs aren't as sweet as they used to be. The sweetness has gone out of the trees because the water's changed. And probably the air bounces differently on trees now, drying them out, and the wind sweeps over them and maybe it gives them a different sort of bark, and the *tyape* might not be able to burrow into the tree because maybe the bark's harder now. Around Mount Undoolya-side there used to be lots and lots of *tyapes*. But not any more, because the *atnyeme*, the witchetty bushes, are only growing in small sizes there now, and there's no *tyape* in their roots.

When you go over the spine of a sandhill, you don't see much *ulyawe* or *ayepe*, the tar vine growing there now, not much *intwerrkere*, the kerosene grass, in fact not much of any grass at all except buffel grass, which has been introduced to us. And the plains are all changed too. They used to be just covered in plants. And the plants that are really native to those places, like *tunpere*, the windmill grass, and *intwerrkere*, they've been taken over. And *irwerlpe*, I don't know whether *irwerlpe* was growing around here before, I'm not sure. That's that parabine grass, do you know it *alere*? I've seen it around, but I don't know whether it grew just right here before. But all these were overtaken by bad grasses like buffel, and by other weeds like couch grass.

We never used to have weeds; cattle and horses are spreading them. First they trample down the windmill grass, and then they spread the other grasses everywhere. They carry the seeds of these new grasses in their feet and these drop off everywhere to start growing and taking over. Maybe the cattle might drop the seeds in their dung, and that's what starts them growing in the first place. Then the dung might dry out, and then the wind comes and blows the seeds away, and they bury themselves in some other place and start growing. These are the things that are creating big trouble for the Land. Now there's just weeds for miles and miles. Windmill grass has almost disappeared.

And the old grasses that used to grow along the river banks aren't there any more. One sort of grass we used to have was *lyentye*, a reedy grass that grows up straight in creeks and sometimes in swamps, there used to be heaps of that around. I've even seen *lyentye* growing around near the high school here in Alice Springs. There used to be a river bank there, but there's no bank and no *lyentye* now. You can't go anywhere to sit down on the sides of the rivers or creeks, or even to go to the other side of the hill to sit down, because foreign grasses have taken over there. You can't even light a fire because the grasses that belonged to here, like the windmill grass, have all disappeared. The buffel grass has taken over now and you can't light a fire because of the great danger of bushfire from the buffel grass. Also the pads that we and our animals used to wander around have been covered over with weeds and choked by those introduced grasses.

The cattle and horses have trampled the plants and the soil so many times that *nothing* can grow in some places any more. When they're walking on the river bank they soften up the sand there, and they powder up the plains. And it softens the soil, that good soil on the surface, making it powdery, and the wind blows that fine topsoil away. And then the soil that's not so good might blow in from somewhere else, and sits on that place where the soil that *was* good used to grow trees and other plants that you can eat, *alakenhe*.

And it wasn't only cattle, it's also goats and sheep as well. And they ate all the grasses and plants that belonged to our own animals, and the trees that our own animals liked to eat, like *arlepe*, the prickly wattle. Now cattle and horses eat all those types of plants. They all eat everything. And so now there's different grasses growing.

The Food Chain is Breaking

That's why there's not much of our animal around any more, because they can't find much of their own food. Bush animals have to go a long way now to find that, the good grasses they have to eat. Kangaroos and other animals like them have to travel a long way now just to get a feed. Emus have to travel very far to get the food that's right for them, and it's the same for goannas, perenties and bearded dragons. *Arlewatyerre*, *ulkerte*, and *ankerte* aren't as healthy now, because of this changed grass. There's none of that good old grass, no good water, and not even much grasshoppers around for them to

that the water's bad and a bit salty nowadays. And there used to be a lot more water in the rockholes. But our wild bush animals, they didn't have any chemicals in them, the kangaroos and birds, they lived on just wild grasses and seeds. Our wild meats haven't got any poisons inside them, they haven't been given needles or anything like that, and nothing special was put on the grass that they ate. Nothing special was needed for them to stay healthy, we never saw any kangaroos or emus with any sort of disease or sickness. People related to those bush animals as part of the Land, as part of us. We come from the same place. So when the kangaroos dug soaks for their water, we just dug those soaks out, and we drank out of them too.

People travelled because there was a backup of water that they could depend on. That's how they could afford to travel to different places, knowing that there's reliable waters in different parts. They really relied on the rockholes that they knew were always there. Where the waters always were, Sacred Waters, those that belonged to that Land. Well, that's *why* they were there, those rockholes and soakages. But they were spoilt and destroyed, these precious waters of ours. Sometimes now people take the Sacred Sites Authority mob to the country, to show them, and to talk about the sites. And when we take them, sometimes instead of water places there, you just find dry plains. And the soil, *ahelhe*, isn't as healthy as it used to be because there's a lot of salt around now.

There's another thing about water places. There might be a small rock at a sacred site, a small rock that's important for creating lots of edible seeds or other type of food, a

---

Teaching Girls How to Dig a Soakage for Water, 2006, acrylic on canvas, photographer *Irrkerlantye* Arts

rock where people do or say something to create that type of food in that area. Anything that gives us food, a woman might rub and sing that rock or whatever it is. The bullocks often destroy something like that, by trampling over the rock or little mound. Now that we're going back to our homelands, we're looking at our waterholes and cleaning them out and fencing them around, so that they can only be used by the bush animals. Lots of people are doing that, so that we can show our kids, both Aboriginal and non-Aboriginal, how it used to be like, what it really should be.

The creek beds have really changed. It used to be pretty wide in creeks, and it seems now to be getting narrower. The creek banks used to hill themselves up, the banks of the river used to be really high, but now it seems to have flattened out, it's only a small hill now. It's not as high as it used to be before, and the creek bed itself used to be really flat. Maybe there's too many people might have sat in the shades in the creek. Us Aboriginal people never used to go back to the same place to sit around, wearing away the sand there. We'd sit here and there under different shades, not all gathered under the one place. Anything like fire, well you'd just make fire under the shade of the tree. We'd dig a small hole to make the fire, and maybe the ash and coals there may have affected the growing of the plants. Whatever it is, the creek bed's changed altogether. It's got hollows here and there now, where it used to be flat before. And all the creeks that used to be good to sit around, other grasses have taken over now, you can't even go walking anywhere.

The Land's really changed. There's introduced trees growing everywhere, and the landscape of the place has all changed too. And they keep on bringing in lots of different sort of cattle and bullocks, like those *irlpe akngerre mape*, the big-ears, and the *aruntyeye mape*, the long-necks, and *amerne-amerne aneme*, those ones with the flaps of skin hanging down from the back of their necks, round like a damper, and also *irlpangkere mape*, the ones with the ears cut short. And they've got different colours now too. The sheep are the ones they brought out first, and they're the ones that destroyed the country in the first place. And then, after the sheep, bullocks and horses came and made it worse. *Pweleke kawe ane pweleke pule. Nanthe mapele akenhe menhengenhenge anyenhengenhenge-arle kine-arle akenge-ilintyeke*, and from them, generation after generation of those animals have continued to destroy the Land. That's who smashed up the soil and made it into the shape the country's in now, made it different, made it all rough and bumpy, not like it was before. And the watercourses are showing strange shapes. Maybe the water comes down just once in a while now, all in a flood, because the water doesn't run as regularly as it used to. And maybe because of that, the ground's so dry now that the wind blows the soil away and changes the shape of the place, changes the direction the creeks run in.

There used to be seasons for water, like a rainy season. That was the natural thing then, in those days when people moved around on country, knowing they could rely on the season and the natural water sources. And now rain comes at all different times, like when there's a cyclone. We never heard of those sort of things before. And that rain becomes just a flood and changes all that water in soaks and rockholes; it stirs it up. And plants have changed because there's a lot of changes in the ground, in the soil, the water, and the wind. And also the sun's changed. *Uterne*'s got a different heat now – that burning heat. It wasn't quite like that before. The summers used to be hot, but we didn't notice it burn like it seems to now. The sun's heat's more bittery now.

There's lots of changes in the seasons that are different to how it was in the early days. And that doesn't fit into the Land.

The Land's really been turned upside down, *ahelhe-arle akngarte-iwelhele*.

Language And Learning

"Our language is sacred to us.
Every Aboriginal language is sacred
For those that speak it.
Words are given to us by the Land
And these words are sacred."

Language

From the Flesh of Our Land

The Land needs words. Otherwise, if we didn't have language to speak with, we'd only have the thoughts that are inside our head. We'd have thoughts, but what good are they without the words to bring them out, so that we can tell each other what those thoughts are, sing our songs, and tell our Stories? So the Land needs words.

Words makes things happen. Words makes us alive, the language keeps us alive. If we didn't have any language, we couldn't have said anything; we couldn't have done anything; we couldn't have sent anything out, you know?

We couldn't have had a meaning for it, the meaning that's in things. That's why our language is really strong and really important to myself and to all the people who speaks it.

It's not only words that's sacred but also it comes from our own Land, and comes from our Ancestors. It's a gift from that Land for the people who join into that Land – fathers, and brothers, and sisters, and brothers-in-law, and also our children. We come from the Land, and the language comes from the Land. And everything that grows from the Land, it really relates to our language as well. Like the hills, creeks, trees, and water. Because they got all the names from the Land. Everything's got a name for it, even ant. Every different ant, every different bird's got a name. Every bird talks different languages, and that comes from the trees from our Land. All the time we relate to the birds' words and the birds' message as well as our own language. *Akarre* is a sacred tongue because it comes from the Land and it's part of us, and because we use it to do things, to say things – give messages, bring out things, you know.

Ane akaltye anthurre angkentye ikwerenheke. Ane angkentye itethe atnerte mpwepe-arenye apeke re. And that person knows his language, and he knows that his language is born out of the living flesh of that Land. No Aboriginal people tells anybody wrongly that his or her language is this or that, *arelhe urrperlele ileme angkentye ikwerenhe arratye anthurre.* Because he never tells lies, because that person is this language speaker. Because *arrenge ikwerenhe*, his father's father, is a language speaker like this, and *aperle ikwerenhe*, his father's mother, she's a language speaker same as this.

My own language is *Akarre*, which I have from my father's father's Land. I also speak *Alyawarr* which is my mother's father's language, and also Central *Arrernte*, *Anmatyerr*, and English. But my knowledge comes through *Akarre*, and that is the way *ayenge-arle akaltyele-antheke, ane akaltye-irrintyeke, ane arintyeke, ane itelarintyeke, nthakenhe-nthakenhe-arle anintyeke*. That's how I got taught these things, how I've learned throughout my life, how I've always seen the world, how I understand it, and how and what in all those ways life has always been. All through my own Sacred Language.

People used to keep language very strong. Never they used to copy any other languages, never really learned any other languages much, *angkentye arrpenheke akaltye-irretyarte aneke. Merne apmere anyente ikwerenge ane unthelte-anemele, ane anpernirrentye anyente ikwerenhe aneke. Ampe-arlke apmerele-arle inteke anyente akwete, anewe-akerrenheke anyente ikwerenge.* They just lived in their own country, speaking the same language. Together they gathered food from that place, held to one kinship line, and their children were born there, always on that one country. They themselves had been born there, lived, grew up, and got married in that same area. They all spoke the same language because of those old people who belong to that country. And the reason they lived like that was because they could see the Ownership of that Land, and saw that they're from that country itself. That's how people used to live in them countries. And not only to have a say in that country, but to make it as their own, make it part of them, and what it is to them, and to their kids, and to the kids to come. So they can grow up in a good environment of understanding. How they can live. That's why they've always wanted to keep them languages straight and strong.

Language is something we *see*, and we know who those people are, and if we hear someone talking the same language as myself, then I know, you know, even a kid might know, "he's talking the language that my parents and my grandparents can talk. He must be our relation too", and that's how people identify themselves. It's really with our language. You can recognise if a person uses different words, and speaks in a different manner that's not exactly in the *Akarre* manner; well, you know they speak another language, come from another *apmereyanhe*. You can also tell who people are just by looking at them. And where they're from. They might really look alike, but in the way that we see it, it's different – different looks, different way of walking or sitting, or action, that's how we see it. *Tyerrtye apmere arrpenhe-arenye alhengke-arerle.* You can tell by their face, even when no words are coming out, even by the way they're dressed, how they are. You can tell them straight out, you can notice them straightaway, "oh this person's that person, and that person's that sort of language-person".

You gotta *akaltyele-anthele ampe ngkwinhe-areye*, you gotta teach your kids what language is, and what language belongs to that country, and what language is tied to the Land, and what is you. 'Being you' is to know your own language from that Land and for the Land, know who is connected to your Land, and know the people who speaks the same language who is really joined from your Land. Language *ngkwinhe angkentye unte-arle angkeme ane angkentye arrpenhe-areye kantreye itweke-itwe-arle aneme mape. Angwenhe-ante-areye apeke angkentye anyente-arle angkeme.* You speak you own language and the language of your closest next-door neighbours, *apmereyanhe-arenye mape, anpernirrentye mape.* They're the ones speaks the same language as yourself. And it's really good you know, your language is from your very own country – it's a real deep country-language. *Unte-arle arrenge akekenge*, or *unte-arle atyakekenge, unte-arle Altyerre akekenge,* it's rooted in your relationships from Creation, in your kinship that cycles from then and there onwards and onwards. Language is just like a root from the tree, 'cause that language is spoken not only *unte*, it's spoken by *ngkwenge artweyele, ngkwenge artweye atherrele, ikwere artweye atherrele,* and *ikwereke artweyeke artweye atherrele angkentyeke.* Not only you speak that language, but generation upon generation upon generation of your families have also spoken it. And so language is really, really important. Your own language. And that language really *recognises* you, gives you identity, and who you are and what is you, and how you're connected to that Land, and how you hold the Land, *alakenhakweye*. *Angkentye*

Language   From the Flesh of Our Land

ngkwinhe. Yanhe-ante-areyele rarle angkentye-arle antirrkweme, those are the things that the language connects and holds. What is to be yourself.

Apmere kantreyenge-ntyele angkentye arrateke angkentye anwekakerrenhe, angkentye Ikngerrekwiperre. Language comes straight out of the country. The *Akarre* language belongs to me and belongs to my family. It comes up from the Land to our Ancestor, then on to our great-grandfathers, *arrengenge akngeye-werne kele anwerne aneme.* And from those old people to me and my other families then. The only way that you can claim another language is by your four grandparents. *Ipmenhe ngkwinhe* might speak that other language, *atyemeye ngkwinhe* might speak that other language, *aperle ngkwinhe* might speak another language, but your very own language comes from your own Land, your father's father's Land, like *akngeye ngkwinhe-kenhe, arrenge ngkwinhe-kenhe, apmere kantreyenge-ntyele. Alakenhe.*

Layake apmere tantyipe nhenhele anemele. Anwerne awerle-aneme angkentye arunthe anthurre angkerrirrerlenge. Because we live with so many other groups now, today we have a better chance of learning other people's languages, which is good for having an understanding of the different Aboriginal people living in a township like Alice Springs. We know now that there are many, many Aboriginal languages. And that's why you gotta learn your own language first, before you learn any other languages – to know it, to understand it, and also to relate to it.

Teaching And Learning

Teaching is a Really Sacred Thing

After they were born, new little babies would be placed in a coolamon. The grandmothers would then warm their hands in the smoke of the fire and touch the little ones' mouths. With the warmth from the smoke, the grandmothers'd speak these words: "Don't talk wrongly, don't speak wrongly with this mouth. Never swear or say anything bad towards anybody, and don't speak wrongly towards elders. Let this mouth to be saying just the right things and the right words. Don't tell other people's stories, and only speak the truth". Then they'd warm their hands and put their fingers on the baby's two ears and say "only hear good stories, don't listen to other people's conversations, nasty gossip, or comments about others. Don't repeat their stories". Then they'd warm their hands and touch the eyes then, and say "use these eyes to see just good things. Don't let your gaze rest upon whatever it is you're not supposed to see, or on anything bad. Don't look at other people's things and want to have them for yourself. You have to always keep your eyes on your own path".

Akaltyele-arle-anthemeye – teaching – is a really sacred thing, because everything that we're learning is sacred, sacred things about our existence: *Nthakenhe amangkenhetyeke*, to grow up how to be, how to continue growing and learning in the right way throughout our lives; *nthakenhe anenhetyeke*, how to live the life stretching out before us, to continue living the life we were born to live; *nthakenhe apeke ilenhetyeke ane arenhetyeke*. And how to see life, and how to know life, and also what life is; the life that keeps on being described to us and seen by us; how that has to be. This is the way they used to learn us, our old people, *alakenhe*.

The old people, the *akngerrepate*, those grandparents that taught the relationship knowledge, they became really top leaders for their families. They were always looked upon really highly. People see them as even much more knowledgeable than their own parents. The *akngerrepate* are right at the forefront, and the parents are halfway along the line. That's how people came to be really literate to know about this stream we're all travelling in. *Iwenhe-ante-iwenhe-ante rarle intenheme itnenhe-arle apentemele ilerle*. Whatever it is that stretches before or ahead, the *akngerrepate* tell the ones that are coming behind about it, handing back that knowledge. So Aboriginal people never skite about how much they know, about how knowledgeable they are. They always just acknowledge those *akngerrepate* that handed down the learning to them. The younger people never say "we are the knowledgeable ones". Because they've always been told: "Be really honest, like your old people, who were really true".

Aboriginal people will always acknowledge and praise-up the ones that taught them. It doesn't matter whether it's men or women. So a bloke might be a really good stockman. He might know all about horses, like fitting the *kapelye* – those jingling hobble chains – or putting on a saddle, or shoes. But there's a lot of people who could do all that who they might've learned from – their daddy, or their uncle, or other relations. Maybe their grandparents. And a young woman might say that she's learned from her mother, or her aunty. Nobody ever exaggerated about how good they were, because if you tell tall stories about yourself, that's really no good. We were always taught to be honest and true, us Aboriginal people. When you've learned something, you have to acknowledge and recognise that person who you've learned from. You cannot tell anybody that you've learned something by yourself, because there's no such thing as learning by yourself. That's why I always acknowledge my mother, my aunties, my old people; because it was them who told me things.

And I'm *Still* Learning

Even though we had a really hard time when we was young, we still used to do all those things which was right, down where we lived. Like when Mum took me and left me at the mission and told me, "you live here now, it's good for you to live here and learn, in this place with all these other young girls and with the Sisters". I didn't say "no, don't leave me here, don't leave me with these others, take me with you". Because I might spoil what she's really wanting for how I should be growing up, I might turn out bad somehow. We used to just live happily there on the mission at Arltunga, going to school with the Sisters and learning; learning how to become Catholics. We also learned from the people who came from Alice Springs to be there at that place. I learned their language, Central *Arrernte*. I'd only known North-eastern *Arrernte* up until then, my *Akarre* language. I also learned from some relatives of mine who were there with me, especially one old woman.

Again, I learned a lot by living with those people that looked after us. My schooling didn't go for very long, and I don't know how much I learned from the school itself. But I knew how to clean houses; I knew how to milk goats and muck out their yards; and I learned about punishment, that if I did anything wrong at the mission, you've gotta get punished. There were useful things that we learned by getting punished, doing certain work as a punishment. And you come free after doing it! These are the things that I learned and we all learned out there. And when I got a bit older, when I became a teenager, I went back to my family.

I learned a lot more again after I went back to my parents. I was about fourteen when I went back to live with my mum and dad at *Apmere Rarlapanpirreke*, that place some people called *Wangkame*. That's where I lived with them. And as I said, I learned lots from them. We walked all the time, but especially we'd walk in the morning, climbing in the hills. I learned so much living their way then, it was a different way. And their language was different to the Central *Arrernte* that I'd been talking, I had to learn *Akarre* all over again. And I learned when them old people used to dance and sing, and about walking only on the women's path, not walking on the men's path. And different way of living styles. That was my growing-up when I was living there with my mum and dad.

I learned a great pile of things from my mother in those early days. Like collecting the seeds of *ulyawe*, a pigweed plant. She used to collect those pigweed seeds and grind them to make into a damper. And she taught me what those seeds represent. We used to lick the dust from the stone when she'd finished grinding! And then my mum would say that the soakage belonged to this country, and she'd tell me whose country we were on. And also she taught me about going hunting, and how to save water when you're hunting; you know, how you don't drink water all the way. We never used to drink plenty water,

Teaching And Learning And I'm *Still* Learning

and we used to save a little bit of water until we got to another patch. Also Mum taught me about trees, what the important trees are. About what the tree holds, like the Sacred Trees, and what connection they had with the country. And she'd point out the different countries. "That country over there, that belongs to this mob, and we relate to that country by this kinship name". Also my mum taught me a lot of things like how to cook meat. Everything, you know, even the littlest thing like making a digging stick, and what tree to get it made out from. You've gotta get a special tree. Some people used to get a stick from *atnyeme*, the witchetty bush. And they'd chop the branch off, clean it down, and then sharpen it. Because people never used to have crowbars, crowbars we have only today now. Back then they'd use those digging sticks to dig out rabbits' burrows and goannas' holes. And also Mum taught about how to look after country. Like this water belongs to us mob, like to my fathers, my brothers and myself. And about the carpet snakes that belong to our country, and the birds. And the grass and other shrubs that grow on our Land, and the fire here that is held by our Land. Because the Land here holds not only us, it holds everything else as well. Those old people knew their country really through and through, and they felt very close to it, it's a very close country to them. Because our Land is part of us.

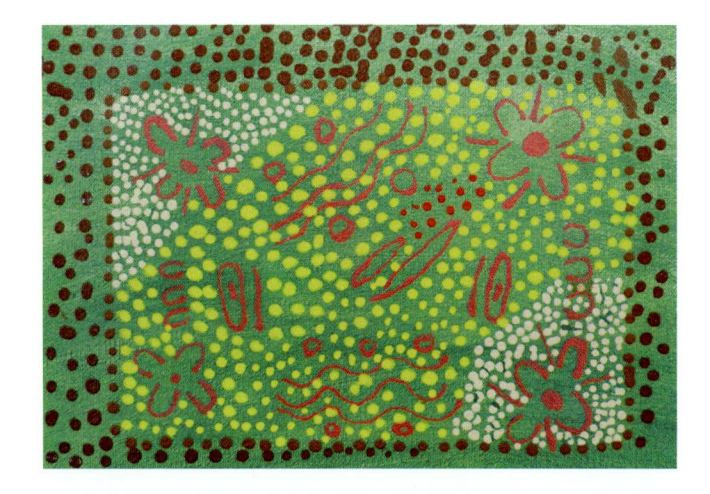

That's the way I learned from my parents, and how my parents learned from their parents, and their parents were learned by their parents. From their grandfathers, their mother's father and from their father's father. Like *arrengenge*, *atyemeyenge*, *ipmenhenge*, *aperlenge* – four families we've all learned from. Well, I learned most with my mum, and also with my aunties, and also with my sisters, and with some other families as well.

Coolamons and Digging Sticks, 2004, acrylic on canvas, photographer Barry McDonald

201

I learned about respect, and what culture is: Relationship; Land; people; what's in the Land, and all about Aboriginal people as families. Relate to brother, and relate to big sister, and to uncles, and to brother-in-laws, father-in-laws, mother-in-laws and their sisters. And relate to people through cultures, and how we relate to our Stories. And also about food in the Land, and sharing, and also caring as well. Because in Aboriginal ways, everything we got we always share. Anything belong to myself or my children has gotta be shared amongst their brothers and sisters, and also amongst my sisters' children. And not only today, 'cause that's in the Legends of Aboriginal people. That's how Aboriginal people were before. When they travelled they used to share everything; kangaroo, emu was divided by the whole camp. Living and having things as one.

I'm really happy that I learnt from my parents, especially my mum. She used to tell us a lot of stories. *Anwerneke-arle iletyarte mamele* everything *rarle ilerle – kwatye-akerte, unthetyeke akngerle,* how to look for water when walking, how you can *kwatye antywerle,* drink water without getting rubbish in your throat, *alakenhe.* How you can *merne iterle,* how you can *kere iterle*. Cook vegetable foods, and cook different meats. How to *arlenge anthurre alhetyeke,* you know, how to walk a long way. And how to save water for that distance. And how you can't drink or eat this or that, like sweet things, 'cause that'll make you go thirsty. Those sort of things my mum used to teach me. If *kere atwemele,* don't *kere akngerrentye arlkwerle,* if you eat at dinner camp, don't gobble up a big mob of meat, because when you're walking back you might want a drink of water, you might get too thirsty. Like when you're walking back home into the sun. You don't really want to walk towards the sun because it's not really good for you, because you're confronting the sun. The best way to walk is by going sideways. Then you might get hit with the sun on the ear from the side the sun is coming out, that's all. But mostly people used to travel at night or in the early morning, so they can stop some of that sun. And also it's cooler to walk then. Those sort of things I was taught by my parents.

A lot of my knowledge I got from my aunties, my dad's brothers' wives. They used to live together with my mum, and they used to take all us children for hunting. That's when they used to tell us everything we know about going hunting – about tracking animals, how to gut a rabbit, or porcupine, or goannas. How if you're gutting a perentie or a goanna, you gotta pull out the throat guts in a certain way. *Atne-ite*, the throat guts, are in the perentie's stomach. You put a little hook up its bum and screw it around and pull it out quickly, and no one's allowed to watch you, to look at it, or the guts will burst and spoil the meat. Even porcupines, you've gotta cut that in the middle stomach. And to see whether the porcupine's fat, you can't see it in their guts, you've gotta cut their little foot, their toe poor things, *akunye*. And also they taught the names of the seasons, what animal comes in what season, what season time they'll get healthy. And what food, what sort of food these animals will get if there's gonna be more of them around. Those sort of stories they used to tell us.

Not only my mum and aunties, but other old ladies as well. We never used to laugh at people, or laugh when somebody's walking, or joke about people. Like today, you see kids, "oh, look at that man with the funny nose!" We never used to say anything like that, or "oh, look at that man with the crooked arm!" You know those sort of things that was really forbidden for us. We never made laughs or made jokes, even though old people used to move around with a lot of walking stick. My brothers and sisters were really funny kids, they used to tease each other a lot. But never teasing old people, Mum and Dad were very strict on that. And never ask for things, never ask when somebody's eating, because that wasn't right. If you ask somebody when somebody's eating – well, sometimes you see a dog eating something and another dog go and rip it off their mouth. That's how we used to see it, *arrakerte-kerle ampakeme merne*, you know, grabbing things from the mouth. And you *never* follow anybody, that's how we were told. You never follow people, unless they ask you to come along.

These stories were told in a special way, and so were other sorts of Stories too. Like when you're laying down at night they'll tell you Stories about the stars, and what's the star in the winter, and what's the star in the summer. When it's wintertime, why the star's over there now when, in the summer, it was over that other way. And how the Milky Way changes, and the Morning Star, and the Evening Star. Because we lived on the Land, that's the sort of Stories we were told, Land Stories. And today, not many people learn about these sort of things. Maybe very few people. Maybe grandmothers now might know about it. Because there's a lot of things in between all our kids now. There's televisions, stereos, games, outfits. Because they've got a new pattern now. New way of living. Cars, alcohol, marriages. So that's why a lot of people like to move back to the homeland, so they can have their own strong Rule in their own Sacred Ground. Where the stars tell their Stories, the flowers of the trees tell *their* stories. Plants give that story. Because not only people live on that Land. Story comes from our own Nature, like from our motherland. Or might be from *arrenge* or *aperle*, father's father or father's mother.

Culture is taught by families as well as by country. Taught in close families, and even by elders who might know someone who knew your parents, and who might know your Stories. You can learn from them as well. Because the culture is always passed around between many people, handed down to related families as well, and certain important people holds Stories for these different families. That's how people learn about their Land, maybe their grandmothers', or their grandfathers'. Every Aboriginal family's got an elder, or important people in them, someone who lived amongst or through their family's generation, to hold the Stories. Not today's stories, but Stories way back. Back when *they* were friends. My mum, she used always tell me: "You know that old aunty of yours? She used to be a good friend of mine, and we grew up together, we lived and married together, and lived our marriage-life with our husbands. She also used to teach me. Now today I'm telling that Story to you". So that's why I always tell my kids what my aunty used to tell me.

To learn is such a really good thing in your life. Things back then wouldn't be taught again, they were taught only once, *akaltyele-anthele anyente-ngare ware*. And you've gotta know it then. Things like going hunting, or shooting or cooking kangaroo, how to keep quiet, or how to dig for *tyape* or *yalke*, how to use digging sticks and what they're all about, and what fighting sticks, *kwetere*s are all about. How to do it when you hit each other with *kwetere*s, those sort of things were taught. Or how to cook with the big shovel-sticks when you've got kangaroo in the coals, you've gotta learn everything like that. And after they're taught, they start doing it themselves then. The girls are taught by women, and the boys are taught by their uncles, mainly.

My younger brothers and sisters and myself were taught everything by our own family elders. To sing sick people with healing *awelye*, to sing for anybody with sores or cuts after fighting, or singing people with diarrhoea. There were different songs to sing people who had different things wrong with them. And they used to really joke a lot when they were playing cards, teasing their *nyurrpe*s. They used to play against their other *nyurrpe*-side, two against two. *Akngerrepate mape*, our old people taught them really well. And my mum taught me. And I'm really happy about it.

That's what I tell other people, the ones that don't know so much. Some of them remember, and some of them don't. But I always tell those others, "surely that's how your families learned as well?" But some people say, "oh no, I didn't learn in that way, my grandmothers and mothers didn't teach me like that, not like the people that are out on communities and learn from their father's and mother's mothers". And today I teach my grandchildren and my nieces and nephews. I teach them how to teach language, how to tell Stories, what to tell non-Aboriginal people the things they should know when they go out onto communities to work. They're the sort of things that I learned when I came to town. How to interpret for the police, and how to interpret in the courthouse. And now I'm teaching here about how we've lived since the earliest times.

I learned more when I was working – working with Land Council, working with people through their Land claims, doing interpreting and telling the lawyers on their behalf. Things like that. I learned a lot from them – how they respect their own country, how their culture is important, how we see it in Aboriginal eyes, and what that Land means to us. I was really happy for those *Anmatyerr* people. I did Land-claim work for them and I really respect them. Some of them were my aunties, some of them were my mother-in-laws, and sister-in-laws, and cousins, 'cause they've got similar skin names as *my* families. I learned a real lot from those people, through their Stories and things like that. About good relationship, and also about listening, and about what is important to them and to myself. But these things that I learned during the interpreting, I didn't take it, I didn't keep it, I didn't use it. That was their knowledge. The knowledge that I learned I left with them, it was theirs. I was a mum then, and a grandmother. But still I was learning what is important to Aboriginal people and to myself. I'm an aged pensioner now, and I'm *still* learning. People always *do* keep learning because they are always looking at the world through different, older eyes. I've learned the same things as a young girl, then as a teenager, then as an adult, then as a grandmother. And that learning's all been different. *Alakenhe.*

When we were young, the older people were followed in their teaching because they were so greatly loved. That's our Rule, and it's a guideline. But it's very strict, we never used to *apale angketyakenhe*. You cannot *apale angkerle*. *Unte nthakenhe apale angketyeke arrangkwe-arle*. That's the leader's learning and rules. We didn't ever talk wrongly to them, and we didn't talk back. We never questioned old people, because *they* had questions for *us*, to tell us what is right and what is wrong. That's some of the rules they had. Old people will teach you at the right time, when they want to teach you. Then they'll tell you: "*These* are the things you've gotta learn".

Like rules for who you could go hunting with. Just with your brother-in-law and your sister, when they go. *Irlkwatherrenge ware.* And sometimes with our parents we used to go hunting, never anybody *mwere apekele alheme-arlenge*, never went with son-in-law. Or like *ampatye-ampatye*, we never used to go with father-in-law. Or son and daughter-in-law, never. *Ulyenyeke*, just only parents we'd go hunting with maybe. And maybe sometimes with our older sisters, *yayenge*, so they can teach us, *ilerle ante akaltyele-anthele*. Sometimes we'd wait at home for our parents if they'd gone hunting without us. They used always bring home special things for us that we liked, *tyape arlperratye*, and *arwengalkere*, whitewood grubs and honey, and maybe bush bananas, *alangkwe apeke*. And we'd always wait 'til Mum gives it out, never grabbed things from Mother's hand, or Father's hand.

I wouldn't do *anything* wrong by my old people, because I love them, and they hold me and I belong to them. When you respect your elders, and obey your elders, which is right, people see you; "gee, you really respect your elders, you never do any wrong things". They'll watch you, you know, people can see you. Sometimes they test you out. You have love and respect for the people who brought you into this world. And for people who teach you, taught you, you have to have respect for them. But mostly for your parents, and also for your big brother and your big sister. Kids today don't really respect elders. But they don't know what knowledge them people's got, them elders've got. And later on when they grow up to be a big man and big woman they'll, "oh gee, I didn't have respect for my old uncle. He had all that knowledge, he was one of the best of the best". And now they feel real sad about it because they don't have that. That's how a lot of people are, they think of that and they take it really serious. *Itelaremele*.

Land is the Real Teacher

We teach our kids language with baby talk first, and then we talk more to them and correct them. The best part is to take your kids back, when they're small, take them back to your own homeland to learn, *akaltye-irretyeke*. You might take them out there for the weekend, you might take them out there for the Christmas holidays, you might take them out there to stay – to move away for a while. Let the kids learn the language, and not only about the language, but also learning about the Land. What language and Land together means, what it is. *Aperle* might not have a language, but *ipmenhe* might have a language. *Arrenge* might not have a language, but *atyemeye* might have a language. That's ways you can learn, that's part of you.

If people don't really know their language well – any people, even grown-ups – they could always go home to learn it back. You learn really well when you're on your homeland, because the country looks after you when you're learning, and the Little People of the Land watch over you while you're learning; they put it into your head. Even though you don't see them, they see *you* while you're learning. They're happy that you're learning, so they help you to hear it properly and to understand, help you to learn well. Sometimes you even realise, "hey, I've learned really well. That old woman, my grandmother, I've really learned well from her. Living at this place I've really learned a lot, because I'm now back home on country, on my homeland, learning". The learning comes from the Land. It comes out of the homeland itself. It might be your father's father's country, or father's mother's country, or mother's mother's, or mother's father's country, it doesn't matter. And learning from people that are still living there, like my families and your families, anybody's families. You learn from the people that are on the Land, those that own the language that really, *really* belongs to you.

If you're *arelhe urrperle, anwerne artepenye urrperle*, well *anwerne alheme apmere anwernekenhe kantreye-werle alpemele*. If you're *arelhe*, well, you *itelarerle atyemeye*, you *itelarerle akngeye*, you *itelarerle ipmenhe*, you *itelarerle arrenge*, and *Arrwekelenye Mape*, you *itelarerle nthakenhe itne-arle aneke apmere kantreyele. Nthakenhe-arle apmere itne antirrkweke*, how the great-grandfathers and great-grandmothers, how they hold the Land, and what the Land is for them, *Apmereyanhe iwenhe itneke aneke. Alakenhe-arle.*

When, as an Aboriginal person you go back to country, you come to realise about your four grandparents, about your great-grandparents, and you come to know how the Ancestors live with the country, how they hold it. Every individual Aboriginal person should know that Land is part of them. They need to be told as kids when they're growing up, and also when they become parents, how to relate. And the best way to do this is on country.

Arelhe arunthe-arle aneme, now today, we are taking a lot of kids back to *apmere arrkene-arle alyelheme iletyeke, ane akwintye-arle arteme ane ilthe-arle arteme, alakenhe mpwaretyeke*. Women are now starting to take kids onto country to teach them singing, or Stories, or how to set up windbreaks, how to build traditional bough-shelters. They're just starting to go back to what Stories they've lost. And some of the kids have lost a lot of language, even the kids who have lived out on the communities. *Arrpenheme-arle angkentye itnekenhe aparlpe-ileme, aparlpe-aparlpe-ileme lyete ulkere*, they're gradually letting go some of their languages. And when they have children, those children will not be as strong a language speaker as even they are. Especially when you're living in a place like this, in the township itself. The language it just wears out. To make it worse, the television is telling its own stories, always *arrparlpe-iweme*, talking over the top of *Arrernte*. That's why we've gotta get those kids to learn back their language from their grandmothers. And then those grandchildren will have a really rare sort of *Arrernte*. We've gotta make sure that the strong language, the solid language is *anerle ngkerneke-arle-arteke*, like if it's planted strongly in the ground, *arne-arle ngkerneke-arteke*, like a tree firmly rooted, or a rock securely propped to make it stand upright, *apwerte-arle ikerrke-iwelhemele antirrkweme-arteke*. Just like that. *Ampe* can *apmere kantreye-werle alpemele akaltye-irrirtnerle*. When they live on the country, the kids can learn it all back. And they'll learn how to not shift stones, or not to move branches, *alakenhe-arle*.

You might learn on the Land of any of your four grandparents, your *ipmenhe*, or *arrenge*, or *atyemeye*, or *aperle*. *Akaltyele-anthenhe-anthenhe rarle apmere rarle*. The Land is the real teacher. That's one of the best ways that you can learn. You might learn your own language in a deeper way, or you might learn other things. You might learn to sing, you might be learning to sing fun songs, you might want to do design of materials, or you might want to learn just to paint yourself for the fun dancing, using ochre. Or you might learn doing feathers, featherwork and headbands you know, for entertainment for women, things like that. And you feel really comfortable because you're in your own Land, or you're in your own country. And you get that lovely feeling in you, that touch of feeling from the Land. May be your grandmother-spirit might be getting happy for you, might be your grandfather-spirit getting happy. You can always feel it when you go.

Land Power and Women Dancing, 2005, acrylic on linen board, photographer Barry McDonald
This painting shows women dancing for their own private ceremony, dancing with their cockatoo-feather headdresses on.

You asked me, *alere*, why I said that kids can 'learn back' these things, why I put it that way. *Unte apeke uye itelareme nhenhe alakenhe-arle the ilerne*. Well, *ngkwenge-arleke apmere kantreye nhenhele-arle lyete iwenhe apeke renhe arraterle ileme unte itelaretyeke. Itirrentye ngkwinhe arrernirtnemele*. Well nephew, maybe you don't recall that I've told you about this before. I told you then that it's Land that reveals things so that people can remember what it is that they've really always known, putting back in what they've forgotten. It's like it says, "well, *unte apmwerrke nhenge awetyakenhe aneke, nhenhe-ante-nhenhe-ante akwele unte itelaretyeke*, you might not have realised before, but these are all the things that you know and should remember". The Land tells you that. *Ingwele apmerele*, at night on the Land it just comes into your head. And when you're sleeping, *intemele*, "oh yeah, *arratye nhenhe-ante-nhenhe-ante kwenhe*, that's right, these are all those things, I remember now".

Alakenhe, so it does, Land teaches you.
And Land *memorises* you.
Itelarentye mpwarerle, it makes you remember.
The Land is the real teacher.

Akngerrepate Mape, the Elders

They Were the Very Highlight to Us

Aboriginal people's way is to respect elders, *akngerrepate itelaremele, anetyeke, ane akngerrepate arrpenhe mape aremele alhengke-aretyeke, ane angkentye apale angketyale, angkentye akurne angketyale akngerrepate-werle. Alakenhakweye* respect *anetyeke. Ane anpernirrentyele-arlenge anetyeke. Itelarentye iwenhe apeke-arle unte ikwere aneme. Ane awetyeke. Awemele anetyeke ane akaltye-irretyeke. Ane anpernirretyeke. Anpernirrentye yanhe-arle renhe apentetyeke.*

Our way is to understand the elders, to be with them, to see and recognise all the old people from around *apmereyanhe*. Never to speak in an improper way to them, and always to live right within your kinship. To understand clearly who you are to them, to sit and listen and learn. But above all to relate, to follow *anpernirrentye*. All that is respect.

The old people, our *akngerrepate mape* were proper happy people, and really knowledgeable. They were wonderful teachers, champions at keeping the relationships and guiding us all in our kinship and showing us our path; they were real champions at that. And also for looking after country, they were outstanding in that way too, and they really lived for it. They loved and respected their son-in-laws, loved their own wives and husbands and their children. And they always used to come together for meals and sing fun songs, entertaining songs together. They had a lot of fun. That's how my mother's fathers were. I didn't get to see my father's father, because I was only a little girl when he passed away. But my mother's father and his wife, my grandmother, they were really happy people.

Those *akngerrepate mape*, they upheld everything for all of us, kept everything together for us. Above all, the elders really *loved* us. The grandfathers might all gather together in the *arnkentye*, the single men's camp, and they never used to get nasty to anybody. Never spoke a bad word about anyone, because they all looked after the country. They had their minds focused on looking after the country, on holding everything together, not pushing things apart. Because they hold all those people, and they're the Land-guiders. And also they were really good to their wives and to their mother-in-laws, and to their father-in-laws. Not only them, but their father-in-laws' brothers and sisters were the very highlight to those old people. And if they see them coming from somewhere they'll always be happy, and they'll tell their wife to cook something, they'll tell their sons to go and hunt something. Those old men really looked after other people when they came visiting. They'd tell someone to go and fetch firewood, or to go and fetch some water and bring it back, that's how those old people were. Very loving, and always playful. And they never used to think of themselves as cleverer than anyone else. They never used to talk like that. Everybody used to be really equal for *akngerrepate mape*. Because they used to regard *everyone* as a champion. All of us were real brilliant people to them, really smart. Who knows and was taught by those elders themselves and by their families, other elders. And also really loveable for everyone. Because they held the Rule, and they know the right ways of living, the lifestyle. That's how the elders used to be.

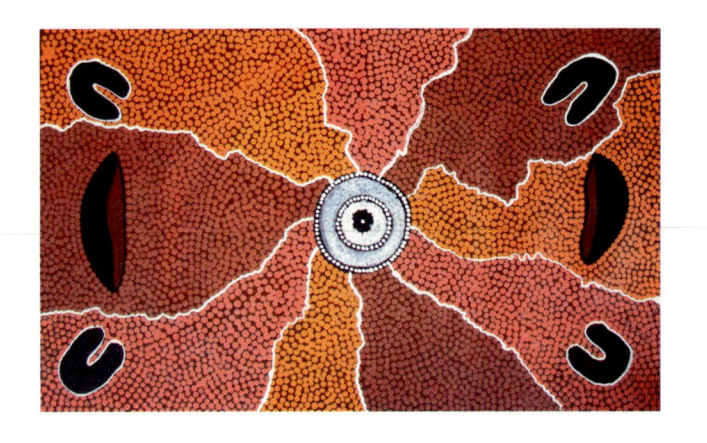

They never spoke a bad word towards anybody, as I've said. All the *kenhenge* in my father's family, all my fathers, they used to really love one another. And they were always happy for us, always loving. Even when we were grown up, they always loved us the same. They never said anything wrong to us. And anyone who visited from another country, they really looked after them when they visited, that's how the old people were. And we're really sorry that we don't have very many *akngerrepate mape* today, not

---

Special Leadership, 2008, acrylic on canvas, photographer *Irrkerlantye* Arts
The elders are sitting around the campfire (u-shapes), talking and making decisions. They represent authority. They are painted up (stripes). It's a special meeting. It's a special protected area with windbreaks (two long lines). There are coolamons (oval shapes by long lines) next to the windbreaks. There is traditional food in the coolamons. This represents goodness and nutrition.

like people used to have, they always had lots of old people. Especially the eastern-side people. Not many left now.

Everyone really loved the *akngerrepate mape* in return. They never used to harm them in any way, they used to really take care of them, giving them whatever they needed, blankets or food. And sometimes those old people'd do something the same for us. They might make us feel really good with comforting or praising words, or they might laugh at us in a special way that made us feel really good for being recognised. We don't get that now these days – we're living in a different ways now, different society. But the hard society – the hard way, and getting things, and you gotta walk things to get it, and when you had to earn things – that was the most loving way. The hard way was a good way of living. Now today's just easy way of living, which really doesn't fit in to our society, *alakenhe*. Those poor old people still had to work, maybe looking after someone's horses or garden, watering the gardens, they probably wasn't getting a pension. Maybe they'd get a little bit of food, and that *merne*'ll be shared around, and if they go hunting they'll share that around too. *Alakenhe-arle aneke*, it was really happy way of living.

I miss *akngerrepate mape* you know, sitting down with them old people-*le-arlenge anetyeke*. I always loved my mum and my uncles, I used to still have 'em in my house, *apmerele anetyeke*, and when they went I really missed them. But we don't have *akngerrepate* like that now. If there's somebody in a family *akngerrepate*, I always *akangkerle aremele* – he must be a really lovable person *iwenhe alakenhe itirremele*, that's how I think. I have really good memories of those happy days *arrwekelenye*. Those times when the old men threw spears and boomerangs, and the old women danced. Sometimes they'd poke each other in the ribs, and then fall over laughing in a big pile. In those times there was lots of funs and jokes and laughs and giggles – it was a really happy gathering *anetyarte*. That's how they were.

There's not many *akngerrepate* left from our side, from my side. Not many *akngerrepate aneme*. Not people who can really teach us what is what, people-*le iletyenhe-arle iwenheke apeke re akaltyele-anthemele*. Maybe *akngerrepate* third-part *ware*, only third-generation *akngerrepate*, not like the fourth and the fifth and the sixth generation, we don't have that now, *anwernekenhe* generation *mape*. *Arrangkwe aneme*. There's none around. We don't have our elders, it's really nothing. The real early *akngerrepate* is great-grandmother. That must've come after the *Akngerrepate Arrwekelenye Mapenge*, the Ancestors. Those old ladies of mine saw *alherntere atherrkenye-arle apetyeke*, the new white people arriving. Those great-grandmothers were the ones who had all the knowledge. I'm just *akngerrepate apmwerrkenye*, 'yesterday's elders', just come lately. *Alakenhe*, and that's a story about *akngerrepate*.

Iwerre Atherrame, Two Cultures

When Shadows Measured Time

Aboriginal people get up real early in the morning, rising with that spreading pale light that brings the dawn. *Tyerrtye mape, anwerne akeme-irreme ingweleme anthurre. Ingweleme anthurre, layake mperlkintyelenge mperlkintyeme yanhe kele aherlkeme-arle.* We can chatter and talk, but people never used to talk really loudly, they just used to talk soft-sound *ware.* Because sometimes – people must have done it sometime before – *arrwekelenye mape akeme-irrerle,* so you're not allowed to *irlkemele-angkerle,* shout out aloud 'cause somebody might *urltatye akwele,* they'll have a little click on the nose, *urltatye.* And then that *urltatye* tells you – somebody might call out, "*alaye!*" – and another somebody might *urltatye-irrerle,* that little thing on the nose clicks, and that hits that person, and that's very wrong. That's how people, when they used to get up in the morning, how they used to light the fire and cook some food to eat, *ure inerle,* and *iterle,* and *merne arlkwerle.* We never used to *aharlperre angkerle,* just sing out in a loud voice for nothing, because that *aharlperre angkeme,* that is not the way. You don't put those things in for no reason. *Aharlperre* is just made for a reason. Like you can put your voice-call for a reason. Like for calling someone to come quickly when it's important, that's the proper way to use it.

When it's starting to become dawn, *akethe-akethe,* we go and collect wood and water. We don't want to wait until the sun, *aherrke,* is really piercing, *nternintyerle.* We don't want that shot of ray on us, 'cause it weakens people's lives you know, like if they want to go hunting. They used to go hunting, or collecting water from the gullies, *ilerrtye,* or the gaps, *arntaye,* when it was cool, *atheperre.* Or cook some meat in that morning cool time. That's at our getting-up time we do those things, when it's almost still dark. People used to *alhele, ingweleme anthurre alhele,* go really early in the morning when it's still cool, tracking down the animals, because the tracks are fresh from their travelling the night before, that's what our time was like. Go early in the morning and hunt the animals so that the dogs' feet don't get too hot when they're chasing kangaroos or chasing emus. Or tracking anything, so it's not hot for their foot.

And by lunchtime, you can be there, sitting in the shade at dinner camp. And as the shade of the trees lengthens you could be cooking something, or lying down having a sleep. And when the shade falls still further from the west and it starts cooling down again, you walk back home then. Because the sun is not as hot. And when it gets later on in the evening, you stretch out a bit early, sometimes as early as the dusk, to lay down and relax as deeply and for as long as you can before the next day. You might tell Stories about the stars, you might talk about the summer and the other seasons, or tell Stories that were 'specially told at night for children, Creation Stories. And you'll drop off to sleep then, and sleep right through the night. And when it starts lightening up the next morning, you get up again then. *Alakenhe*, that's how it was.

People used to follow the cool of the day, track the coolness. You can't travel back home into the sun, it's too hot and piercing for that. You might catch the brunt of that sun on your chest. You've gotta wait until the shade gets really long in the cool of the evening. So people used to keep an eye on the shadows; "we'd better go before the shade gets any longer or the shade falls further, *arlpentye-athathe-irreketye*". Or if it's in the morning, "let's go before the shadows get shorter, *urteke-athathe-irreke*. Let's go before the sun gets higher in the sky and shortens the shade". They used to go by the shadow of the hills, they used to measure time by shadows. *Alakenhe*. That's how our people followed time.

Urekethureke, it's a Problem Life Now

That's why you see people in town nowadays *ingweleme anthurre alhelenge* bank-*werle*, going off to the bank really early. It's not gonna open until 9.30. So they just sit there. And another mob sit there, and then another mob come and sit there. You see them *prape arlpentye anthurre anerle-alperlenge*, all sitting in a long line waiting for the bank to open. 'Cause we haven't woken up to the time that we're s'posed to you know, like time machine-*le-arlenge aneme-arlenge*, like clock time-*le-arlenge*. We haven't been able to fit ourselves into the time that the machines make it, the clock times: You gotta get up at *this* time and get ready. Then by the time you get over there that thing'll be open for you to go in, instead of going lazing yourself by waiting on *anerle-anetyeke akarelhemele*, which'll take all day, whole day of your life, you could be home by now, *alakenhe*.

But going by machine time is breaking the Law of the Land, and breaking the Law of yourself, you know? You're not that person to be that thing, *itelaraye*. It disturbs your part of life, but you're doing it because you have to do it because this is *itnekenhe* rule *aneme anwerne apenteme*. We gotta follow their rules now. *Itnekenhe iwerre aneme anwerne apenteme*, we have to follow their road now. Nephew, when you mob go back *intetyeke akwele*, when white people go back home to sleep, they reckon some people work 'til about 8 or 9-*nge*. Or even 10 at night. How many hours do they have before they get up in the morning? "Oh, my stomach feels no good, I must be getting ulcers". 'Cause you don't have enough eating time and resting time. Today we all take it really short now.

And like with *tyerrtye anwerne*, we *irrpenhelte-iwerle anerlte-anetyeke*, we Aboriginal mob just arrive somewhere in the morning nowadays, go inside, and sit down all day! *Arrwekele kenhe tyerrtye mape akeme-irretyarte iwenheke*. But we gotta walk! The old people started walking almost as soon as they got up in the morning. *Arlenge-arle kereke alhele, arlenge-arle apetye-alperle*, walking a fair distance to hunt for meat and a fair way back home again. And then they lay down to sleep. You put that body to sleep, and it sleeps and relaxes all the way. And then it's up the next morning and the same round starts again. Our kids today aren't getting the good teaching from older people that they did in earlier times. They go to school that's true, but what sort of teaching we got at home? We can't go hunting anymore, we don't go and sit down the creek now, because if people are just sitting around in the creek, the police come and hunt you away. There's no rights here, not like in the old days or when we're living out on a community. The old people in the old days used to sit around in the rivers here without any problems. Go down and sit in the river until evening time, cooking food and sitting under the shade of a tree. Nowadays you can't do that any more. You learn your knowledge when you're out on communities, and when you come into town, sometimes you lose it. What they've learned about their lifestyle, the lifestyle that they learned for out bush, it's forgotten about. Because there's a big problem here in town now. There's a lot of motorcars around, the food's different, the people's different, the language is different, even the time's different, you know?

Arrernte people are only just learning how to deal with it. Even the very old people are still learning, but their learning now is about today's life, about modern life. They still remember what they've learned from long ago, so it's a different way of learning for old people nowadays. All of us, we've all got a different way of learning when we come into a town from the community, but especially the old people. They're used to community ways, and once they get to town it's another way of life and learning. Like on communities they lived close together, and also there's no problems much out there. They never lived badly out on the communities, but when they come into town they have all these problems. *Urekethureke* – it's a problem life. *Urekethureke* is just like 'shaking here and shaking there'. *Alakenhe*, it's not a settled life. And that's how coming into town is. People have to know who to be with in town, because there's drinkers and there's non-drinkers. And the old people have to start learning about all that. We also gotta talk to our kids every day about these things. About life in town, about the old people and their ways, but also about trees, rivers, hills, what Land is. Even about sticks and woods and fire. Because if people like me and the other grandmothers we don't teach them now, then they probably won't get much more chances to learn.

Grandmothers Teaching, 2003, acrylic on canvas, photographer Barry McDonald
"This painting shows the grandmothers teaching young girls about patterns, like for painting on the body. The girls come from different skin groups, and each skin group has a different pattern because they come from different countries. In the background are the bright lights from the fires and the patterns they are learning".

Two Cultures Can Hold Each Other

I think that white people, their language is a loveable language, and that loveable language fits in their culture, how they run it, how they live with it, how they get on. Well, our language, our *anpernirrentye*, and our culture's like that too. So I've been thinking, let's get together, every one of us, and hold these two languages and things together. And teach them, and teach each other. We can't have blaming business today, now. We can't do that, because we're living together. We're eating the same food, we're drinking the same water, we breathe the same air, *alakenhe*. The Land can't support us like it used to, and there's not much bush tucker any more. But today we buy vegetables to make up for that. Two cultures can hold each other very strong.

That's what it's like for me as a Catholic. As a Catholic person, I really love my Land. You've asked me a couple of times, *alere*, just how I see God and the Land fitting in with each other. Well, that's a very hard question. We just see how God's created us and God created everything, and how our Creation is to the Land, and how we treat Land in the eyes of those Beings in the Land, you know, the Little People of the Land. Always it's really hard to have a question like that. And we just know like, how *Ngkartele anwernenhe mpwareke arntarnte-aretyeke*, how He created us to look after the Land. *Ngkartele anwernenhe mpwareke ntange mape apeke*, *mape arlwiletyeke*, how He made us to work in with the Land to harvest seed, or caterpillars. *Ngkartele antheke apmere anwernekenhe*, God gave us our Land to look after it, to guide it. God will also Himself guide the Little People of our grandfather's Land so that they can look after us, *arrenge-kenhe Ngkartele irrerntarenye anwernenhe arntarnte-aretyenhenge-arlke*. So that we're just like joint guardians of the country maybe, joint custodians. *Alakenhe anwerne itelareme*, you know, that's how we understand it. But it is a really difficult question.

Anwerne, layake, alyelheme, we *akngarte-iwerle*. *Iwerre anwernekenhe itelaremele* way. *Layake Ngkarte-werle alyelhetyeke. Utnenge arratye iletyenhenge Ngkartele aretyenhenge.* So that God can see our spirit, given in our own way, and so that He can see us in *His* way, we say it and sing it in a different style to the white people, how we see God. Different to how *alherntere mape* sees it. It ties in to how we see our Land. It's like 'the Creation of the Creator have put us in'. To be there. But, it's a very hard question, and it's a really difficult answer. Unless we sit down and translate it properly. We *iwenhe anthurre anwerne itelareme akngarte-iwetyeke*, like we could sort all those words out, but we really just want to leave it as it is, you know? As myself, as a Catholic person, I cannot stop loving my Land. And I really like my Catholic faith, and what I've learned. And I still keep myself as *arelhe urrperle*, a true-believing Aboriginal person, and I keep our ways of relating through our skin names, and how we relate to people. And that's really important for Aboriginal people. I'm saying here that I'm strong in Catholicism, and I'm strong in my own culture. But I've changed things around so that I can worship God in my own language, with my own words. And not only me, a lot of people are doing that as well. That's the way I'll always see it, and that's the way I'll teach my children and my grandchildren and my great-grandchildren. *Alakenhe*.

Two cultures *can* hold each other. I understand that because I know how I can relate with non-Aboriginal people as well as with my own. Not only me, but other Aboriginal people as well. The *alherntere mape* that I've worked with in my life, there's a different, special way of feeling for those people that share the knowledge, and the people that continue to get together to give it. Like that *Penangke* man who worked on the big *Arrernte* dictionary. There's a different feeling for people when you learn, like you're really close. Not really close that you're sitting holding hands with your arms around each other, *akwaketye-akerreme*, not like that. But it's something like being related to someone in a way that's almost as though they're your own parents. A real close feeling in a different, *ikirrentye* way. That's how I feel when I work with this *alere* of mine, I really recognise and respect him just as I would my other nieces and nephews. Really close. It's not like you want someone to sit close to you all the time, but because of the skin system, *anpernirrentye*, you have a different feeling, like the other-side-skin feelings, an *ikirrentye* feeling, but it's a loveable *ikirrentye* feeling for that person. The feeling brings you into the system somehow, even non-Aboriginal people, joining them together with us in *anpernirrentye*. It's a really good relationship, and it's in a really respectful way. That's how I feel, and you make that feeling and that person to be like your close friend, or your sister, like that *Kemarre* woman I've known for such a long time. Or make it like people you can rely on, and say things with, and joke. Not an angry joke, but just a good laughing joke.

The people that I work with, I always recognise and acknowledge them and work in well with them, because that's the relationship I'm in with them according to *anpernirrentye*. That's the feelings we have towards each other. And the feeling goes directly from me to those people, and it also comes back straight, and to me. I wouldn't let anyone talk badly about these feelings I have for those people, or the feelings that come from them to me. The people that I work with are really good, and we're in a good learning relationship, because you learn from one another when you do this type of work together. If you're a good teacher, then the person that learns from you gets really good knowledge. That's what I think about myself, after working with these people.

I used not be very knowledgeable before, but I learned how to interpret, and from there I learned more and more, and then I started to teach *Arrernte* language, and now I'm doing this book work and I'm really happy. I'm working with my *alere*, and we have jokes all the time, and I recognise him just like I do my own children. I wouldn't say anything bad towards him, or anything that might make him think, "why is Aunty saying this thing about me, how can my aunty talk like that?" I recognise him as my nephew, they've given him the same skin name as my other nephews in my *anpernirrentye* network. *Alakenhe*.

All the work that I do, I make sure I do it in a professional way, for professional people. That's how I see myself, especially when I'm interpreting for people like police, or lawyers, doctors, Land Council. I would never interpret for *nyurrpe*s, because it's not right for *my* culture, or through my skin group. That's being professional in the Aboriginal way, recognising kinship, knowing about it, and following its path. Sometimes, as Aboriginal interpreters, we have to stand back and let someone else do the work. I see the group of interpreters that I work with, no matter what language they speak, I see us all as good friends. I recognise them as having good strong language, and as knowing their culture right through. And I see a similar thing for some of the *alherntere mape* that I've worked with. Aboriginal and non-Aboriginal people working together as real champions for language; for culture; for Land, and for relationship. *Alakenhe athewe*.

IAD PRESS

PO Box 2531
Alice Springs NT 0871
phone +61 8 8951 1334
fax +61 8 8951 1381
sales@iad.edu.au
www.iadpress.com

Published by IAD Press in 2010

© *Arrernte* language and cultural information: *Arrernte* people
© Original story: Margaret *Kemarre* Turner
© Compilation: Margaret *Kemarre* Turner and Barry McDonald
© Translation: Margaret *Kemarre* Turner, Veronica *Perrurle* Dobson and Barry McDonald
© Artworks: Margaret *Kemarre* Turner
© Photographs: As indicated in captions

This book is copyright. Apart from any fair dealings for the purpose of private study, research, criticism or review as permitted under the *Copyright Act 1968* and subsequent amendments, no part of this book may be reproduced, stored in a retrieval system, or transmitted in any form or by any means electronic, mechanical, photocopying, recording or otherwise, without prior permission.
Please forward all enquiries to IAD Press.

National Library of Australia Cataloguing-in-Publication entry

Turner, Margaret Kemarre.
Iwenhe Tyerrtye: what it means to be an Aboriginal person / Margaret Kemarre Turner OAM; compiler, Barry McDonald.
ISBN 9781864650952 (pbk.)

Aranda (Australian people)
Aranda (Australian people) – Kinship.
Aranda (Australian people) – Social life and customs.
Aranda (Australian people) – Folklore.
Aboriginal Australians – Ethnic identity.
Other Authors/Contributors: McDonald, Barry Matthew John.
305.89915

© Cover painting: Margaret *Kemarre* Turner; photographer Michael Watson, University of New England, Marketing Services and Publications Office
© Front flap portrait: Photographer Barry McDonald
© Back flap portraits: Photographer Barry McDonald and Tamsyn Jones

Editor: Jill Walsh
Design: Tina Tilhard
Inside cover: Design Tina Tilhard, based upon *Everything comes from the Land*, © Margaret *Kemarre* Turner, IAD Press 2005
Printing: Hyde Park Press, Australia

Acknowledgements

Bob Roden and Jim Vickers for generously donating their time to photograph selected paintings;
Tamsyn Jones for generously donating her time to provide photographic images;
Jason Gibson and Ada Nano for ongoing personal support;
Gavan Breen of IAD and John Henderson of the University of Western Australia for advice on *Arrernte* language;
Kevin Bradley and Mark Cranfield of the Oral History and Folklore Section of the National Library of Australia for their initial support and encouragement;
Patrick Sullivan and Tony Boxall of AIATSIS for their support;
Manda McMillan of *Irrkerlantye* Arts for her assistance with images and captions.

Australian Government
Department of the Environment, Water, Heritage and the Arts

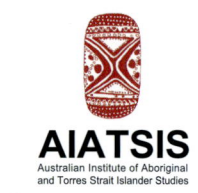

This activity is supported by the Australian Government under the Indigenous Culture Support Program of the Department of Environment, Water, Heritage and the Arts.

The authors gratefully acknowledge the National Library of Australia for its support for the research undertaken as part of this project.

The authors gratefully acknowledge AIATSIS for its support for the research undertaken as part of this project.